Women, gende
in Europe

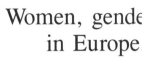

MANCHESTER
UNIVERSITY PRESS

Women, gender and fascism in Europe, 1919–45

edited by
Kevin Passmore

Manchester University Press

First published in Great Britain 2003
by Manchester University Press
Oxford Road, Manchester M13 9NR, UK
www.manchesteruniversitypress.co.uk

First published in the United States 2003
by Rutgers University Press
New Brunswick, New Jersey

British Library Cataloguing-in-Publication Data
A catalogue record for this book is available from the British Library

ISBN 0 7190 6083 4 hardback
0 7190 6617 4 paperback

11 10 09 08 07 06 05 04 03   10 9 8 7 6 5 4 3 2 1

Typeset in Times
by Action Publishing Technology Ltd, Gloucester
Printed in Great Britain
by Bell & Bain Ltd, Glasgow

Contents

Notes on contributors

Melissa Bokovoy, Associate Professor of History at the University of New Mexico, has published *Peasants and Communists: Politics and Ideology in the Yugoslav Countryside* (Pittsburgh, PA, University of Pittsburgh Press, 1998) and has edited, with Carol Lilly and Jill Irvine, *State–Society Relations in Yugoslavia, 1945–1992* (Basingstoke, Macmillan, 1997).

Maria Bucur, Assistant Professor, is John Hill Chair in East European History at Indiana University, Bloomington. Her recent publications include *Eugenics and Modernization in Interwar Romania* (Pittsburgh, PA, University of Pittsburgh Press, 2002) and *Staging the Past: The Politics of Commemoration in Habsburg Central Europe, 1848 to the Present*, of which she was co-editor with Nancy Wingfield (La Fayette, IN, Purdue University Press, 2001). Her research interests range from the cultural history of modern Eastern Europe to gender analysis, eugenics in Romania, and memory and nationalism.

Martin Durham is Senior Lecturer in Politics at the University of Wolverhampton. He is author of *Women and Fascism* (London, Routledge, 1998), and has written extensively on gender and the right. He is currently working on the extreme right in both Britain and the USA.

Kirsten Heinsohn received her Ph.D. in 1992 and since 1995 has been Academic Assistant in the History Department at the University of Hamburg. She is also a member of the Gender History of Politics research group. She has published widely on German women's history in the nineteenth and twentieth centuries, feminist theory and German conservatism in the twentieth century.

Dobrochna Kałwa, completed her Ph.D. dissertation on 'A model of the active woman in Poland between the wars' at Jagiellonian University, Poland, in 2001. Her essays include 'Kobiety w miedzywojennej Polsce w sprawie planowania rodziny 1929–1932' (Women in Poland of 1920s and 1930s and the question of birth control 1929–1932), in A. Zarnowska and A. Szwarc (eds), *Kobieta i kultura zycia codziennego wiek XIX i XX* (Women and Everyday-life Culture) (Warsaw, Wydawn DiG, 1997).

Cheryl Koos is Assistant Professor of History at California State University, Los Angeles. She received her Ph.D. from the University of Southern California. She has authored several articles on gender, the family, and pro-natalism in inter-war France.

Mária M. Kovács is Professor of History at the Central European University and is director of its Nationalism Studies Programme. She holds a Ph.D. from the ELTE University of Budapest, and has published works on nationalism, Jewish history and legal history, including *Liberal Professions and Illiberal Politics: Hungary from the Habsburgs to the Holocaust* (Oxford, Oxford University Press, 1994).

Mara I. Lazda is completing her Ph.D. dissertation, 'Gender and totalitarianism: Soviet and Nazi occupation in Latvia, 1940–1945', at Indiana University, Bloomington. Her research interests include the relationship between gender, nation and memory and oral history. She has published 'Latvian women and identity: oral history and memoirs of Soviet deportation', in Ilze Koroleva (ed.), *Invitation to Dialogue: Beyond Gender (In)equality* (Riga, Latvian Academy of Sciences, 1997).

Carol S. Lilly is Associate Professor of History at the University of Nebraska at Kearney. The author of *Power and Persuasion: Ideology and Rhetoric in Communist Yugoslavia, 1944–1953* (Boulder, CO, Westview Press, 2001), her current research is on women, nationalism and war in Serbia and Croatia, 1991–2001.

Kevin Passmore is Lecturer in History at Cardiff University. He is the author of a number of books and articles on history and theory and on political history in France and Europe, including *Fascism* (Oxford, Oxford University Press, 2002). He is currently completing a history of the French right.

Daniella Sarnoff is Assistant Professor of History at Xavier University. She received her Ph.D. in history from Boston College in 2001. She is currently revising for publication her dissertation, 'In the cervix of the nation: women in French fascism, 1919–1939'.

Mary Vincent is Senior Lecturer in History at the University of

Sheffield. She is the author of *Catholicism in the Second Spanish Republic* (Oxford, Oxford University Press, 1996) and of various articles on religion and gender in 1930s Spain. As co-editor of the journal *Contemporary European History*, she recently produced a Theme Issue on 'Gender and War' (November 2001). Her current project is a study of Franco's Crusade.

Perry Willson is Senior Lecturer in Italian History at the University of Edinburgh. Her publications include *The Clockwork Factory: Women and Work in Fascist Italy* (Oxford, Oxford University Press, 1993) and *Peasant Women and Politics in Fascist Italy. The Massaie Rurali* (London, Routledge, 2002).

Preface

The historiographical pace in the study of women, gender and fascism has been set by historians of Germany, among whom there was by the 1980s a thriving debate. That decade also witnessed the publication of the first international comparative research, including work on Spain, France, Austria and Italy.[1] Since then historians of Eastern Europe have begun to ask questions about women, gender and fascism, and the field has been redefined by the impact of gender history. Historians of women, gender and fascism outside Germany are not driven by the same sense of moral urgency as those studying Nazism. Debates concerning the participation or victimhood of women in the extreme right are less sharp. Yet without in any way denying the uniqueness of the Nazi regime and of its biopolitics, historians have recently reassessed the strength of racist tendencies in other countries and the extent of complicity in the Holocaust. The time is ripe to revisit old debates and subsequent methodological developments in the light of international comparison.

This book is also comparative in the sense that it is concerned with both fascist movements or regimes and non-fascist movements of the extreme right. Inevitably, given the weight of historical research and the place occupied by fascism in contemporary methodological discussion, fascism is more central to this volume than the non-fascist extreme right, and this is evident in the historiographical discussion in the introduction. While non-fascist extreme-right movements are often evoked primarily to show what is distinctive about fascism, the book aims nonetheless to illuminate the role of women and gender in less well-known anti-democratic conservative movements and regimes.

1 Rita Thalmann (ed.), *Femmes et fascismes* (Paris, Tiercé, 1986).

The book deliberately focuses on women *and* gender. True, there has been a methodological shift away from women's history with its unproblematic assumption of natural gender identities. Yet many of the issues debated by women's historians in the 1980s remain pertinent today, even if we must now ask, rather clumsily, 'what was the position in relation to the extreme right of those defined as "women", to whom "feminine" characteristics were conventionally ascribed?', rather than simply 'what did women do?' or 'what was done to women?'. Furthermore, the distinction between women's and gender history should not be construed in terms of a sharp binary opposition. Often, what counts as women's, gender, or men's history depends upon the observer's perspective. Accordingly, whilst the contributions to this volume are methodologically diverse, none can be easily categorised.

The book deliberately focuses on *women* and gender too. There is little explicit consideration of men or masculinity and the extreme right. Of course, men and masculinity are present throughout as a subtext and as the essential counterpart to women and femininity.

This book could not have been written without the help of a number of people. I would like to thank the participants in the conference 'Women, gender and the extreme right in Europe, 1919–1945', held at Cardiff on 4–6 July 2001, for their excellent range of papers and stimulating discussion. Liz Walker acted as co-organiser of the conference, and has helped make this book possible in many other ways. Garthine Walker read the manuscript and provided more intellectual stimulus and support than she can imagine. Alison Whittle was a sympathetic and helpful editor, while anonymous readers provided generous criticism and constructive comment.

1

Introduction

Kevin Passmore

The study of women, gender and fascism lies at the confluence of two areas of contemporary scholarly interest, yet the controversies of each have not resonated equally in the combined field. Taking the study of women and gender first, Claudia Koonz's *Mothers in the Fatherland* in 1986 crystallised antagonism between major tendencies in women's history as it was written at that time.[1] Koonz's book was intended to remedy the near absence of women from academic discussions of Nazism. It showed that contrary to received opinion, women had played significant roles in the movement and regime. Indeed, women had used the Nazis' idealisation of the family to empower themselves, and had been primarily responsible for the social component of Nazi policies. In keeping with one of the dominant strands of contemporary women's history, she sought to *recover* women's historical experience and demonstrate that women's *agency* was significant. Koonz suggested that Nazi women achieved some of the goals of the pre-Nazi German women's movement, and in one of her early works went so far as to describe the leaders of Nazi women as 'heroines'.[2]

For two reasons Koonz's findings were unsettling. First, feminist efforts to recover women's agency had hitherto been used to demonstrate that women had played roles regarded positively by most feminists – as foremothers of the contemporary feminist movement, or as leading figures in the labour movement, for example. Yet Koonz (paradoxically, given her view of Nazi women as quasi-feminist)

1 Claudia Koonz, *Mothers in the Fatherland: Women, the Family, and Nazi Politics* (New York, St Martin's Press, 1987).
2 Claudia Koonz, 'The fascist solution to the women question in Italy and Germany', in Renate Bridenthal and Claudia Koonz (eds), *Becoming Visible: Women in European History* (Boston and London, Houghton Mifflin, 1977), pp. 499–534.

declared that women were partly responsible for what decent people regard as the greatest crime in history.

Secondly, Koonz's contention that women had justified their participation in Nazism *as women* – as a product of Nazism's idealisation of motherhood – provoked a reaction from a rival school of feminism. For many feminists men's oppression of women within a 'patriarchal' society was *the* constant of human history. From this perspective, the task of the historian was not to demonstrate women's agency, but to chronicle patriarchal oppression of women, and the object of feminism was not to permit women to enter the man's world on equal terms, but to build a separate female sphere as an alternative to patriarchy. Difference feminism takes many forms, but the one in which we are interested idealised motherhood as the ethos of a morally superior women's sphere. In other words, this difference feminism emphasised permanent differences between men and women while Koonz thought in terms of future equality.

The best-known critic of Koonz's book, Gisela Bock, owed something to difference feminism. In her study of compulsory sterilisation, published in 1986, she had denied that Nazism was a maternalist regime, arguing that it had in fact radically undermined women's control over their bodies by sterilising the 'racially inferior' and by invading the privacy of those mothers who were considered fit to reproduce. She saw Nazism as fundamentally anti-feminist and patriarchal, and, like Jill Stephenson before her, she argued that women were largely resistant to Nazism. Bock's positive view of motherhood makes it understandable that she was concerned to refute Koonz's contention that women participated in Nazi racial policies as women, or rather as actual or potential mothers. Bock accepted that some women had been involved in Nazism – no one disputed that. But those women who were implicated, she says, were usually single women, and they were positioned within professional structures created and defined by men, while the victims of gassing were in majority female. These arguments preserved the notion of a feminine sphere as a positive goal for feminists.[3]

3 Gisela Bock, *Zwangssterilisation im Nationalsozialismus: Studien zur Rassenpolitik und Frauenpolittk* (Opladen, Westdeutscher Verlag, 1986); Gisela Bock, 'Die Frauen und der Nationalsozialismus: Bemerkungen zu einem Buch von Claudia Koonz', *Geschichte und Gesellschaft*, 15 (1989), 563–79; Gisela Bock, 'Equality and difference in National Socialist racism', in Gisela Bock and Susan James (eds), *Beyond Equality and Difference: Citizenship, Feminist Politics and Female Subjectivity* (London, Routledge, 1992); Jill Stephenson, *The Nazi Organisation of Women* (New York and London, Barnes and Noble, 1981). See Lerke Gravenhorst and Carmen Tatschmurat (eds), *TöchterFragen: NS-Frauengeschichte* (Freiburg, Verlag Traute Hensch, 1990).

In a rather more restrained manner, similar debates characterised women's history in other countries. There is insufficient space to examine each national history individually. Suffice it to note that Victoria De Grazia's influential *How Fascism Ruled Women*, published in 1992, was methodologically similar to Koonz's book, in that it was motivated partly by the desire to remedy inadequate treatment of Italian Fascism's female subjects. De Grazia examined the complex ways in which women negotiated the Fascist years, and argued that some women in Italy too used separate spheres ideology to justify a claim for female control of social policy and thereby realise some of the goals of the pre-Fascist women's movement. But she was more pessimistic about the extent to which women were able to overcome the weight of anti-female prejudice.[4]

By the time that De Grazia published her book, the traditions within which women's history had hitherto been written were being (partially) recast by the rise of gender history. Although as the Koonz–Bock debate progressed both sides became influenced by the new ideas, the antagonists had nevertheless assumed that 'woman' and 'man' were self-evident categories, and both, in their different ways, sought to 'reconstruct' the lost female experience.[5] Gender theorists, in contrast, questioned the naturalness of gender identities. Ideas about gender were not, they said, determined by biology or psychology, but constructed by languages and cultures, and so the meanings of male and female were historically variable. Furthermore, influenced by poststructuralist linguistic theory, gender historians suggested that gender identities were both opposite, in that female and male tend to be defined in contradistinction to each other, but also mutually interdependent, in that the definition of each relied on the other.[6] The implications of these rather abstract points for the study of women and fascism have been fourfold.

First, because gender historians insist that one cannot reduce a text

4 Victoria De Grazia, *How Fascism Ruled Women: Italy 1992–1945* (Berkeley, University of California Press, 1992).

5 For the shift from women's to gender history in this debate I have drawn upon Atina Grossman, 'Feminist debates about women and National Socialism', *Gender and History*, 3 (1991), 350–8; Ralph M. Leck, 'Conservative empowerment and the gender of Nazism: paradigms of power and complicity in German women's history', *Journal of Women's History*, 12 (2000), 147–69.

6 The key texts are Joan Wallach Scott, 'Gender: a useful category of historical analysis', *American Historical Review*, 91 (1986), 1053–75; Joan Wallach Scott, 'Deconstructing equality versus difference; or, the uses of poststructuralist theory for feminism', *Feminist Studies*, 14 (1988), 33–50.

to a purpose exterior to it, a little of the political heat has gone out of the debate. Historians are now less likely to ascribe political attitudes to historians on the basis of their views of the past, or to claim that such and such an interpretation of the past necessarily dictates a particular political project. Although some still see gender theory as intrinsically 'anti-feminist', the connections between different schools of feminism and views of the past have become more complex, and research on women, gender and fascism is more likely to be treated on its merits. Interestingly, the contributors to the present volume rarely evoke explicitly the implications of their arguments for feminist practice, but many do explore the complex continuities and discontinuities between the women's movement in all its variety and the equally diverse extreme right. 'Political' controversy has not died out, but it has come, we shall see, from outside the ranks of those principally interested in women's and gender history.

Secondly, gender theory provided a new angle on the problem of women's agency. In this area gender theory tended to be read in two mutually contradictory ways, which perpetuated older debates in different ways. Some historians took up Joan Scott's point that ideas about gender are normally 'expressed in religious, educational, scientific, legal and political doctrines and typically take the form of a fixed binary opposition'. Ideas about gender might at particular times be contested, but one position eventually emerges as dominant and 'is stated as the only possible one'.[7] Femininity might then be expressed as the negative term of a binary opposition, and women might be seen as imprisoned within linguistic structures. Female agency (and indeed male agency) becomes a linguistically created illusion. This formulation of gender theory potentially reinforced the view that women's position in extreme-right movements and regimes was determined by patriarchal structures, as Bock argued it was.

There is, however, another way to read the treatment of agency in gender history. Scott also insisted that 'real men and women do not always or literally fulfil the terms either of their society's prescriptions or of our analytic categories'.[8] So patriarchal discourse might constrain women in theory, but whether it did so in practice was a matter for historical investigation. This approach had a precedent in the later work of Michel Foucault, who contended that the same identities which positioned some as the holders of power could be used by the subordinated to constitute their own identities and contest the

7 Scott, 'Gender: a useful category', pp. 1067–8.
8 Ibid., p. 1068.

dominant discourses.[9] This second approach to gender is not easy to reconcile with poststructuralist theory, in that it appears to reinstate the autonomous historical subject, but it has proved fruitful for historians, and it is well represented in this volume.[10]

The latter conception of agency potentially underpinned Koonz's suggestion that women were able to use the notion of domesticity as a basis for intervention in society and even formulate demands for equality. Koonz's own argument that separate spheres provided a discourse common to the Nazi leadership and female activists, but which was used in a manner differentiated by gender, already owed something to gender theory in one of its formulations. Gender theory's second view of agency opened the way to subtle interpretations in which women became both victims and victimisers.

Thirdly, this break with the 'either/or' polarities of earlier debates was part of a wider critique of essentialism. Whereas earlier interpretations tended to measure women's experience in terms of categories assumed to be objective and timeless, such as equality/inequality, progressive/conservative, or modern/traditional, gender theory problematised these oppositions. Attention now focuses more upon how they have been constructed and perceived in different historical circumstances.

Fourthly, just as gender historians have insisted that ideas about gender structure all aspects of social relations, so they have stressed that other forms of identity simultaneously structure gender discourses. Historians have therefore turned their attention to the way in which different identities intersect with one another. Again, this concern can be detected in the Koonz–Bock controversy. Gisela Bock proved to be a highly subtle practitioner of gender history. She perceptively criticised those who assumed that while ideas about gender were historically variable, biology remained fixed. Biology itself was a cultural construct, used to legitimate inequalities between men and women which did not derive from biological differences.[11] From a political perspective this formulation had the advantage of suggesting that women need not 'liber-

---

9 Michel Foucault, *Discipline and Punish: The Birth of the Prison* (London, Penguin, 1991), pp. 59–60.

10 I have suggested elsewhere that the linguistic theory of M. M. Bakhtin provides a good theoretical basis for much contemporary gender history. Kevin Passmore, '"Planting the tricolour in the citadels of communism": women's social action in the Croix de Feu and Parti social français', *Journal of Modern History*, 71 (1999), 814–51.

11 Gisela Bock, 'Women's history and gender history: aspects of an international debate', *Gender and History*, 1 (1989), 7–30.

ate' themselves from biology, as equality feminists advocated, for everything depended upon how biology was defined and how it was related to
other forms of social difference. From a historical perspective Bock's
approach permitted analysis of the interlinkage of Nazi racial and gender
discrimination. The Nazis distinguished between women on racial
grounds, regarding only Aryan women as sufficiently 'evolved' to play
a maternal role. Non-Aryan women were not regarded as fit to reproduce, and like non-Aryan men they were subject to sterilisation and
extermination, although in ways still differentiated by gender. 'National
Socialist racism', Bock concludes, 'was by no means gender neutral and
more than National Socialist sexism was race neutral.'[12] Recent work
on gender history has taken up this point, exploring the mutual construction of gender, race, religion, marital status and other sources of
identity.

To sum up so far, the specific historical questions raised in the
debate are as follows:

1 Are fascist movements intrinsically anti-feminist and/or anti-
   women?
2 What continuities and discontinuities are there between women's
   movements, feminist and non-feminist, and fascism?
3 Was fascism maternalist and/or familialist?
4 To what extent was women's role in fascist movements and
   regimes determined by patriarchal and/or gendered linguistic structures, and to what extent did separate spheres ideology provide an
   identity through which women could demand equality?
5 How did gender and political identities intersect with other forms
   of identity, such as class, religion, and above all nation and race?

The purpose of this book is to re-examine these controversies through
comparison of different national contexts – remembering gender
history's contention that national and gender identities are mutually
'constructing'. The book is also comparative in that it seeks to
examine the role of women and gender in both fascist and non-fascist
movements of the extreme right, in order to illuminate the distinctiveness of each.

This brings us to the second set of debates with which we are
concerned: what is the nature of generic fascism and how does it
differ (if at all) from the non-fascist extreme right? For the moment
it is sufficient to re-state a widely accepted distinction between on the
one hand non-fascist authoritarian movements and regimes, which are

---

12 Bock, 'Equality and difference in National Socialist racism'.

based on established institutions such as armies, civil services, monarchies and churches on the one hand, and on the other hand fascist movements and regimes which seek to bring to power a new elite organised in a mass party.

There is a methodological disjuncture between the two historiographical fields under consideration, in that whereas the study of women and gender in fascist movements has been increasingly influenced by poststructuralism, the study of generic fascism has not. Until the 1980s, Marxist and neo-Weberian approaches to fascism held sway. Marxists, whatever qualifications they added, held that fascism was 'ultimately' meaningful because of its relationship to capitalism. Neo-Weberians substituted the 'pre-industrial elites' (especially neo-feudal aristocrats) for capitalists as the orchestrators of fascism. However opposed these approaches were politically, both interpreted fascism as primarily conservative and saw it as subservient to the interests of powerful elites – both represented 'top-down' views of history. Marxists were at least interested in the history of the working class (usually conceived as resistant to fascism). But neither was especially interested in women or gender (it was this deficit that Bock, Koonz and others sought to fill). Insofar as Marxists and neo-Weberians were interested in gender relations, they emphasised the conservatism of fascisms' family policy, and they did not clearly distinguish between the place of women in fascist and non-fascist movements of the extreme right. Marxists saw women as instrumentalised by capitalists,[13] while neo-Weberians assumed that fascists' aim was to restore women to their pre-modern 'natural' domestic sphere. These interpretations tended to reinforce the view that fascism, like the non-fascist extreme right, was essentially misogynist, and that women played little role in it. As Kirsten Heinsohn suggests, historians, like historical protagonists, were swayed by prevailing prejudices about the 'apolitical' nature of woman, and their predilection for the domestic sphere.[14]

13 Annmarie Tröger, 'The creation of a female assembly-line proletariat', in Renate Bridenthal, Atina Grossmann and Marion Kaplan (eds), *When Biology Became Destiny* (New York, Monthly Review Press, 1984), pp. 237–70; Dave Renton, 'Women and fascism: a critique', *Socialist History*, 20 (2001), 71–81 argues that women were attracted to fascism because they were open to its use of sexual imagery. Thus while men join fascism for rational economic reasons, women do so because they are motivated by irrational desires and are easily manipulated.

14 M. Goot and E. Reid, 'Women: if not apolitical, then conservative', in J. Siltanen and M. Stanworth (eds), *Women and the Public Sphere* (London, Hutchinson, 1984), pp. 122–36.

In the 1990s theorists of generic fascism turned their attention away from underlying social forces towards the structures of fascist ideas. Notably, Roger Griffin has suggested that fascism has at its core a form of populist ultra-nationalism and a myth of national resurrection after a period of alleged decadence. Fascist movements are revolutionary in that they attempt to revitalise the decadent old order through a process of permanent mobilisation of the population in a nationalised, totalitarian society. In this view fascism is radically different from authoritarian conservatism, for the latter seeks to preserve established institutions.[15]

The idea that fascism is a form of revolutionary ultra-nationalism might have stimulated convergence between the study of generic fascism and the history of women and gender, and generated new understandings in each. No such cross-fertilisation has occurred. One reason is perhaps that those who see fascism primarily as a form of ultra-nationalism have revived the once-forgotten concept of totalitarianism, with its assumptions about control from above. Despite the view that fascism is revolutionary, recourse to totalitarian theory reaffirms the assumption that women were essentially victims of fascism.

Another potential reason why historians of generic fascism neglect women and gender is that they distrust the poststructuralist method that underlies so much recent work in the latter field. This suspicion is understandable, given that some have charged that poststructuralist relativism leaves the door open to far-right historians who wish to depict the Holocaust as 'just a story'.[16] If we take poststructuralist theory as espoused by Jacques Derrida, or by some historians and literary critics, there might be some truth in this, for taken to its logical conclusion, poststructuralism arguably deprives us of any means of distinguishing between more and less valid accounts of the past. Yet poststructuralism as practised by historians, including most gender historians, generally has only a tenuous link with poststructuralist theory proper. This history generally combines some aspects of poststructuralism – the critique of essentialism and the deconstruction of binary oppositions and grand narratives – with a historical method which in practice is rather similar to that advocated by earlier

15 Roger Griffin, *The Nature of Fascism* (London, Pinter, 1991); Kevin Passmore,
    Fascism (Oxford, Oxford University Press, 2002).
16 Richard J. Evans, *In Defence of History* (London, Granta, 1997), pp. 238–43. See
    also the essays by Saul Friedlander, Hayden White, Hans Kellner, Wulf Kunsteiner
    and Beryl Lang reprinted in Keith Jenkins (ed.), *The Postmodern History Reader*
    (London, Routledge, 1997), pp. 387–443.

critics of Marxist and other grand narratives, such as Karl Popper and Imre Lakatos.[17] These empiricists advocate a method of 'objectivity from a point of view'. It transcends the simplistic binary opposition between the relativism of poststructuralist theory and the 'reconstruction' preached by some 'defenders of history'. Ironically, in poststructuralist historical practice, radical and conservative critiques of positivist history converge – another salutatory warning of the complex relationship between scholarly debates and political positions. It is also worth noting in passing that there are some similarities between the gender history of fascism and the researches of German historians of 'everyday life' (*Alltagsgeschichte*). Although the latter start from a different philosophical position, their histories demonstrate difficulties of using simple oppositions between consent and resistance to understand the position of workers under Nazism.[18]

In practice, then, 'practical poststructuralism' and gender history might have something to offer the study of generic fascism. First, for example, just as gender historians problematised the meaning of the category woman within fascism, one might re-think the relationship between fascism and 'underlying' social forces of any kind. The fascist desire to remake a decadent world through radical nationalism, rightly emphasised by Roger Griffin, might be as much a notion constructed by fascist militants as the product of a genuine decay of accepted values.

Secondly, gender historians have deconstructed the binary oppositions in terms of which women's position within fascism was traditionally understood. Women are no longer seen simply as such as victims or victimisers, but as both simultaneously. *Mutatis mutandis*, it might be possible to re-think the terms in which generic fascism more broadly has been understood – modern/traditional, revolutionary/ reactionary, resistance/oppression. Fascism, after all, is notoriously contradictory, preaching order and practising disorder, denouncing capitalists yet enriching them, calling for the return of women to the home, yet encouraging them to join political organisations. Historians of generic fascism have tended to dismiss one side of fascism as 'secondary', 'tactical' or 'less important'. Marxists explain away the radical side

17 Karl Popper, *The Poverty of Historicism* (London, Routledge, 1986, first published 1957); Imre Lakatos, *The Methodology of Scientific Research Programmes: Philosophical Papers*, Vol. 1 (Cambridge, Cambridge University Press, 1978).
18 For example, Alf Lüdtke, 'The appeal of exterminating "others": German workers and the limits of resistance', *Journal of Modern History*, 64 Issue Supplement: 'Resistance against the Third Reich', (1992), S46–S67.

of fascism as a device to fool the workers into supporting it, while those who see fascism as a form of radical nationalism see its alliances with conservatives as merely 'tactical'. Following gender historians, we might attempt to grasp fascism in its contradictions.

2

Italy

Perry Willson

Italy, as the pioneer of European fascism, found itself in a unique position in the panorama of far-right movements and regimes discussed in the other chapters of this book. Women in the National Fascist Party (Partito Nazionale Fascista, PNF) lacked specific role models to follow and when Mussolini came to power in 1922 the way in which gender roles would be shaped under the regime of the blackshirts was not a foregone conclusion. The new party's gender ideology was still, to an extent, fluid.

Italian Fascism remained in power for over twenty years (far longer than the Nazis in Germany) and some of the dynamics that shaped shifting gender relations were produced by the need to maintain governability over time in a changing situation. Although many male Fascist hierarchs had quite clear views on what were proper gender roles – fairly traditional, misogynist views on the whole – the international situation, economic developments and the fear of a resurgence of class conflict gradually increased the importance of women's role within the party.

This role was primarily in welfare activities. In this respect women in the PNF did not behave in a fundamentally different way from many non-fascist female activists in other European countries in this period. Indeed, Fascist women displayed a great deal of interest in the activities and achievements of foreign women, and despite the regime's emphasis on nationalism and autarky, delegations of Fascist women attended international women's conferences throughout the *ventennio*. But although women's involvement in nascent welfare states (and indeed in populationist policies) was by no means confined to Italy during the inter-war years, the way in which Italian women followed this broader European trend was heavily conditioned by the specific context in which they found themselves. The context was dictatorship and the suppression of free speech and civil liberties, extreme nationalism leading to imperialism and war, and the virtual powerlessness of women within the political hierarchy. Ultimately Italian Fascism was a regime made by and for the interests of men. Within this unpromising context, however, certain, largely middle-class women were able to carve out new roles for themselves in the name of service to the state.

The first decade: 1919–29

Initially it was by no means clear whether women were going to have any sort of role in the party. The vast majority of early PNF members were male. Right from the start, however, there were women who attempted to claim a place in the new movement. Initially numbers were small. There were only nine women at the founding meeting of the blackshirt movement in Piazza San Sepolcro in Milan in March 1919, and only tiny numbers of largely young, petty bourgeois women who became involved in *squadristi* activities such as strikebreaking.[1]

Soon, however, some Fascist women began to organise separately. Although at first women like the young 'Fascist *squadrista* heroine' Ines Donati[2] had joined mixed (almost all-male) groups (the Fasci di Combattimento), it was not long before women-only groups (the Fasci Femminili) appeared. The first was founded in March 1920 in Monza (Milan) and was soon followed by others, mainly in northern and central urban areas. Like the male 'Fascists of the first hour', the members of these women's groups were fairly diverse. They included both those who saw the new movement as one which would radically transform Italy as well as more conservative elements, largely from the traditional elites, who valued the movement essentially as a means of defeating the 'red threat'. The early Fasci Femminili had many urban lower-middle-class members but even at this stage the leaders tended to come mainly from a higher social milieu, being upper-middle-class or, in many cases, aristocrats.[3] Many of these early

---

1 On female *squadristi* see D. Detriagache, 'Il fascismo femminile da San Sepolcro all'affare Matteotti (1919-1925)', *Storia contemporanea*, 14:2 (1983), 225–30.

2 See I. Rinaldi, 'Ines Donati: realtà e mito di un'"eroina" fascista', *Quaderni di Resistenza Marche*, 13 (1987), 48–89.

3 Much research still remains to be done on the lives of prominent female Fascists. A few biographical works exist. See, for example, H. Dittrich-Johansen, 'Strategie femminili nel ventennio fascista: la carriera politica di Piera Gatteschi Fondelli nello "Stato degli uomini" (1919-1943)', *Storia e problemi contemporanei*, 21 (1998), 65–86; D. Detriagache, 'Du socialisme au fascisme naissant: formation et itinéraire de Regina Terruzzi', in R. Thalmann (ed.), *Femmes et fascismes* (Paris, Tièrce, 1986); F. Taricone, *Teresa Labriola: Biografia politica di un'intellettuale tra Ottocento e Novecento* (Milan, Angeli, 1994).

leaders were not particularly young and already had some previous experience of public life, whether in political or philanthropic organisations. For some of them the events in Fiume had proved formative in drawing them to right-wing politics, and indeed some of the women involved in early Fascism saw themselves primarily as irredentists rather than Fascists. Many were unmarried or widowed or with children already grown up. In keeping with their generally higher social status their average level of education tended to be somewhat higher than that of the male hierarchs of this early period.[4] A substantial number of the early leaders were feminists.

The conversion of these feminists to Fascism is one reason why Italian historians have proved generally reluctant to study this topic.[5] Indeed, until recently, much of the historiography has been written by foreigners who tend to feel less emotionally tied up with the question.[6] Although now a number of younger Italian scholars[7] have begun to turn their attention to the role of Fascist women (the members of the Fasci Femminili), many Italian feminist historians have (quite understandably) preferred to concentrate on the more inspiring, heroic topic of the role of female anti-fascists.[8]

Many feminists were, nonetheless, present in the early period of

4 On the class composition of the early leaders see H. Dittrich-Johansen, 'Le professioniste del PNF', *Studi storici*, 42:1 (2001), 190–4.

5 As Dittrich-Johansen has argued, research on this topic has also been held back by the fact that many historians have dismissed the need to study local party hierarchs (whether male or female) and by the problem of sources, including a dearth of autobiographical material written by the female hierarchs themselves. Ibid., 182–6.

6 Undoubtedly the most influential work on this topic is by an American: V. De Grazia, *How Fascism Ruled Women. Italy 1922–1945* (Berkeley, California University Press, 1992). See also R. Pickering-Iazzi (ed.), *Mothers of Invention: Women, Italian Fascism and Culture* (Minneapolis, University of Minnesota Press, 1995). Italians have not, however, been totally absent in this field. See, for example, the pioneering, if now somewhat dated, P. Meldini, *Sposa e madre esemplare: ideologia e politica della donna e della famiglia durante il fascismo* (Florence, Guaraldi, 1975).

7 In particular the work of the young historian Helga Dittrich-Johansen (who, despite her name, is Italian) should be noted here.

8 There is a good Italian-language historiography on this topic, some hagiographic, some more analytical. Two recent interesting examples are P. Gabrielli, *Fenicotteri in volo: donne comuniste nel ventennio fascista* (Rome, Carocci, 1999) and G. De Luna, *Donne in oggetto: l'antifascismo nella società italiana (1922–1939)* (Turin, Bollati Boringhieri, 1996). See also M. Gibson, 'Women and the Left in the shadow of Fascism in Interwar Italy', in H. Gruber and P. Graves (eds), *Women and Socialism, Socialism and Women: Europe Between the Wars* (New York and Oxford, Berghahn, 1998).

the Fascist movement. For many of them, the catalyst for involvement was quite clearly the First World War. During the war, although some feminists had opposed it, arguing that women were by nature pacifist beings, others had moved over to an interventionist position. They began to portray women's role on the home front as an essential element of modern mechanised warfare. Consequently, they argued, female suffrage and equal legal rights were necessary to ensure that women felt fully part of the nation they were called upon to serve.[9] For some of these women it was but a small ideological step from this patriotic stance to the new blackshirt movement. Their new roles during the war had given many a taste for an active public life. Many middle-class and upper-class women who rallied to the Fascist cause had done various types of welfare work during the war and some, mainly aristocrats, had been Red Cross volunteer nurses.[10]

In general, however, the small numbers of women who became Fascists in the early period, whether feminists or not, chose to do so essentially as members of their class rather than of their gender. Undoubtedly many middle-class women were, quite simply, convinced by Fascist politics and, together with others of their class, believed that Mussolini and his followers could save them from the Bolshevik menace and restore the honour of the nation. Moreover, none of the other political parties had so far managed to deliver substantial improvements to female rights. For many nationalist and irredentist women who also thought of themselves as feminists, this new movement must have seemed as good as the rest on gender questions.

Indeed, at first the new movement did not seem to be particularly misogynous and its first programme even promised the core feminist demand of suffrage. But many male 'Fascists of the first hour' were far from encouraging towards the new women's groups. They regarded Fascism as a fundamentally masculine movement and propaganda frequently stressed supposedly 'virile' virtues such as war heroism, action and so on.[11] Such men wanted women to confine

9 See E. Schiavon, 'L'interventismo femminista', *Passato e presente*, 19:54 (2001), 59–72. See also S. Bartoloni, 'L'associazionismo femminile nella prima guerra mondiale e la mobilitazione per l'assistenza civile e la propaganda', in A. Gigli Marchetti and N. Torcellan (eds), *Donna lombarda* (Milan, Angeli, 1992).

10 On Italian Red Cross nurses in the First World War see S. Bartoloni (ed.), *Donne al fronte: le infermiere volontarie nella Grande Guerra* (Rome, Jouvence, 1998).

11 On Italian Fascism and masculinity see B. Spackman, *Fascist Virilities: Rhetoric, Ideology and Social Fantasy in Italy* (Minneapolis, University of Minnesota Press, 1996).

themselves entirely to support roles.[12] This was, to a degree, a reflection of the broader post-war backlash against women's increased participation in the public sphere. Many women were being expelled from wartime employment to make way for returning soldiers.[13] In 1921, when the Fascist movement officially constituted itself as a political party for the first time, draft regulations were drawn up for the women's groups that defined them as internal sections of the Fasci di Combattimento. They were to be under the control of the male heads of each Fascio and their task was to be confined essentially to propaganda and welfare work.

Despite this, somewhat paradoxically, the general disinterest of the hierarchs in women's political role gave early female Fascists a certain degree of autonomy. They were left to organise their own conferences and even to lobby for feminist demands such as the vote. Their press in this period, when open debate was still possible, is a rather odd mix of patriotism and feminism, and, as Stefania Bartoloni has noted, often expressed 'positions that were later persecuted by the regime'.[14] At the end of 1924, in the aftermath of the Matteotti affair, Mussolini appointed the former Red Cross nurse and 'Fascist of the first hour' Elisa Majer Rizzioli to the new position of Inspectress of the Fascist Women's Groups with a seat on the Party Directorate. Majer Rizzioli was a patriot and moderate feminist who aspired to real power for PNF women.

Regardless of her moderate position, however, Mussolini's choice of someone from the 'feminist' wing of the movement was immediately opposed by most male hierarchs. Their hostility to her viewpoint was reflected in the new Fasci Femminili regulations that were drawn up by the Party Directorate. Although a congress of Fascist women held in Milan in June 1924 had drawn up its own draft regulations which would have given women far more equality with male PNF members, this proposal was simply ignored and a different document imposed which removed the last vestiges of female autonomy. The

---

12 On women and early Fascism see the detailed and careful reconstruction in Detriagache, 'Il fascismo femminile da San Sepolcro'. See also S. Bartoloni, 'Dalla crisi del movimento delle donne alle origini del fascismo: "L'Almanacco della donna italiana" e la "Rassegna femminile italiana"', in A. Crispino (ed.), *Esperienza storica femminile nell'età moderna e contemporanea* (Rome, UDI, 1988).

13 On women's employment in the First World War and post-war attempts to expel women from the labour force see B. Curli, *Italiane al lavoro 1914–1920* (Venice, Marsilio, 1998).

14 Bartoloni, 'Dalla crisi del movimento delle donne', p. 130.

vote, furthermore, central to the demands of even the most moderate of the feminists, was granted, in a cruel gesture, to certain, very limited categories of women in November 1925, just as democracy itself was in the process of disappearing.

Majer Rizzioli herself did not last long after this. At the end of 1925 Party Secretary Roberto Farinacci moved against the women's groups. He closed down Majer Rizzioli's newspaper the *Rassegna femminile italiana*[15] and in January 1926 abolished the Women's Inspectorate, forcing Majer Rizzioli herself to resign. From this date on the women's Fasci were directly controlled by the Party Secretariat. To reinforce this a man – Serafino Mazzolini – was put in charge. The attack on party feminists was not confined to Majer Rizzioli. Others were deemed similarly too troublesome by the male hierarchs and during the mid to late 1920s a number of local leaders, such as Maria Spinelli Monticelli of Milan and Pia Bartolini of Bologna, were purged. Their crime had been to attempt to resist the sidelining of women in the party.[16]

Augusto Turati, who succeeded Farinacci in March 1926, was not much more encouraging to the women's groups. His attitude can be seen in a circular he sent round to all the Fasci Femminili secretaries in May 1926, rebuffing a demand from Fascist women to be allowed to wear black shirts. This stated bluntly that: 'The black shirt is the virile symbol of our revolution and has nothing to do with the welfare tasks that Fascism has given women'.[17] Turati appointed Angiola Moretti, previously Majer Rizzioli's clerical assistant, as Secretary to the Women's Groups. Only twenty-seven years old, Moretti was too young to have dabbled much with feminism and ambitious enough not to cause trouble.

This clampdown on feminist ideas among female Fascists was

---

15 Although it was supposed to be the official organ of the Fasci Femminili, the newspaper was entirely personally financed by Elisa Majer Rizzioli herself. On Majer Rizzioli and her newspaper see S. Bartoloni, 'Il fascismo femminile e la sua stampa: la "Rassegna Femminile Italiana" (1925–1930)', *Nuova DonnaWomanFemme,* 21 (1982), 143–69; Bartoloni, 'Dalla crisi del movimento delle donne'; E. Santarelli, 'Protagoniste femminili del primo Novecento', *Problemi del socialismo,* 4 (1976), 249–50.

16 H. Dittrich-Johansen, 'Per la Patria e per il Duce: storie di fedeltà femminili nell'Italia fascista', *Genesis,* 1:1 (2002), 125–56. Bartolini was one of the more radical of the Fascist women who spoke explicitly of 'Fascist feminism'. See Detriagache, 'Il fascismo femminile da San Sepolcro', 231.

17 Circular from Turati, 14 May 1926, conserved in Archivio di Stato di Treviso, Fondo PNF Conegliano, Busta 26.

accompanied by an ideological backlash. In 1927 the demographic campaign was launched with the 'Ascension Day Speech' in which Mussolini called on Italians to reverse the falling birth-rate. In this period his speeches and other Fascist propaganda referred increasingly not to rights but to duties to the nation, duties which were separate and specific according to gender. For women this meant maternity, which was relentlessly stressed.

Here feminists found themselves caught in a slippery trap since pre-fascist feminism had also been much preoccupied with the social value of maternity. Many of its political demands had been couched in social maternalist language. Thus when Fascism founded the National Organisation for Mother and Child (Opera Nazionale per la Maternità ed Infanzia, ONMI) in 1925 and launched the demographic campaign two years later, dubbing the falling birth-rate 'the problem of problems', some women felt that at last things for which they had long campaigned were being granted.[18]

It is important to stress that far from all feminists became Fascists (it was largely the more moderate and conservative among them who did so), and that, of those who did, not all continued to support Fascism after the abolition of the last vestiges of democracy in 1925. Others, however, continued to be involved, although often at the cost of a certain amount of torment and confusion. Many felt betrayed by new laws limiting female professional employment and by the fact that Mussolini had promised them the vote and then taken it away. Some former feminists, such as Teresa Labriola, however, managed to rationalise their conversion to Fascism by dubbing their party activities, after a few ideological gymnastics, 'Latin feminism'. This was supposedly an Italian reformulation of feminism. It stressed, unlike 'sterile foreign doctrines' which emphasised individualism and equal rights, the importance of women's maternal duty to family and nation. As De Grazia has argued, however, male and female Fascists saw these things differently, for 'Latin feminists saw [sexual] difference as meaning complementarity and collaboration between men and women, whereas Fascist men understood it to mean sexual hierarchy and female subordination'.[19]

18 On ONMI see A. Bresci, 'L'Opera nazionale maternità ed infanzia nel ventennio fascista', *Italia contemporanea*, 192 (1993), 421–42. On the demographic campaign see, for example, C. Ipsen, *Dictating Demography: The Problem of Population in Fascist Italy* (Cambridge, Cambridge University Press, 1996); M. S. Quine, *Population Politics in Twentieth Century Europe* (London, Routledge, 1996), ch. 1.
19 De Grazia, *How Fascism Ruled Women*, p. 238.

The progressive control exerted over PNF women in the mid to late
1920s can be seen quite clearly in their press. Lively debate gradually
disappeared. This process continued in the following decade. By the
late 1930s the three party women's newspapers – *La donna fascista*
(which had become the official Fasci Femminili newspaper in 1929
under its former name *Giornale della donna*),[20] *La massaia rurale*
(for rural women) and *Lavoro e famiglia* (for workers) – were all drab
official publications filled with dull propaganda.[21]

The 1930s

The next step in the process of subordinating the women's groups to
the male hierarchy came in 1930 when even Moretti's post was abolished, leaving the women's groups effectively leaderless. Central
party control was further reinforced in May of the following year,
after which all nominations for local fiduciaries became subject to the
approval of the male hierarchs in party headquarters in Rome.

Once control was firmly in place, it was safe to allow women's
activities to expand. The background to this was the transformation of
the PNF itself in the early 1930s, the period when it became increasingly bureaucratic and depoliticised. Under the guidance of the
unintelligent and unimaginative Achille Starace (Fascist party leader
for most of the decade), a massive membership drive was launched
for the party and its ancillary organisations. In the new policy of
'going to the people', the women's groups proliferated rapidly. From
1932, it was compulsory for every local party branch to have a Fascio
Femminile. One was to be automatically created wherever the local
party had at least ten female members over the age of twenty-two.
Each local Fascio Femminile was run by a Secretary and she was
supervised by a Provincial Fiduciary. This all-female chain of
command was, however, always subordinate to the male party hierarchy and the tasks and duties of Fascist women were simply assigned
them from above.

With this structure, the PNF was poised to become the first Italian
political party with a truly mass female membership. The novelty of

---

20 Previous to this Turati had allowed the *Rassegna italiana femminile* to reopen
temporarily but only in a more propagandistic and less feminist guise.
21 On *La massaia rurale* see P. R. Willson, '"Domus rustica" e "L'Azione delle
massaie rurali": due riviste per contadine negli anni del fascismo', in S. Soldani and
S. Franchini (eds), *Donne e giornalismo: politica e cultura di genere nella stampa
'femminile'* (Milan, Angeli, forthcoming).

the mobilisation in the 1930s, as many commentators have noted, should not be underestimated. For all its rhetoric about women's role being primarily as 'exemplary wives and mothers', with this attempt to recruit millions of women the regime was clearly doing something new. Women now were asked to demonstrate their active support for Fascism and play a role in forging the 'consensus' that the regime desired. This meant, essentially, various types of welfare work.

Fascist welfare

One factor that needs to be taken into account when seeking to explain the conversion of some feminists to Fascism was the seamless continuity of many of the Fasci Femminili activities with women's philanthropic role before Fascism. Even feminists had been deeply engaged in welfare work in the name of so-called 'practical feminism'.[22] Fascist welfare frequently differed from such initiatives more in its propagandistic messages and the sheer scale of its operations than in its precise activities. It is clear that many Fascist women engaged in running party welfare programmes did genuinely believe that they were doing 'good work', offering a helping hand to those in need. Many of the causes Fascism asked them to support, such as running the much publicised holiday camps for poor and sickly children, must have seemed a perfectly worthwhile outlet for their energies. Fascist welfare was, however, stripped of any emancipationist ideology. It was to be selfless service by an army of dutiful women carrying out orders for the greater good of the state and nation.

Fascist women were engaged in party welfare work during the entire *ventennio*. In the 1920s this was deemed largely a peripheral activity of the party, something considered relatively unimportant, which could be safely left to the women's Fasci.[23] In the context of the world economic depression, however, welfare took on new importance as a central plank in the regime's attempts to forge a consensus or at least to prevent the eruption of open social unrest. From the early 1930s party women provided the volunteer labour required to enable the Fascist propaganda machine to sing the praises of how

22 For a case study of 'practical feminism' see A. Buttafuoco. *Le Mariuccine: storia di un'istituzione laica. L'Asilo Mariuccia* (Milan, Angeli, 1988).
23 For a general description of the sorts of welfare activities in which Fascist women engaged in this early period see Partito Nazionale Fascista, *Fasci Femminili* (Rome, Libreria d'Italia, 1929).

caring the regime was. This made them essential agents of Fascist domestic policy: without their voluntary work party welfare schemes would have collapsed. This potentially could have had far-reaching consequences for the regime's 'consensus' strategy and affected the durability of the dictatorship itself. A number of historians have noted this aspect but generally without any real recognition of the gender dimensions of this shift in the role of the party. Massimo Storchi, for example, (writing about the Reggio Emilia PNF Federation in the early 1930s) has argued that:

> The PNF was changing, due to the urgency of the situation, from a political and military organisation to a welfare-charitable structure. The goal was, after all, to take on a role which could be defined as almost maternal, assisting the defenceless and needy masses. Once they had perceived how impossible it was to do anything about the causes of misery and the crisis, individual fascists became the charitable arm of a State, which, nonetheless, did not want to miss anyone out. In return for a daily bowl of soup, it obtained grateful support towards the hand that gave it. This was, essentially, already effectively the core of the idea of the 'bread card'. This idea did, nonetheless, represent a real innovation for those social strata normally neglected by those in power and who were used to lives constrained by day to day survival.[24]

Welfare activities played a role in a number of other Fascist policies such as the 'Battle for Births' (the campaign to stem the decline in the birth rate) and the ruralisation campaign which sought to keep the peasantry on the land. Welfare, furthermore, provided a useful channel into poorer homes. Whilst distributing powdered baby milk or layettes or packets of vegetable seeds, the *visitatrici fasciste* (Fascist home visitors) could bring propaganda into the heart of millions of families. As the new directives from Rome summed this up in 1932:

> The Fasci Femminili are entrusted with the task of putting into practice the programme of welfare initiatives organised by the party. This is an extremely powerful means of propaganda and a good way of reaching out to the people. In particular the Fascist women are assigned the work of providing the direct assistance to humble folk which is offered daily in the local Fascio headquarters or, by means of the Fascist home visitors, in the homes of the poor and abandoned.
> These complex and varied initiatives of moral and material assistance

---

24 M. Storchi, 'Un Ventennio Reggiano: attività e organizzazione del PNF a Reggio Emilia', *Contributi*, 10:19–20 (1986), 210.

are exquisitely feminine and could not be entrusted to other organisations with a greater chance of success.[25]

In the field of welfare, Fascist women were very active. Even in
the late 1920s their activities already included organising the girls'
groups, running sewing workshops, teaching domestic science
courses, visiting pregnant women in their homes, handing out milk
and layettes to impoverished mothers and staffing children's holiday
camps. In the 1930s their responsibilities increased vertiginously. A
Fascist woman might find herself engaged in, amongst other things,
running nurseries for olive pickers' children or information centres
for peasant women or domestic servants, or teaching child-care
methods to the girls' groups to prepare them for their future 'maternal mission'. She might work with migrant rice-workers by inspecting
their dormitories, running refreshment stalls for them at railway
stations, or organising morally suitable recreation activities to keep
them from the 'dangers' of local dance halls. Her tasks could involve
visiting the homes of welfare recipients, assisting medical staff in
paediatric or obstetric clinics, raising funds through lotteries or lucky
dips, inspecting chicken coops for national poultry competitions or
supervising collective radio listening sessions for peasant women.

Particularly in northern and central areas many sections were a
hive of activity. The level of activity is particularly impressive given
the fact that most of it was run on an absolute shoestring, for the party
offered virtually no funding to the women's Fasci. Most of their
budget, apart from the income from membership fees, had to be raised
by running lotteries, begging for donations from local wealthy
persons, requesting special levies from the Fascist women themselves,
and so on.

War

The Ethiopian War, and the series of 'Fascist wars' which followed
it, brought Fascist women a further range of new challenges.
Fascism's glorification of warfare was, of course, related closely to
notions of manliness in Fascist propaganda.[26] Man as warrior would

25 'Organizzazioni Femminili Fasciste', Foglio d'Ordini no. 81, 26 May Fascist Year
IX (1931/32).
26 See, for example, on the notion that Ethiopian War was construed by Mussolini as
a kind of proof of Italian virility, S. Falaschi-Zamponi, *Fascist Spectacle: The
Aesthetics of Power in Mussolini's Italy* (Berkeley, California University Press,
1997), p. 181.

reclaim the nation's honour that had been lost at the Battle of Caporetto and in the failed imperialist ventures of the Liberal period. Such Fascist attempts to restore the reputation of Italian masculinity, however, inevitably also led to an expansion of female roles on the 'home front' and a shift in both activities and the language used to address women. Much recent historiography of the impact of wars on gender relations has, of course, tended to stress the highly transitory nature of the upheaval in gender roles brought by warfare while men are at the front and women take over tasks previously not seen as in their sphere. In the case of Fascist Italy, however, the consequences may have been more far-reaching since the period of warfare was so lengthy (effectively from 1935 until the fall of the regime).

Easily the best known aspect of women's mobilisation for the Ethiopian War, the public sacrifice of their wedding rings in the 'Day of Faith' ceremonies,[27] seemed only to confirm them in traditional roles as wives and mothers. But the war effort also opened up a far greater public role for Italian women, called to the service of the nation in response to the League of Nations sanctions. Party activists attempted to mobilise all Italian women, both as consumers and as producers, for the autarky campaign, and propaganda stressed their central role to the national cause. They also were to bring assistance, solace and propaganda to soldiers' wives. Special women's committees threw themselves into an organisational frenzy to manage all these new activities and the party women's press was swept along in a flood of war-faring rhetoric and patriotism. Women were exhorted to make sacrifices, including sacrificing their own sons. To pick but one example from many, as one writer, Lucilla Arciello, wrote in *La donna fascista* in April 1936, there was no greater glory for a true Fascist woman than to give her sons to the nation:

> How sad, how very sad it is to be barren at a time when the mother-land is asking for sons! And how proud it makes a mother, rich in children, who is able to offer her country not one but two or three sons. The smile of glory enters homes where brave youths have left empty spaces ... A mother who, today, bent over an unfolded newspaper, reads of the victorious advance and in her soul follows the route of her soldier son, is happier than a childless woman who watches the others' fervour as if it were nothing to do with her and smiles: but her soul is far away.[28]

---

27 The name of this day – '*giornata della fede*' – is ambiguous. It can be translated as either 'day of faith' or 'wedding ring day'.
28 L. Arciello, 'La donna fascista', *La donna fascista*, 18:7 (1 April 1936), 3.

Even after the actual sanctions ended, the autarky campaign, which had proved a useful mobilisation tool, was not abandoned and women continued to be urged to do their bit for the nation. This period also saw the creation of courses to prepare Fascist women and girls from the party youth groups for 'colonial life' in the new Empire, instructing them in things like specialised types of first aid and camping skills. The proliferation of activities continued after this, and during the early part of the Second World War Fascist women were given a role in civil defence and the mobilisation of the civilian population on the 'home front'.

As time went on, the limitations of amateur voluntarism became increasingly apparent and training of various types was introduced. For most this meant only short courses such as those for 'Fascist home visitors' and those for 'assistants and directors of children's holiday camps'. More in-depth residential education for a few was available at the elite female sports academy in Orvieto and in the three party women's colleges in Rome which trained domestic science teachers, rural primary school teachers and factory social workers.[29] These offered residential training and issued their own diplomas at the end of the courses that each lasted a year. Shorter forms of training were also increasingly developed for those already in leadership positions. One method was the *'turni di servizio'* (service rotas) whereby Provincial Fiduciaries were briefly (usually for a week in July during school holidays) transferred to another province to observe its organisational methods. It was only in 1940 that a more formal training programme emerged when a two-month national training course was run in Rome for ninety women aspiring to take up provincial leadership positions. The following year this was repeated, this time preceded by local courses.[30]

Class and hierarchy

The class composition of the Fasci Femminili members has never been subject to systematic historical analysis but all the evidence

29 On the Orvieto academy see M. Rossi Caponeri and L. Motti (eds), *Accademiste di Orvieto: donne ed educazione fisica nell'Italia fascista 1932–1943* (Perugia, Quattroemme, 1996). On the colleges in Rome see, for example, Anon., 'Le tre Scuole Superiori Femminili del Partito si riapriranno nella prima decade di ottobre', *Giornale della donna*, 15:18 (15 September 1933), 1–2.

30 See Anon., 'Il primo corso nazionale di preparazione per dirigenti delle Organizzazioni femminili del PNF', *La donna fascista*, 22:23 (17 November 1940), 6; Anon., 'Il secondo Corso Nazionale di Preparazione per dirigenti delle organizzazioni femminili del Partito Nazionale Fascista', *La donna fascista*, 22:44 (30 September 1941), 11.

suggests that it was predominantly middle- or upper-class. In the 1930s, as the number of members increased, the class base of the mass membership does seem to have widened slightly but even in this period aristocrats continued to monopolise many of the higher-ranking leadership positions. Many Provincial Fiduciaries came from this class. There were also many professionals (mainly teachers) and middle-class housewives who took organisational roles at all levels. Particularly in rural areas the mainstay of the organisation at lower levels was an army of primary school teachers. In the provinces of Reggio Emilia, Belluno, Pavia and Cosenza, for example, almost all the local section secretaries were primary school teachers.[31]

Despite the expansion of their duties, Fascist women never obtained any actual political power and were not allowed to formulate any of their own policy except at the most local level. After 1930 they did not even have a proper national leadership. Admittedly, in the late 1930s, such was the increased level of activity, created in particular by the autarky campaign and the growth in membership numbers, that National Inspectresses eventually became necessary to deal with the rapidly spiralling demands of running the women's organisations. But although much research remains to be done on their role,[32] it seems clear that even they, the highest ranking of the Fascist women, remained excluded from the real corridors of power. Their main task was to ensure that central policy was carried out locally. Those appointed to these new, salaried positions were, at least initially, all party stalwarts with years of unpaid service as local federation leaders behind them.

After the outbreak of the Second World War Fascist women made other, albeit small, political gains. They got a seat on PNF Provincial Directories for the first time in 1940 and in December of the same year they even moved into local corporative bodies. The Fasci Femminili Provincial Fiduciaries secured a seat on the committees which helped oversee local economic affairs.[33] The

31 A. Zavaroni, 'La donna del fascio: I La donna che comprese il buon cuore del Duce', *L'almanacco*, 32 (1999), 35–79; V. Cappelli, *Il fascismo in periferia: il caso della Calabria* (Rome, Riuniti, 1992), p. 143; E. Signori, 'Il Partito Nazionale Fascista a Pavia', in M. L. Betri et al. (eds), *Il fascismo in Lombardia* (Milan, Angeli, 1989), p. 87; F. Vendramini, 'Guerra e donne nel giornale Bellunese "Dolomiti"', *Protagonisti*, 39 (1990), 4.

32 De Grazia, *How Fascism Ruled Women*, does not even list their names, although she gives some useful information on the careers of a few of them.

33 Foglio di Disposizioni no. 24, 18 December Fascist Year XIX (1940/41).

importance of this, in symbolic terms at least, should not be missed, for the corporate state was theoretically the Fascist substitute for democracy. It was also in this period, just after the outbreak of the Second World War, that the women's Fasci for the first time got their own central committee.

Such slight widening of their political influence did not, however, substantially change their subordinate position in the party pecking order and the only sphere where Fascist women ever had real power was over other women, the poorer women who were the recipients of party welfare. Eventually it was decided to recruit such women too into the party. The class composition of the Fasci Femminili was safeguarded by channelling new recruits into two special separate, dependent sections: one for peasants and one for working-class women. The first to be set up was for peasant women. The foundation of this section marked a turning point as previously the PNF (in common with most other political parties before it) had shown little interest in rural women, apart from the relatively small numbers who worked as waged farm-labourers, like rice-weeders. But such waged workers, many of whom had previously been members of socialist trade unions, represented only a small percentage of the millions on the land and eventually Fascist attention turned to wider categories of rural women, such as sharecroppers, smallholders and small tenant farmers. In 1933 a special federation was founded for them as part of the Fascist farmworkers' union. Headed by a retired schoolteacher, the former socialist *sansepolcrista* Regina Terruzzi, the following year it was absorbed into the party itself to become the Rural Housewives Section (Massaie Rurali, MR) of the Fasci Femminili.[34]

This section developed an extensive training programme that aimed to improve the lives of rural women without altering rural class relations, land tenure arrangements or the gender hierarchy of the rural household. Peasant women were trained to carry out 'women's agricultural and household activities' in a 'modern and rational' manner, supposedly following the tenets of the 'rational farming' movement

---

34 On the MR see P. R. Willson, *Peasant Women and Politics in Fascist Italy: the Massaie Rurali* (London, Routledge, 2002); P. R. Willson, 'Cooking the patriotic omelette: women and the Italian Fascist ruralisation campaign', *European History Quarterly*, 27:4 (1997), 531–47. See also V. De Grazia, 'Contadine e "massaie rurali" durante il fascismo', *Annali Cervi*, 13 (1991), 151–76; S. Salvatici, *Contadine dell'Italia fascista: presenze, ruoli, immagini* (Turin, Rosenberg & Sellier, 1999); A. Amoroso, 'Le organizzazioni femminili nelle campagne durante il fascismo', *Storia in Lombardia*, 1–2 (1989), 305–16.

(the application of Taylorism to agriculture). To encourage the take-up of training, numerous competitions were held. Most of the courses and competitions focused on domestic science, hygiene and child-care and on what were seen as female roles in agriculture such as poultry and rabbit farming, handicraft manufacturing and vegetable gardening. The farming courses were taught mainly by men from the agricultural corporative organisations since few of the female middle-class organisers were suitably qualified for this task. Nonetheless, the Fascist women did take part in training activities. They offered instruction in domestic science and child-care methods as well as subjecting the peasant members to lectures on political themes.

From 1935 onwards, the section was heavily mobilised for autarky: peasant women were urged to play a key role in the anti-sanctions campaign. Members were exhorted to increase production for the national cause in a whole range of ways including raising greater numbers of rabbits and chickens to replace imported meat, gathering wild herbs and berries to be used for medicinal purposes, and increasing their output of sunflowers, honey, silkworms and so on. They were also trained in new 'autarkic' craft and cultivation techniques.

An analogous section for female workers, the Section for Women Workers and Homeworkers (Sezione Operaie e Lavoranti a Domicilio, SOLD) was belatedly created in 1937. As its name suggests, its target recruitment group included factory workers and women engaged in domestic manufacturing, but it also paid particular attention to domestic servants, a category virtually untouched by the other Fascist mass-mobilising organisations. Membership was also open to working-class housewives.[35] SOLD was quite clearly modelled on what was seen as the successful example of the MR. Its members could participate in sports and short holidays, go on outings, enter competitions, receive handouts and cut-price goods and follow training courses. Similar to the courses for rural women, these combined propaganda with practical instruction, mostly in domestic science, child-care and hygiene but in some cases offering professional training or basic literacy education.[36]

Although training and welfare heavily dominated the day-to-day

35 Partito Nazionale Fascista, *Fasci Femminili, Sezione Massaie Rurali, Sezione Operaie e Lavoranti a Domicilio. Regolamenti* (Rome, Ist Poligrafico dello Stato, 1929), p. 19.
36 On SOLD see P. R. Willson, 'Sezione operaie e lavoranti a domicilio', in V. De Grazia and S. Luzzatto (eds), *Dizionario critico del fascismo* (Turin, Einaudi, 2003).

activities of both sections, in practice the party hierarchs saw these aspects as no more than enticements to encourage women to join. The real aims of both sections were quite clearly political. It is worth noting that a number of their activities, such as domestic science courses for women workers taught by Fascist women, or sewing workshops for unemployed women, long predated the foundation of either of the sections. This suggests that they were established at least in part to formally recruit the beneficiaries of party welfare programmes. The sections were part of Starace's broad plan to gradually find a niche in the PNF for every single category of Italian according to class, gender and economic sector. He, quite literally, aimed to put the entire nation into some sort of Fascist uniform. In many respects, of course, such blanket mobilisation could only be achieved at the expense of any real sense of political commitment. Starace, however, was optimistic: he argued that the sections could enable the party to bring Fascist politics right into the heart of poor urban and rural families. This was an interesting proposition in its own right since it portrayed women as a key to the political mobilisation of whole families and households. This was quite new, for pre-fascist politicians had made little or no attempt to court female support, seen as of little relevance since women were not able to vote.

Joining the party

The extent to which Starace's plan really succeeded is highly debatable. In purely numerical terms, however, it was wildly successful. In 1929 Fasci Femminili membership was only about 100,000 but by 1940 this had soared to around 750,000 and over a million in 1942. Even larger numbers joined the MR: its membership grew rapidly from 225,094 in 1935, to 895,514 in 1937, nearly 1.5 million in 1939 and over 2.5 million by the end of 1942, making it one of the largest of all the Fascist mass organisations overall. Even the latecomer SOLD had signed up an impressive 1,514,860 by July 1942.

The reasons for this huge rush to join the party were varied and differed according to the period and to women's class and position in the organisation. In the case of poorer women, who constituted numerically the majority of these recruits, the meaning of membership is far from clear as women who joined the MR or SOLD were offered only a passive role in the party. Many of them, in particular peasant women and domestic servants (often from rural families themselves), were politically totally inexperienced. This, of course, was less true of urban industrial workers who were more likely to come from left-wing families.[37] Although some members of both sections may have joined out of a sense of loyalty to the regime, many others may have not had much understanding of the issues at stake or even joined in spite of the political message. In many cases, opportunism or material necessity were clearly significant motives. Both sections offered a good range of material incentives and social opportunities. Some women clearly joined to obtain employment: servants seeking work in labour exchanges, for example, were vetted by SOLD organisers who, under the guise of offering professional and 'spiritual' guidance, scrutinised their political and moral suitability. Some categories of workers, such as rice-weeders, needed the card to secure employment. More broadly, by the late 1930s the party card had become a prerequisite for access to welfare benefits and services previously open to all, earning it the nickname of the 'bread card'. Although considered equivalent to a full PNF card, membership of the sections was extremely cheap and entailed the purchase of only a neckerchief and badge (with different designs for each section) rather than the expensive tailored Fasci Femminili uniforms (one for summer and one for winter).

Without denying that there were at least some committed Fascists among the members of the sections for poorer women, it is, undoubtedly, among the middle- and upper-class Fascist women that the greatest number of 'true believers' were to be found. In the 1930s and 1940s propaganda increasingly depicted Fascist women as almost mesmerised by the glories of Fascism and the godlike person of the Duce. They were frequently praised for their disciplined devotion, their blind and unswerving loyalty to the regime and their desire to serve it with any sacrifice that might be required.

It is indeed possible to find women who fit this picture, women who had what can only be termed fanatical levels of belief in Mussolini, the regime and its politics. This was true, for example, of Laura Marani Argnani, Provincial Fiduciary in Reggio Emilia and eventually National Inspectress, whose writings were drenched with the Cult of the Duce and declarations of total unquestioning loyalty to him. Testimonies of people who met her in person confirm that these really do seem to have been heartfelt convictions. In the words of one former student from the teacher training college where she worked: 'she had an obsession that filled her whole head: her head was full of

37 On this question see P. R. Willson, *The Clockwork Factory: Women and Work in Fascist Italy* (Oxford, Oxford University Press, 1993), ch. 10.

the Duce, she adored him. She was in love with the Duce.'[38] That there were also other women as deeply dedicated to Mussolini and the regime is undeniable. In the final doomed phase of the regime, the Republic of Salò, there were women who remained loyal despite the inevitability of defeat, and even some who were keen to take up arms for it.[39]

It does need to be stressed, however, that not all Fascist women were so wholeheartedly devoted to the politics of the regime. For some middle-class women too, opportunism and material factors could be significant factors – teachers and others working in the public sector, for example, could not be employed without proof of party membership. In the early period commitment to the Fascist cause was always conditional since many Fascist women hoped at last to get forms of recognition denied them by previous political parties, particularly the vote. In this period it is still possible to talk of women making clear choices to support the regime, for alternative political paths were still open to them. This is less true of the 1930s when many Fasci Femminili members came from a whole new generation. They had more or less grown up under the regime and been indoctrinated with propaganda in the education system and by the party youth groups from an early age.[40] By the time they moved up into the adult party the regime seemed completely normal, just a fact of life, immovable and unchanging. In this context anti-fascism of any sort seemed hard to imagine and, for many of the rank-and-file members, simple conformism, the hallmark of the 1930s, certainly played an important role.

Opportunism and conformism, however, are perhaps not enough to explain why women sought leadership positions. As Helga Dittrich-Johansen has argued in a recent article,[41] even among female leaders levels of commitment were far from uniform and the motives for taking up organisational positions in the party varied over time as well

38 Testimony of 'Clorinda C' in M. Mietto and M. G. Ruggerini, '"Faber est suae quisque fortunae": gli studenti del Liceo Classico e dell'Istituto Magistrale a Reggio Emilia', *Contributi*, 21–2 (1987), 359. On Marani Argnani see also Zavaroni, 'La donna del fascio I'.
39 See M. Fraddosio, 'The fallen hero: the myth of Mussolini and Fascist women in the Italian Social Republic (1943–5)', *Journal of Contemporary History*, 31 (1996), 99–124; L. Garibaldi, *Le soldatesse di Mussolini* (Milan, Mursia, 1995).
40 On the PNF youth organisations and the 'fascistisation' of school education see T. Koon, *Believe, Obey, Fight: Political Socialisation of Youth in Fascist Italy 1922–1943* (Chapel Hill, University of North Carolina Press, 1985).
41 Dittrich-Johansen, 'Per la Patria e per il Duce'.

as according to generation, class, region and rank in the party hierarchy. Some who took leadership positions doubtless did so out of a real desire to support the aims of the regime. For others, the incentive may have been more related to the potential for social advancement that the party could offer.[42] For many, moreover, the real spur may have been simply the desire to find some valid extra-domestic activity to absorb their energies. As the regime took over and refashioned charities and other welfare organisations to its own ends, many of the sorts of activities women had done voluntarily in a variety of contexts in the Liberal period increasingly became party work. Very few of the positions open to women were, however, paid. This means that, for many, the primary motive for seeking organisational responsibility in the party was not an economic one.

Admittedly some opportunities for paid employment did emerge, but this was mostly only towards the end of the *ventennio*. Before this there were a few women employed by the central Fasci Femminili office in Rome and party responsibilities could open the door to various other forms of paid employment which stemmed from the increasing professionalisation of certain welfare initiatives, such as directorships for children's summer camps. From 1938 the party also employed salaried 'Rural Housewives Technical Leaders' trained in the party Sant'Alessio College in Rome,[43] and the National Inspectresses, appointed from 1937, also received a monthly wage for their work.

At lower levels, however, the party seems to have considered a sense of importance and the satisfaction of doing their 'duty' to the nation sufficient reward for women's time. All over Italy thousands of local Fasci Femminili section secretaries, MR and SOLD secretaries or 'nucleus leaders' (the lowest rank in the pecking order) soldiered on, often in difficult circumstances with little financial support from above, without any remuneration.[44] Some of them may have accepted these positions because they found the challenge genuinely interesting. Others may have found it hard to refuse, particularly teachers in tiny rural schools who were dreaming of a transfer elsewhere and could not afford to offend the authorities. All the

42 Ibid.
43 On the Sant'Alessio College, which until 1937 had trained rural primary school teachers, see Willson, *Peasant Women and Politics*, ch. 7.
44 Although Dittrich-Johansen has suggested that economic motives were paramount for many lower level leaders, I have found no evidence that any of these people were actually paid. (Dittrich-Johansen, 'Le professioniste del PNF', 200.)

archival documentation that I have seen suggests that only a very small number of organisers were paid. The heads of the Fasci Femminili in each province – the Provincial Fiduciaries – worked for absolutely nothing (apart from fairly miserly expenses) until late 1940 when they were, at last, offered monthly salaries. Even the veteran campaigner Regina Terruzzi, who dedicated a considerable amount of her time and energy to founding and running the Massaie Rurali Federation in 1933, was paid nothing whatsoever for her labours. It needs to be noted, furthermore, that even those who took on paid positions were not necessarily economically driven. In the case of the Inspectresses, for example, some, like Clara Franceschini, former Provincial Fiduciary in Pavia, really needed the money, but there were still quite a few extremely wealthy women who rose to this rank, for whom non-economic motives must have been foremost. A good example is Countess Laura Calvi Roncalli, the aristocratic Provincial Fiduciary of Bergamo, who simply donated her entire salary as National Inspectress to charity in 1942.[45]

Conclusion

Despite a huge expansion in their party activities, Fascism never accorded women any real power in the PNF hierarchy, and, as their difficult funding situation demonstrates, offered little official recognition to the growing importance of their role. Nonetheless, the mass recruitment of millions of women into the Fascist Party eventually had an impact on both the role of women and the history of the regime itself.

In engaging in an ever-expanding range of welfare and organisational activities, middle- and upper-class women were clearly carving out new spaces for themselves. In order to preach the value of domesticity, motherhood, autarkic housekeeping and the importance of national pride to the poor, they themselves were required to leave their own homes and hearths. Clad in their smart tailored uniforms, Fascist women became an unprecedentedly visible female presence at political events such as party rallies. Although it is much less easy to take this 'widening sphere' approach to the much more passive role of poorer women in the party, even the two dependent sections were not without significance in the history of female politicisation in Italy. This was the first time that a

---

45 Archivio Centrale di Stato, Partito Nazionale Fascista, Direttorio Nazionale, Servizi Vari, Serie II, Busta 39, Fascicolo 'Laura Calvi Roncalli'.

political party seriously attempted to recruit all female Italians into its ranks. The precise meaning of membership may have varied according to factors such as class, region and position in the party hierarchy, but the sheer scale of the recruitment was undoubtedly an important precedent for the mass recruitment of women by the Communists and Christian Democrats after the Second World War. It helped women get used to the idea of political party membership and, indeed, was not without influence on the types of activities women did in post-war political parties and movements.

In terms of the history of the regime, the Fascist mobilisation of women was more important than many historians have admitted. The lack of real female influence on policy-making has led many quite wrongly to dismiss women's role in the party as of little significance. In practice, however, in spite of the fact that male hierarchs wanted women relegated to 'merely welfare', which they saw as a safe, 'traditional' female role, women were brought to the fore by the circumstances of the time, in particular by the series of Fascist wars from 1935 onwards and by the changing importance of welfare in the context of the world economic depression. None of this means, of course, that women should be somehow considered as 'responsible' as men for Fascism in Italy, for men held firmly on to the reins of power. It does suggest, however, that women's activism is one factor which should be taken into consideration when attempting to account for the longevity of Mussolini's period of rule.

3

Germany

Kirsten Heinsohn

Translated by Helen Lowry

For many years in Germany the history of 'women and right-wing politics' was seen exclusively as a history of women's oppression.[1] The
conservative idea of women's place in society, symbolised by the three
'Ks' ('*Kinder, Küche, Kirche*' – children, kitchen, church), was often
analysed critically, but its practical effects were not adequately investi-
gated. Consequently, women appeared only as objects in the history of
right-wing groups. More recent women's and gender history points more
strongly to the 'agency' of women. This development allows the bringing together of two tendencies of current historiography: on the one hand
interest in the actions, ideas and political ambitions of women, and on the
other hand one of the great questions of German history – how could
there have been so much support for the Nazi regime?

Investigation of 'women, gender and fascism' as an aspect of *German*
history implies the analysis of continuities and breaks before and after
1933. The contribution of women to the maintenance of the Nazi dictatorship is still intensively debated.[2] There has been one generally

I would like to thank Anne Fleig and Birthe Kundrus for their supportive comments.

1 R. Thalmann, *Frausein im Dritten Reich* (Frankfurt a. M., Hanser, 1984); Renate
Wiggershaus, *Frauen unterm Nationalsozialismus* (Wuppertal, Hammer, 1984). S.
Ottens, 'Rechtsextremismus – ein Männerproblem?', in R. Bitzan (ed.), *Rechte Frauen:
Skingirls, Walküren und feine Damen* (Berlin, Elefanten Press 1997), pp. 166–77.

2 Frauengruppe Faschismusforschung, *Mutterkreuz und Arbeitsbuch: Zur Geschichte
der Frauen in der Weimarer Republik und im Nationalsozialismus* (Frankfurt a. M.,
Fischer, 1984); R. Bridenthal, A. Grossmann and M. Kaplan (eds), *When Biology
Became Destiny: Women in Weimar and Nazi Germany* (New York, Monthly
Review, 1984); C. Koonz, *Mothers in the Fatherland: Women, the Family, and Nazi
Politics* (New York, St Martins Press, 1986) (*Mütter im Vaterland: Frauen im
Dritten Reich*, Reinbek b. Hamburg, Rowohltt, 1991); L. Gravenhorst and C.
Tatschmurat (eds), *Töchter-Fragen: NS-Frauen-Geschichte* (Freiburg, Kore, 1990);
A. Grossmann, 'Feminist debates about women and National Socialism', *Gender*

accepted gain from the extremely polarised debate about whether 'women' should be viewed more as victims or as perpetrators of Nazism: both women and men were affected by Nazism in a myriad of ways. Women, in particular 'non-German' women, could be the victims of persecution. But women could also act as onlookers and bystanders, and as profiteers. They could decide to make a career or not; they could decide to support or participate actively in the regime or to resist. Women are not a homogenous social and political group. And finally Nazi racism was prior to any other social difference. Two fundamental themes of women's and gender history were renewed in the debate about guilt: first, the polarity of equality and difference; and secondly, the relationship between the private and public spheres. The Nazi dictatorship erased various contrasts between men and women. Because the regime assigned primacy to 'race', men and women were declared equally 'Aryan', whereas 'non-Aryan' women and men were persecuted. Within these groups of equals and others, the question of gender still mattered, but it was secondary.[3] The relationship between private and public was altered in a similar fashion. No political system politicised and made public the private sphere like Nazism did, for it offered many different possibilities for political involvement in both spheres.

These considerations oblige us to reassess the problem of breaks and continuities between the Weimar Republic and the National Socialist dictatorship, and indeed the history of women's organisations of right-wing and extreme right-wing origin in this period. But what was 'right-wing' in Germany? The right was less a clearly defined group than a heterogeneous political force gravitating around common values and symbols.[4] The right legitimises social inequality, while the left preaches

---

and History, 3 (1991), 350–8; G. Bock, 'Ein Historikerinnenstreit?', *Geschichte und Gesellschaft,* 18 (1992), 400–4; K. Heinsohn, U. Weckel and B. Vogel (eds), *Zwischen Karriere und Verfolgung: Handlungsräume von Frauen im nationalsozialistischen Deutschland* (Frankfurt and New York, Campus, 1997); A. T. Allen, 'The Holocaust and the modernisation of gender: a historiographical essay', *Central European History,* 30 (1997), 349–64.

3 G. Bock, 'Nazi gender policies and women's history', in Georges Duby and Michelle Perrot (eds), *A History of Women in the West,* Vol. 5: *Toward a Cultural Identity in the Twentieth Century* (Cambridge, Belknap Press, 1994), pp. 149–76, 617–21. G. Bock, 'Gleichheit und Differenz in der nationalsozialistischen Rassenpolitik', *Geschichte und Gesellschaft,* 19 (1993), 277–310; G. Bock, 'Challenging dichotomies: perspectives on women's history', in K. Offen et al. (eds), *Writing Women's History: International Perspectives* (Basingstoke, Macmillan, 1991), pp. 18–39.

4 S. Breuer, *Ordnungen der Ungleichheit: Die deutsche Rechte im Widerstreit ihrer Ideen 1871–1945* (Darmstadt, Wissenschaftliche Buchgesellschaft, 2001).

equality, and liberals defend freedom. In modern society the right-wing notion of inequality requires new justifications, which can be either drawn from memories of pre-modern times or derived from modern principles such as 'race'. The use of anti-modern references is not however *eo ipso* a rejection of the modern, but rather is itself a part of modernity.[5] Historically, the right has struggled to decide where the parameters of inclusion and exclusion lie. One side called for a political elite to lead the dependent people, while the other side saw the inclusion of all social groups into the 'German *Volksgemeinschaft*' as the most important means to strengthen the nation.

Bearing these points in mind, we can address the values and symbols of the right. Belief in the need to strengthen the 'German nation' and faith in the 'German people' were important common denominators in the right. However, some democrats, liberals and social democrats also adhered to this basic value. What differentiated the right definitively from the left was its strategy of exclusion: the emphasis was placed on Germanness, and therefore exclusion of all 'non-Germans'. Exactly who should be excluded was a contentious issue, although anti-Semitism was generally accepted.[6] The right-wing milieu espoused a social vision based upon racism and the rejection of democracy and equality. Under this banner, party-politically affiliated conservatives were organised in the German National People's Party (Deutschnationale Volkspartei, DNVP) and the German People's Party (Deutsche Volkspartei, DVP) as well as the *völkisch* groups and the National Socialists.

'*Völkisch*' was a collective term for an extra-parliamentary movement dedicated to a search for the sources of the 'German-Germanic', and opposed to an allegedly 'racial foreign infiltration' (*rassische Überfremdung*) of Germany. It was in the *völkisch* milieu that authoritarian, anti-urban, anti-modern, and above all anti-Semitic ideas were

---

5 C. Klinger, *Flucht Trost Revolte: Die Moderne und ihre ästhetischen Gegenwelten* (Munich and Vienna, Hanser, 1995).

6 S. Volkov, 'Antisemitismus als kultureller Code', *Leo Baeck Institute Yearbook*, 23 (1978), 25–5; G. Eley, *Reshaping the German Right* (New Haven, Yale University Press, 1980); J. Kocka, 'Ursachen des Nationalsozialismus', *Aus Politik und Zeitgeschichte*, B25 (1980), 3–15; J. Flemming, 'Konservatismus als "nationalrevolutionäre Bewegung": Konservative Kritik an der Deutschnationalen Volkspartei', in D. Stegmann et al. (eds), *Deutscher Konservatismus im 19. und 20. Jahrhundert* (Bonn, Verlag Neue Gesellschaft. 1983), pp. 295–331; M. Broszat, 'Zur Struktur der NS-Massenbewegung', *Vierteljahreschrift für Zeitgeschichte*, 31 (1983), 52–76; K. Sontheimer, *Antidemokratisches Denken in der Weimarer Republik* (Munich, Nymphenburger Verlagshandlung, 1962) analyses the ideological basis of the right.

advocated.[7] The *völkisch* milieu comprised a mixture of small, elite associations and a few larger unions, including the Pan German League (Alldeutscher Verband), the German-*Völkisch* League of Defence and Defiance (Deutsch-Völkischer Schutz- und Trutzbund), and the Stahlhelm – Veterans' Organisation (Stahlhelm – Bund der Frontsoldaten). All these groups were bound by belief in the association of *men* and the authority of the leader; male bonding was meant to be the constitutive nucleus of the state. Some of these organisations merged into Nazism at the end of the Weimar Republic. However, they should not be understood exclusively as precursor organisations, but primarily as a part of the *völkisch* milieu[8] that was later used for its own purposes by National Socialism.

A number of women and women's organisations were active in the right-wing milieu. These groups addressed the relationship between equality and difference in society on various levels. In terms of the gender order, right-wing women's associations tended towards inclusion and equality, and they wanted to influence the questions of 'general' politics *together* with men. Women were expected to use all political means at their disposal to this end. Most right-wing women rejected 'women's liberation' (*Frauenrechtlerei*), however, as well as any fundamental challenge to the bourgeois social order. Nevertheless conservative and *völkisch* women's groups were required to justify their right of existence even in their own political milieu, for the conservative and *völkisch* conception of the world commonly advocated a strict separation between the social sphere of men (state and public) and women (family and private). Not surprisingly, the *völkisch* milieu, with its orientation toward the authoritarian principle and the comradeship of

---

7 G. L. Mosse, *The Crisis of German Ideology* (London, Weidenfeld and Nicolson, 1964) (*Die völkische Revolution: Über die geistigen Wurzeln des Nationalsozialismus*, Frankfurt a. M., Hain, 1991); U. Puschner, W. Schmitz and J. H. Ulbricht (eds), *Handbuch zur 'Völkischen Bewegung' 1871–1918* (Munich, Saur, 1996), pp. ix–xxiii. The terms völkisch and extreme right are used synonymously in this chapter.

8 F. Walter and H. Matthiesen, 'Milieus in der modernen deutschen Gesellschaftsgeschichte: Ergebnisse und Perspektiven der Forschung', in D. Schmiechen-Ackermann (ed.), *Anpassung, Verweigerung, Widerstand: Soziale Milieus, Politische Kultur und der Widerstand gegen den Nationalsozialismus in Deutschland im regionalen Vergleich* (Berlin, Hentrich, 1997), pp. 46–75; D. Lehnert and K. Megerle (eds), *Politische Identität und nationale Gedenktage: Zur Politischen Kultur in der Weimarer Republik* (Opladen, Westdeutscher Verlag, 1989); Megerle Lehnert, (ed.), *Politische Teilkulturen zwischen Integration und Polarisierung: Zur politischen Kultur in der Weimarer Republik* (Opladen, Westdeutscher Verlag, 1990); S. Marquardt, *Polis contra Polemos: Politik als Kampfbegriff der Weimarer Republik* (Cologne, Weimar and Vienna, Böhlau, 1997).

men, had great difficulty with the inclusion of women.

Völkisch women's organisations' strategy of inclusion accepted the gender-specific organisation of the world, and at the same time used that order to postulate equal tasks for women and men: man and woman should work together for the people and the fatherland. All right-wing women's associations saw nation and the fight for German values as founding principles for the political community of the sexes. Only by accepting these basic right-wing values could women establish a political room of their own. Yet this community of the sexes was connected with an extreme notion of racial and political exclusion which applied to women as well as men. Anti-Semitic and anti-democratic values functioned therefore among the majority of right-wing women as a common cultural code, which excluded the 'foreign races' or 'non-Germans' as well as Liberals and Social Democrats.[9] This cultural model explains why the few feminist-leaning right-wing women, like Käthe Schirmacher or Sophie Rogge-Börner, had such a difficult position within the right: they criticised the bourgeois gender order too obviously. Less clear-cut is the extent to which women's groups in the right-wing milieu changed the right unintentionally – simply because they existed. Did they undermine the gender hierarchy in spite of professed intentions to the contrary?

This chapter will consider some exemplary, broadly right-wing women's groups and their self-images. Due to the state of research this compilation must be incomplete. The history of men still dominates, especially histories of right-wing extremist men.[10] The self-image of right-wing groups as preservers of 'German manliness' contributed substantially to this one-sided historical perspective. Right-wing politics was depicted as a world in which, even on the fringes, women were spoken of uniquely as mothers and guardians of the family. Women themselves do not emerge as political subjects. This bias was exacerbated by two further factors. For many years the dominant strand of feminist history searched for the 'heroines' of history or for the history of lost opportunities, with which female researchers could identify positively or negatively. Only in most recent times have historians, even feminist historians, turned towards

---

9 Volkov, 'Antisemitismus'. U. Planert, *Antifeminismus im Kaiserreich: Diskurs, soziale Formation und politische Mentalität* (Göttingen, Vandenhoeck and Ruprecht 1998).

10 R. Chickering, *We Men Who Feel Most German: A Cultural Study of the Pan-German League 1886–1914* (Boston and London, Allen and Unwin, 1984); K. Theweleit, *Männerphantasien* (Reinbek b. Hamburg, Rowohlt, 1980).

right-wing women.[11] Secondly, not only contemporaries but also historians and political scientists were influenced by the dominant discourse about the allegedly apolitical 'nature' of woman, and by the bourgeois notion of the 'separate spheres' of the sexes.[12] Consequently the activities of organisations such as the Home and Country Women's Associations (Haus- und Landfrauenvereine) were understood to be mainly non-political, although their activities represented a contribution to political conservatism. Both factors reinforce the blindness of established historiography regarding the political autonomy of conservative and extreme right-wing women.

The following contribution will attempt nevertheless to illuminate the political influence of extreme right-wing women's organisations in the Weimar Republic. It will show that a *völkisch* women's milieu emerged from the conservative association and party spectrum at the very moment that extreme-right men's organisations fought against democracy and equality.[13] Protestant women's organisations and the DNVP provided an important point of departure and field of recruitment for the *völkisch* women's movement.[14] Meanwhile, the *völkisch* women's milieu became

11 See also the contributions in U. Planert (ed.), *Nation, Politik und Geschlecht: Frauenbewegungen und Nationalismus in der Moderne* (Frankfurt and New York, Campus, 2000); R. Scheck, 'German conservatism and female political activism in the early Weimar Republic', *German History,* 15 (1997), 34–55; R. Bridenthal, 'Organised rural women and the conservative mobilisation of the German countryside in the Weimar Republic', in L. E. Jones and J. Retallack (eds), *Between Reform, Reaction and Resistance: Studies in the History of German Conservatism from 1789 to 1945* (Providence and Oxford, Berg, 1993), pp. 375–406; Bitzan (ed.), *Rechte Frauen*; J. Gehmacher, '*Völkische Frauenbewegung': Deutschnationale und nationalsozialistische Geschlechterpolitik in Österreich* (Vienna, Döcker, 1998); C. Streubel, 'Völkisch-nationale Feministinnen in der Weimarer Republik', in E. Schöck-Quinteros and C. Streubel (eds), '*Ihrem Volk verantwortlich': Frauen der politischen Rechten (1890–1933). Organisationen, Agitationen, Ideologien* (Berlin, forthcoming).

12 M. Goot and E. Reid, 'Women: if not apolitical, then conservative', in J. Siltanen and M. Stanworth (eds), *Women and the Public Sphere* (London, Hutchinson, 1984), pp. 122–36.

13 K. Bruns, 'Völkische und deutschnationale Frauenvereine im "zweiten Reich"', in Puschner et al. (eds), *Handbuch*, pp. 376-95; R. Chickering, '"Casting their gaze more broadly": women's patriotic activism in imperial Germany', *Past and Present,* 118 (1988), 156–85; Planert (ed.), *Nation*; Schöck-Quinteros and Streubel (eds), '*Ihrem Volk verantwortlich'*.

14 U. Baumann, *Protestantismus und Frauenemanzipation in Deutschland 1850 bis 1920* (Frankfurt and New York, Campus, 1992); Koonz, *Mütter*, pp. 267–325; D. Kaufmann, *Frauen zwischen Aufbruch und Reaktion: Protestantische Frauenbewegung in der ersten Hälfte des 20. Jahrhunderts* (Munich, Piper, 1988); On Catholics, see D. Kaufmann, 'Vom Vaterland zum Mutterland: Frauen im katholischen Milieu der Weimarer Republik', in K. Hausen (ed.), *Frauen suchen ihr Geschichte* (Munich, Beck, 1983), pp. 250–75.

more differentiated in the 1920s, as new groups were founded which were part of right-wing male associations such as the Stahlhelm-Bund. Within this milieu a small number of *völkisch* women authors distinguished themselves, such as Käthe Schirmacher and Sophie Rogge-Börner, whose influence extended well beyond the organisations to which they actually belonged.[15] *Völkisch* women's associations were connected by the Ring of National Women (Ring Nationaler Frauen) – an umbrella group for extreme right-wing women.[16] It is still not possible to calculate conclusively the social position and numbers of members. Several indications lead one to suspect, however, that the conservative and extreme right-wing women's groups were influential in bourgeois circles.

The chapter will also examine Nazi policies towards women, and will pay particular attention to the incorporation of the extreme right-wing women's milieu into the Nazi regime. This will reveal continuities and discontinuities before and after the Nazi seizure of power in 1933. We shall see that extreme right-wing women's groups were successfully absorbed by National Socialism. The Nazis deprived these groups of power in order to sustain the primacy of the party and the re-establishment of the allegedly 'natural' gender order. This process was accompanied by extreme politicisation of the private and, ominously, by racism.

Extreme right-wing women's groups in the Weimar Republic

The end of the monarchy in Germany in 1918 and the establishment of a parliamentary democracy, accompanied by civil war, plunged the right into crisis. Subsequently the right recreated itself in strict opposition to the 'Weimar System' and became politically influential. In the first months of the Republic grief over what had been lost reigned among right-wing women too, often packaged as a denunciation of the 'home front' for its alleged lack of resistance and self-sacrificial spirit.

15 L. Crisp, '"National-feministische" Utopien: Pia Sophie Rogge-Börner und "Die deutsche Kämpferin" 1933–1937', *Feministische Studien*, 8:1 (1990), 128–37; E.-M. Ziege, 'Sophie Rogge-Börner – Wegbereiterin der Nazidiktatur und völkische Sektiererin im Abseits', in Heinsohn et al. (eds), *Zwischen Karriere*, pp. 44–77; A. Walzer, *Käthe Schirmacher: Eine deutsche Frauenrechtlerin auf dem Wege vom Liberalismus zum konservativen Nationalismus* (Pfaffenweiler, Centaurus, 1991); J. Gehmacher, 'Käthe Schirmachers Auto/Biographie der Nation', in S. Kemlein (ed.), *Geschlecht und Nationalismus in Mittel- und Osteuropa 1848–1918* (Osnabrück, Fibre, 2000), pp. 99–124.
16 Streubel, 'Völkisch-nationale Feministinnen'.

Paula Mueller, head of the conservative German-Evangelical Women's Association (Deutsch-Evangelischer Frauenbund, DEF) and member of the executive committee of the Union of Conservative Women (Vereinigung konservativer Frauen), claimed at the end of October 1918 that 'the front was not breached from the outside, but rather the homefront was breached'.[17] She thus made an influential female contribution to the 'stab in the back legend'. Nevertheless, a few weeks later she was using the freedoms offered by the new democratic state and attempting to recruit female members for the newly formed DNVP from the DEF. In her first editorial after the November revolution, Mueller urged DEF members to understand the new women's suffrage not as a right, but as a duty, requiring the voter to espouse of a 'true German disposition' and an 'evangelical conviction'.[18] Less than one year later, Mueller-Otfried, now Reichstag member for the DNVP, argued that the DEF was part of a 'political direction', namely, that of the 'nationally-minded right-wing parties'.[19] Female Protestant organisations displayed a cohesion which male conservatives valued. The integration of Protestant women's groups into the party-political battle could be justified either by the need to defend the nation and Germanness, or by the importance of Protestant values to society. The integration of women into politics was legitimised through two main points: fighting for the *German* nation and fighting for a *Protestant* nation, i.e. re-establishing the narrow relationship between state and Protestant church, which was lost with the implementation of the democratic Weimar Constitution. But the common denominator and the most important reason for women's political activism on the right was the fight for *Germany*. Germany was understood as a great Protestant nation, now oppressed by the French and the Allies. Germany was meant not to be a part of the Western world, but a nation with its own unique nature and significance.

The DNVP, suffrage and the organisation of women
The DNVP was founded after the war as a conservative coalition party, unifying various social and political positions: Prussian conservatives and monarchists as well as representatives of the young

---

17 Paula Mueller, 'Vertrauen', *Evangelische Frauenzeitung*, 19:3/4 (November 1918), 10.
18 Paula Mueller, 'Was nun?', *Evangelische Frauenzeitung*, 19:5/6 (December 1918), 18.
19 Paula Mueller, 'Die nächsten Aufgaben des DEF', *Evangelische Frauenzeitung*, 20:1/2 (October 1919), 1. In 1929 the DEF had approximately 200,000 members. N. Hartwich (ed.), *Handbuch für evangelische Frauen* (Berlin, Vereinigung der Evangelischen Frauenverbände Deutschlands, 1929), p. 87.

'Conservative Revolution', the *völkisch* movement and the German national commercial clerks' groups.[20] The *völkisch* group began as early as 1920 to question the fragile consensus of the party, when it insisted that only 'Germans', i.e. 'non-Jewish' citizens, should represent the party in the Reichstag elections.[21] In 1922 some of the *völkisch* members broke away from the DNVP and founded the German *Völkisch* Freedom Party (Deutschvölkische Freiheitspartei), which would later join the National Socialist Party (Nationalsozialistische Deutsche Arbeiterpartei, NSDAP).

Already in 1918 the role of women was significant in the reconstitution of the right. Whether or not there had truly been a new beginning for the DNVP, political rights for women were welcomed. According to Paula Mueller, there was no contradiction between traditional, conservative women's roles on the one hand, and the political rights of the Weimar Constitution on the other. Rather, women's suffrage could be used as a political weapon and for this reason alone was considered acceptable by conservatives.[22] The DNVP presented itself to women voters and members as the party of the Christian community of men and women. In the party's guidelines for women's political work, it is stated that the female German citizen should 'confess to the organic idea of state, based on Christian principles, as the German National People's Party represent them'. National welfare was therefore paramount for the woman: 'she considers all questions of public life and therefore also women's questions not from the standpoint of an individual, but from the standpoint of the totality'.[23]

With this denunciation of individualism and liberalism the DNVP could successfully recruit female members and voters. Although no reliable data about the composition of German national membership are available, there are a few indications that bourgeois women were

20 L. Hertzmann, *DNVP: Right-Wing Opposition in the Weimar Republic* (Lincoln, University of Nebraska Press, 1963); A. Chanady, 'The disintegration of the German National People's Party 1924-1930', *Journal of Modern History*, 39 (1967), 65–91; D. P. Walker, 'The German Nationalist People's Party: The conservative dilemma in the Weimar Republic', *Journal of Contemporary History*, 14 (1979), 627–47.

21 J. Striesow, *Die Deutschnationale Volkspartei und die Völkisch-Radikalen 1918-1922* (Frankfurt a. M., Haag & Herchen, 1981).

22 Scheck, 'German conservatism'; K. Heinsohn, 'Im Dienste der deutschen Volksgemeinschaft: Die "Frauenfrage" und konservative Parteien vor und nach dem Ersten Weltkrieg', in Planert (ed.), *Nation*, pp. 215–33.

23 'Grundsätze deutschnationaler Frauenarbeit', *Der deutsche Führer: Nationale Blätter für Politik und Kultur*, 1-8 (1922), 235–6.

greatly interested in the DNVP, at least during the early phase of the Weimar Republic. Women were preponderant in the party's electorate until the end of the Weimar Republic,[24] and in the beginning its membership seemed to be predominantly female. Contemporary accounts suggest that women constituted 54 per cent of all party members in Danzig in September 1921 and 43.2 per cent in Hamburg in January 1925.[25] The high number of female members could have resulted from the DNVP's successful mobilisation of the conservative milieu of bourgeois women's associations such as the DEF and Evangelical Women's Aid (Evangelische Frauenhilfe).[26] Internally conservative women organised themselves in women's committees, at national as well as regional and municipal levels. Many heads of these women's groups came from evangelical women's associations and brought their organisational experience with them.

The right's opposition to Weimar democracy expressed itself in an extremely negative position regarding parliamentary proceedings and the search for compromise between the parties – all this was 'horse-trading' and 'party bickering', contrary to the true interests of the 'German people'. The woman in her 'natural' function as guardian of the family and moral values was called upon to save the people and that which was 'German'. DNVP representative Käthe Schirmacher advocated that the suffrage, although extended to all adult women and men by the social democrats, should be used in the sense of '*völkisch* Germanness'. She presented the DNVP as the political group in which Germanness was in the safest hands. The German nationalists were the only party which required 'the national (not international) politicisation of the woman, as German woman and mother'. But Schirmacher was a feminist too. She updated the hierarchy of

24 H. Boak, 'Women in Weimar politics', *European History Quarterly*, 20 (1990), 369–99; J. Falter, T. Lindenberger and S. Schumann, *Wahlen und Abstimmungen in der Weimarer Republik: Materialien zum Wahlverhalten 1919–1933* (Munich, Beck, 1986), pp. 81–5.

25 W. Liebe, *Die Deutschnationale Volkspartei 1918–1924* (Düsseldorf, Droste, 1956), p. 130, note 71. It is uncertain whether these figures were representative of the party as a whole. The composition of the DNVP's predecessor, the German Fatherland Party in 1917 and 1918, shows that the figures are indeed representative. See H. Hagenlücke, *Deutsche Vaterlandspartei: Die nationale Rechte am Ende des Kaiserreiches* (Düsseldorf, Droste, 1997) p. 184. New data is presented in R. Scheck, 'Die Partei als Heim und Familie: Frauen in den Ortsvereinen der DNVP und DVP in der Weimarer Republik', in Schöck-Quinteros annd Streubel (eds), '*Ihrem Volk verantwortlich*'.

26 Baumann, *Protestantismus*, p. 260.

women's political concerns, so that *völkisch* issues were valued more highly than 'women's issues':

> [Women] will assert their claims perhaps more easily sometimes on the left. But in the German National People's Party they are surely in better hands in other respects. The German National People's Party is markedly Christian, markedly not social democratic and markedly '*German*'. For us this is crucial.[27]

In her pamphlet *Women and the Parties*, Schirmacher formulated two concerns. First, she outlined a legitimisation strategy for women's groups with respect to conservative and extreme right-wing men on the basis of *völkisch* views. The reconstruction and preservation of the German people and the German nation was to be the highest object of all 'German feeling women and men' – this priority legitimised women's political activities. Secondly, Schirmacher discussed the programme of conservative and extreme right-wing female politicians. She wanted the inclusion and recognition of women in the political sphere to be based on the acceptance of a higher value: 'Germanness'. Equality and difference between women and men were therefore based on the same principle as the exclusion of 'non-Germans'. Women and men were supposed to protect and enlarge their '*Volkstum*' (national characteristics) together, but they were meant to undertake different tasks. This credo marked a fundamental break with the bourgeois women's movement, which wanted to bring specific female interests and cultural tasks into politics. Conservative women and their *völkisch* colleagues did not recognise any particularly female interests. They saw only specifically German cultural tasks which both genders had to pursue. Schirmacher outlined a *völkisch* order founded on the principle of race, which determined equality and difference in the gender order.

How far this *völkisch* order should be realised within the DNVP was a contentious issue among women. On the occasion of a debate about the addition of *völkisch* regulations to the party statutes, some criticised the older 'leaders' of the party Women's Committee. The objects of these attacks, notably Margarete Behm, member of the German parliament and head of the DNVP National Women's Committee, originated from evangelical women's circles.[28] Their

---

27 K. Schirmacher, *Die Frauen und die Parteien* (Danzig, Sauer, 1918) p. 12.

28 Behm had condemned the *völkisch* impulse. For her attitude to DNVP anti-Semitism see Striesow, *Deutschnationale Volkspartei*, p. 148. The general manager of the DNVP, von Lindeiner-Wildau, later published an official answer in which he repudiated *völkisch* attacks and emphatically supported Behm. *Deutsche Zeitung*, No. 536, 26 November 1920.

younger opponents charged that the Women's Committee, which co-ordinated the women's political work in the party, was biased towards the 'old' women's liberationism of the democrats. The Committee therefore worked against the men in the party rather than with them. In November 1920 Martha Voß-Zietz elucidated her criticism of the Women's Committee of the DNVP:

> A serious error might yet now appear in allowing women to work in separate committees without thinking that politics is the work of the entire people, and that there cannot be one single area where men's and women's work must not proceed as complementary![29]

Voß-Zietz pleaded for abolition of the women's committees, and for women to be granted an 'apprenticeship' under the direction of 'reasonable' men. Subsequently the critical voices became more radical. They professed to detect a lack of clear national goals in women's work. Since, it was said, DNVP women politicians emulated the democrats, the natural order of the genders would suffer as much as the national interest. One anonymous letter insisted that the 'mission of national women's politics' is not 'boundless insisting on justice' (*uferlose Rechtlerei*), as it was called, but rather the support of men, from the 'natural feeling that the area of "high politics" is the domain of men and further that men, as they have done until now, should make history'.[30]

Martha Voß-Zietz's attack was surprising. She was after all an old women's liberationist who started her political activity in Hamburg. Together with Lida Gustava Heymann, she founded the left-wing liberal association Frauenwohl in 1899 and in 1902 the German Association for Women's Suffrage (Deutscher Verein für Frauenstimmrecht).[31] Publication of an investigation into 'women's parochial suffrage' (*kirchliche Stimmrecht der Frau*) made her widely known within the women's movement. During the war she worked on the advisory council of the War Ministry of Food and was one of the founders of the German Federation of German Housewives

---

29 M. Voß-Zietz, 'Die Frauenarbeit in der DNVP', *Deutsche Zeitung*, No. 529, 22 November 1920.

30 'Ziele deutschnationaler Frauenarbeit', *Deutsche Zeitung*, No. 561, 11 December 1920.

31 On Voß-Zietz see Richard Evans, *The Feminist Movement in Germany* 1894–1933 (London, Sage, 1976), pp. 211–13; K. Heinsohn, *Politik und Geschlecht: Zur politischen Kultur bürgerlicher Frauenvereine in Hamburg* (Hamburg, Verein für Hamburgische Geschichte, 1997), p. 393.

Associations (Reichsverband Deutscher Hausfrauenvereine, RDH).[32] From 1910 to 1919 Voß-Zietz was the executive-committee secretary of the Alliance of German Women's Associations (Bund Deutscher Frauenvereine), the umbrella organisation of the bourgeois women's movement. In 1917 she crossed over from the left-wing liberal Progressive People's Party to the extreme right-wing German Fatherland Party (Deutsche Vaterlandspartei). In 1918, alongside Karl Helfferich, she jointly headed the Hamburg DNVP list. She also belonged to and frequently spoke for the extremely anti-Semitic German-Völkisch League of Defence and Defiance (Deutsch-Völkischer Schutz- und Trutzbund).[33] The RDH believed that these propaganda activities compromised Voß-Zietz's political neutrality, and forced her to give up the chair of the organisation.[34] This *völkisch* background prompted Voß-Zietz to criticise her own party and its women's committees. She wanted a 'strengthening of *völkisch* ideals' through women because she assumed that women must 'prepare the way for our leaders, and create the necessary men and women voters for them, so that the German National People's Party can become the birthplace of a newly established Germanness'.[35]

Schirmacher and Voß-Zietz were known representatives of *völkisch* circles within the DNVP. While Schirmacher remained in DNVP women's politics until her death in 1930, Voß-Zietz distanced herself from the party and drew nearer to the Nazis. Like the well-known publicist Sophie Rogge-Börner, Voß-Zietz was rejected by the National Socialists because of her women's liberationist past.[36] The political activities of these women, however, contributed to the undermining of parliamentary democracy in the Weimar Republic while at the same time opening a *völkisch* position for women.

32 R. Bridenthal, '"Professional" housewives: stepsisters of the women's movement', in Bridenthal et al. (eds), *When Biology Became Destiny*, pp. 153–73.

33 U. Lohalm, *Völkischer Radikalismus: Die Geschichte des Deutschvölkischen Schutz- und Trutzbundes 1919–1923* (Hamburg, Leibniz, 1970).

34 Bundesarchiv (BA) Berlin-Lichterfelde, R 8083/3, Reichsgemeinschaft Deutscher Hausfrauen, Sitzungen des geschäftsführenden Vorstandes, Protokoll 24/25 August 1933, p. 3.

35 M. Voß-Zietz, 'Die Frauenarbeit in der Deutschnationalen Volkspartei', *Deutsche Zeitung*, No. 50, 5 January 1921.

36 BA, R 8083/3, Beschwerdebrief des Deutschen Frauenwerks gegen Voß-Zietz, 1934.

Women's groups: the New Land Movement and the Queen Luise Alliance
Guida Diehl pursued similar goals to Schirmacher and Voß-Zietz in her
New Land Movement (Neulandbewegung, NLB), founded in 1916. She
too wanted to strengthen the nation by establishing a *völkisch* gender
order.[37] Diehl had close contacts with the bourgeois, evangelical women's
movement and the Christian social movement, and she aimed to mobilise
Protestant women outside the existing political context.[38] Her NLB saw
itself as working for the 'inner renewal' of Germany in the Protestant-
völkisch sense. Starting from small Bible and discussion circles for
'refined' girls, Diehl built a network around her newspaper *Neuland*. She
advocated women's 'spiritual fight' alongside men in the field and
declared the normal duties of everyday female life to be a contribution to
the war effort. Like the conservative and *völkisch* women of the DNVP,
Diehl and her NLB saw women's social and political duties as a contribution to the 'people as a whole'. They condemned the liberal thinking of the
Enlightenment as the cause of advancing secularisation. Nevertheless, the
collapse of 'Christian culture' was to be stopped above all by an 'inner
renewal' of the *individual*. The organisational structure of the movement
also reflected this personal promise of salvation. Guida Diehl set herself
up as the 'leader' (*Führerin*) to whom an oath had to be sworn as a condition of admission to the movement. Individual groups built concentric
circles around the 'leader' and her headquarters, the 'Neulandhaus' in
Eisenach. Comparable to the bourgeois youth and *völkisch* movements,
this *bündisch* organisational structure was used to create an intense relationship between the group and the individual person in order to strengthen
the team spirit. The NLB was an elitist movement that sought to establish
itself as the core of a 'women's renewal movement' (*Frauenerneuerungs-
bewegung*) based on the primacy of the nation.[39] In 1920 approximately

37 This portrait of the NLB is based upon S. Lange, *Protestantische Frauen auf dem
    Weg in den Nationalsozialismus: Guida Diehls Neulandbewegung 1916–1935*
    (Stuttgart Weimar, Metzler, 1998); S. Lange, 'Protestantismus, Nationalismus und
    frauenpolitische Konzepte der Neulandbewegung in der Weimarer Republik', in I.
    Korotin and B. Serloth (eds), *Gebrochene Kontinuitäten? Zur Rolle und Bedeutung
    des Geschlechterverhältnisses in der Entwicklung des Nationalsozialismus*
    (Innsbruck, Studienverlag, 2000), pp. 53–70.
38 On Guida Diehl see Lange, *Protestantische Frauen*, pp. 16-24.
39 See also Elizabeth Harvey, '*Serving the volk, serving the nation: women in the youth
    movement and the public sphere in Weimar Germany*', in L. E. Jones and J. Retallack
    (eds), *Elections, Mass Politics, and Social Change in Modern Germany* (Cambridge,
    Cambridge University Press, 1992), pp. 201–21; Elizabeth Harvey, 'Gender, genera-
    tions and politics: young Protestant women in the final years of the Weimar Republic', in
    M. Roseman (ed.), *Generations in Conflict: Youth Revolt and Generation Formation in
    Germany 1770–1968* (Cambridge, Cambridge University Press, 1995), pp. 185–209.

10,000 female members and sympathisers were registered, a number which sank to approximately 2,000 by the end of the Weimar Republic.[40]

The NLB saw itself as part of the 'national opposition'. In 1926 it founded the 'German Women's *Kampfbund* against degeneration in the life of the people', which pleaded for the 'establishment of a German-Christian womanhood'.[41] By 1928, thirty-nine organisations comprising 183,000 members and approximately 1,400 individuals had joined this '*Frauenkampfbund*'. Among its members were representatives of the conservative associations of the Alliance of German Women's Associations, like Countess Keyserlingk for the German Federation of Agricultural Women's Federations (Reichsverband Landwirtschaftlicher Frauenverbände), the DNVP delegates Margarete Behm and Annagrete Lehmann, Elisabeth Boehm as chair of the German Federation of Country Women, some evangelical women's associations, as well as morality associations and finally Nazi women's groups such as Elsbeth Zander's German Order of Women (Deutsche Frauenorden). The success of the '*Frauenkampfbund*' demonstrated the alienation of a large part of the women's movement from the Weimar Republic and its inclusion in the 'national opposition'.[42]

The activities of the NLB within the 'national opposition' prompted Diehl to revise the alliance's objectives. In her 1928 book, *Deutscher Frauenwille* (German Women's Will), she presented the NLB as part of the *völkisch* movement, yet also criticised the *völkisch* movement.[43] Seeing the bourgeois women's movement as insufficiently patriotic, neglectful of religion and too influenced by male standards, Diehl proposed a radical autonomy of gender spheres: both school and vocational training for girls and women was to be offered exclusively in women's institutions. Married women and mothers should be legally prohibited from paid employment since women were mothers above all else, and their education should be based on this premise. Unmarried, childless women, meanwhile, would be educated as 'spiritual mothers' for the 'female professions'. The autonomy of the separate spheres would be established politically through separate municipal councils and parliaments for men and women. Diehl's suggestions were all subject to the 'people's well being' (*Volkswohl*), which determined the genders' 'natural' duties, and dictated the need

40 Lange, *Protestantische Frauen*, p. 46.
41 Ibid., pp. 41 ff.
42 Ibid., p. 42.
43 Also ibid., pp. 29–36 and 118–27, and Lange, *Protestantismus*, pp. 58–61.

for 'racially' perfect offspring. 'Mothers' education' would serve these ends.

Diehl's writings owed something to the bourgeois women's movement – the concept of 'spiritual motherhood', for example, connected bourgeois feminism with *völkisch* thought and radicalised her propositions concerning the social spheres of the genders.[44] Bourgeois liberals, like the evangelical women's movement, reacted negatively to Diehl's writings.[45] When the NLB enthusiastically embraced the national opposition's campaign for a 'No' vote in the Young Plan referendum in 1929, a break with the women's movement became unavoidable. The NLB became an integral part of the *völkisch* milieu, and now represented itself as the 'women's renewal movement'.

At this time Diehl moved closer to the increasingly important Nazis, seeing Hitler's movement as a welcome partner in the struggle to realise the NLB's own programme.[46] Diehl joined the party in 1930 and in 1931 became the Cultural Speaker in the National Women's Leadership of the NSDAP (Reichsfrauenleitung der NSDAP). She portrayed the NLB as a 'female parallel movement to Nazism', hoping that she, her groups and her programme would be of use to the party. Her *Deutscher Frauenwille* became the unofficial textbook for party women, and later provided some points of the programme of the Nazi Women's Group (NS-Frauenschaft, NSF), founded in October 1931. Diehl herself contributed to the creation of the NSF, and promoted Nazism in lectures to middle-class women's groups. After October 1932 Diehl left the National Women's Leadership because of conflicts with her superiors, Elsbeth Zander and Gregor Strasser. Thanks to the Nazi policy of 'co-ordination of institutional powers' (*Gleichschaltung*), the NLB could no longer develop in parallel with Nazi women's organisations (the *Frauenkampfbund* was even dissolved in 1933 as a result of *Gleichschaltung*). From 1935 Diehl and the NLB's journal, *Neulandblatt*, withdrew from politics, and in 1940 the latter ceased publication. From the mid 1930s, the NLB became ever more strongly connected with Protestant associations, but failed to win much influence in the Evangelical Women's Union (Evangelisches Frauenwerk).

The NLB used the *bündisch* organisation principle to encourage girls and women of the 'educated classes' to advocate an elitist *völkisch*

---

44 A. T. Allen, *Feminism and Motherhood in Germany 1800–1914* (New Brunswick NJ, Rutgers, 1991).
45 Lange, *Protestantische Frauen*, pp. 118–27.
46 Ibid., pp. 101–95.

policy. Like male *völkisch* groups, the NLB was organised around a (female) leader to whom members swore an oath of allegiance. One could not simply join the groups, one had to be co-opted. This form of recruitment differed substantially from that of other right-wing associations. The latter organised women into large group contexts, often based upon hierarchical military principles with strict service obligations. The great conservative National Women's Associations (Vaterländische Frauenvereine), which prepared women for war service and had approximately 600,000 members before the First World War,[47] or even the smaller federations like the German Women's Association for the Eastern Provinces (Deutsche Frauenverein für die Ostmarken),[48] the German Women's Naval League (Flottenbund Deutscher Frauen)[49] with 129,000 members (1918) or the Women's League of German Colonial Society (Frauenbund der Deutschen Kolonialgesellschaft)[50] which reputedly had approximately 25,000 female members after the war, were organised in this way. Although these right-wing groups lost members after the war, the milieu of the conservative and *völkisch* women's associations managed to hold itself together in the early years of the Weimar Republic and later re-formed itself into the 'national opposition'.

The Queen Luise Alliance (Königin-Luise-Bund, KLB), founded in 1923, was one of these *völkisch* women's associations.[51] Inspired by the legends about Prussian Queen Luise (1776–1810), under the motto 'I serve', the alliance sought to serve as a 'concentrating force' (in

47 Chickering, 'Casting', pp. 162–7; Andrea Süchting-Hänger, 'Gleichgroße mut'ge Helferinnen' in der weiblichen Gegenwelt: Der Vaterländische Frauenverein und die Politisierung konservativer Frauen', in Planert (ed.), *Nation*, pp. 131–46; H.-J. Arendt, 'Frauenverbände gegen Frauenemanzipation: Rechtskonservative und faschistische Frauenorganisationen in der Weimarer Republik', *Wissenschaftliche Studien der Pädagogischen Hochschule Clara Zetkin*, 3 (1990), 86–102.

48 Chickering, 'Casting', pp. 167–71; E. A. Drummond, '"Durch Liebe stark, deutsch bis ins Mark": Weiblicher Kulturimperialismus und der deutsche Frauenverein für die Ostmarken', in Planert (ed.), *Nation*, pp. 147–64.

49 Chickering, 'Casting', pp. 172–4; D. Fricke et al. (eds), *Lexikon zur Parteiengeschichte: Die bürgerlichen und kleinbürgerlichen Parteien und Verbände in Deutschland (1789–1945)*, 4 vols (Leipzig, Bibliographisches Institut, 1983–1986), Vol. 2, pp. 67–89.

50 Chickering, 'Casting', pp. 174–83; L. Wildenthal, 'Mass-marketing colonialism: the career of Else Frobenius in the "Weimar Republic" and Nazi Germany', in Planert (ed.), *Nation*, pp. 328–45.

51 BA, Berlin 61 Sta 1 – 1832: Bund Königin Luise; E. Schöck-Quinteros, 'Für's Vaterland, für's Vaterland' – der Königin-Luise-Bund in der Weimarer Republik', in Schöck-Quinteros and Streubel (eds), *'Ihrem Volk verantwortlich'*.

the sense of rallying the troops) in the national opposition. The KLB regarded itself as a 'sister organisation' of the 'Stahlhelm', an extreme right-wing coalition of veterans and Freikorps fighters.[52] Reappropriating the soldier's ethos, the KLB declared: 'Our battlefield is the family, our weapons are toughness, patience, tenacity, love, according to the gifts which God has bestowed upon us'.[53] Like other women's *völkisch* organisations, the KLB counted especially upon female relatives of male organisers and expected 'that [male] comrades support us here and ensure that their women and girls align themselves with us completely'.[54] Attempts to recruit 'female comrades' were very successful, for according to some accounts the KLB had over 100,000 members in 1932.[55] Practically, the KLB organised a myriad of activities around the home and family, many of which would be useful in the eventuality of war, such as nursing. In May 1933, on the tenth anniversary of its founding, the KLB chair, Baroness Charlotte von Hadeln, who had been active in the DNVP women's committee and the Evangelical Women's Aid in Cottbus, set the KLB squarely in the tradition of the Nazi 'Freedom Movement' (*Freiheitsbewegung*). The KLB was not, she said, founded

> to create a new parliamentary or party tool, but in the most difficult of times, amidst the misery of wide sections of the population, it endeavours to create a *Volksgemeinschaft* on a new foundation of trust. . . . Only a corporate national will can achieve freedom. Today the national freedom movement marks as its highest goal the creation of the new German man. In addition to this, however, equally placed and closely connected with it, exists the duty of the national women's leader: to create the new German woman.[56]

This defintion of the KLB's task ostensibly served Nazi policy, but behind it lay an attempt to protect the organisation's autonomy *vis-à-vis* the NSF. Although remaining technically independent of parties, the KLB had in May 1932 been placed 'unconditionally' under Nazi authority, or rather the authority of the 'Führer Adolf Hitler', in order to encourage the 'formation of the German women's front' and assist 'in the construction of a new state'.[57] After the installation of the Nazi dictatorship, some

---

52 Volker Berghahn, *Der Stahlhelm 1918–1935* (Düsseldorf, Droste, 1966).
53 Marie Netz, 'Was will der Königin-Luise-Bund?', in, Schöck-Quinteros, 'Für's Vaterland'.
54 Ibid.
55 BA, Berlin 61 Sta 1 – 1832: *Der Tag*, 1 April 1932.
56 Ibid., *Der Tag*, 13 May 1933.
57 Ibid., 'Die neue Deutsche Frauenfront', *Berliner Börsen-Zeitung*, 9 May 1932.

members of the KLB proposed self-dissolution and complete integration into the new NSF. The leader of the Westphalian chapter of the KLB demanded: 'Our mission is accomplished. We must come to terms with having been pioneers and trail blazers.'[58] Internal arguments and the unauthorised dissolution of several subgroups indicated how strong the pressure was on groups that had not yet 'co-ordinated'. In these circumstances the KLB decided to dissolve itself on 1 April 1934 and recommended that its members cross over to the NSF.

No more than Diehl's NLB could the KLB escape Nazi 'co-ordination'. With the primacy of the 'people' and 'Germanness' embedded in their politics of women for women, *völkisch* women's organisations successfully pursued the fight against the Weimar Republic. Although the political male elite was directly responsible for freeing the way for Hitler to assume state power, the actions of the *völkisch* women's groups were part of the conditions that made this possible. *Völkisch* women's associations, like conservative party women's groups, helped undermine democratic structures. They used for themselves the possibilities offered by democratic constitutions – the right to vote, freedom of association, and free speech – but they directed these freedoms against the Republic. In accordance with an allegedly 'natural' gender order, women's groups worked for an autonomous sphere within the right-wing camp.[59] The emphasis on the 'national' legitimised women's political activities, and conservative and *völkisch* men's groups accepted any support which served the 'national' purpose – including the politicisation of women. The success of the Nazi movement resulted from this profitable combination of contradictory forces. The Nazis explicitly emphasised the male-bonding character of party politics while simultaneously pushing for politicisation of the private sphere, which concerned women as much as men.

National Socialism, women and politics

The paradoxes in Nazi policies have often been emphasised, and attention has been drawn particularly to their policies on women and the family.[60] On the one hand they preached the 'natural' role of

58 Ibid., *Berliner Tageblatt*, 9 February 1934.
59 For example, Dora Hasselblatt, *Wir Frauen und die nationale Bewegung* (Hamburg, Agentur des Rauhen Hauses, 1933) with contributions by female DNVP, DVP and Nazi politicians.
60 Bernd Jürgen Wendt, *Deutschland 1933–1945: Das 'Dritte Reich'* (Hannover, Fackelträger, 1995), pp. 247–63.

woman as housewife and mother, while on the other they strove to bring women together in Nazi organisations outside women's 'domestic sphere'. Moreover, mandatory service for all women, introduced during the war, was meant to be universally applied, but in practice there were social differences in application. No one wanted to disturb the 'home front' too much. Clearly, there was no genuine Nazi policy on women, but rather an *ad hoc* range of programmes supposedly determined by the higher goal: create a mass movement, align state and society, organise for war and win it. Central to all the regime's policies, however, was the realisation of an extreme 'racial policy' and policies towards women were subordinate to this priority.[61]

The peculiar development of Nazi women's groups can be explained by the aforementioned ambivalences. Before the Nazi movement won power, an array of women's groups felt bound to the party and some of them competed with each another.[62] In 1928 Elsbeth Zander's German Order of Women (Deutsche Frauenorden) was recognised as the Nazi women's organisation and was assimilated into the party. The party's increasing institutional complexity led to the formation of the Nazi women's group, the NSF, in October 1931, and the simultaneous dissolution of all other party-based women's organisations. All female party members were automatically members of the NSF. By this time the party had increased the proportion of women among members from 4.4 per cent in 1923 to around 6 per cent. In January 1933 the proportion amounted to 7.5 per cent, at a time when the total party membership had increased dramatically from around 130,000 men and women in September 1930 to 840,000, of which 63,000 were women.[63] The NSF was subordinate to male leaders at all levels of the party, who chose female leaders of individual NSF groups. At the beginning of 1934 Gertrud Scholtz-Klink was made leader of the NSF, thereby ending a two-year rivalry between Diehl, Zander, Lydia Gottschweski (leader of the League of

---

61 Gisela Bock, *Zwangssterilisation im Nationalsozialismus: Studien zu Rassenpolitik und Frauenpolitik* (Opladen, Westdeutscher Verlag, 1986).

62 L. Wagner, *Nationalsozialistische Frauenansichten: Vorstellungen von Weiblichkeit und Politik führender Frauen im Nationalsozialismus* (Frankfurt a. M., Dipa, 1996); H.-J. Arendt, S. Hering and L. Wagner, *Nationalsozialistische Frauenpolitik vor 1933: Dokumentation* (Frankfurt a. M., Dipa, 1995); Frauengruppe Faschismusforschung, *Mutterkreuz*; Jill Stephenson, *The Nazi Organisation of Women* (London, Croom Helm, 1981); M. H. Kater, 'Frauen in der NS-Bewegung', *Vierteljahreshefte für Zeitgeschichte*, 31 (1983), 202–41; Koonz, *Mütter*.

63 Arendt, *Nationalsozialistische Frauenpolitik*, p. 325.

German Girls, or Bund Deutscher Mädel) and Paula Siber (head of
the Division for Women's Issues in the Reich Interior Ministry) for
control of Nazi women's organisations.

In May 1933 Charlotte von Hadeln of the KLB defined the task of
women in the 'national freedom movement' as 'the creation the new
German woman'. Many other *völkisch* and conservative women's
organisations welcomed the Nazi regime as the fulfilment of long-
standing goals. Like Paula Mueller-Otfried, they hoped for a 'national
government' which would struggle for 'cleanliness in public life,
[and] against unemployment, hunger and need'.[64] Some conservative
and *völkisch* women's groups had already aligned themselves with
Nazism by early 1933. During 1934 the others followed one by one
as in the framework of the policy of 'co-ordination', all opposition
was eliminated. The Nazis succeeded in incorporating the existing
women's network and in using this network and its goals for their own
purposes. The male associative character of the NSDAP was not abandoned; on the contrary it was successfully defended against right-wing
women's demands for inclusion.

Continuities

From the end of 1931, in pursuit of its desire to create a mass movement, the NSDAP adopted a more open attitude towards women's
political ideas. Only then was a sustained and focused – and successful – attempt made to attract women to Nazism. Before that an
NSDAP women's policy was not a priority for male leaders. On 5
September 1931 the Reich's organisational leader, Gregor Strasser,
argued that if the party was to win state power, women must be won
over:

> If the conquest of power is the concern of men, the preservation of
> power is the duty, obligation and responsibility of German women. ...
> Today we face the great responsibility that the National Socialist move-
> ment has become Germany's largest party and has good prospects for
> getting Germany's largest women's movement off the ground.[65]

Hitler and Goebbels, like *völkisch* women, saw woman as 'man's
sexual and working companion'. Both spoke of the common and

---

64 P. Mueller-Otfried, 'Rückblick und Ausblick', *Evangelische Frauenzeitung*, 35
    (January 1934), 49–50, cited in Koonz, *Mütter*, p. 276.
65 Cited in Arendt, *Nationalsozialistische Frauenpolitik*, p. 193. The meeting at which
    Strasser spoke announced the disbanding of the women's order in favour of the NSF
    on 6 September 1931.

equivalent tasks of the genders, and thus moved closer to the gender-political ideas of the *völkisch* women's movement. They proposed a modernised conception of the working couple legitimised by references to the traditional rural life. The gender hierarchy remained intact and female actions were deflected away from male authority:

> Woman is the sexual and working companion of man. She always has been and always will be. Formerly in the fields, today in the office. The man is the organiser of life, the woman his helper and his executive. These views are modern and take us high above all German *völkisch* resentment.[66]

Thus Nazism presented itself also as a modern movement open to women and attempted to repress its anti-woman image. It depicted a community of men and women working together for a national good that stood above all other issues. Equal rights for women were to be protected in a Nazi state, it was said, and the goal became the creation of a 'single German women's movement' founded on the NSF. The NSF programme of March 1932 addressed *völkisch* and Christian women's associations' fears that there would be a return to traditional women's roles. The Nazis accepted 'the great transformation of women's lives in the last fifty years as a necessity of the industrial age'.[67] The programme added that 'education and integration of women's powers are for the good of the nation, insofar as they cannot perform their most obvious service to society in marriage, family and motherhood', the most urgent goal of women's politics. This programme also included the racist definition of *Volk*: 'German should be the spirit, German the language, German the law and German the culture'. Protestant and Catholic women were reassured by the claim to 'support the preservation of the Christian faith'. The programme concluded with a call to fight the 'Jewish-Marxist spirit'. In this programme the Nazis expressed a clear claim to leadership of parts of the bourgeois women's movement, the *völkisch* women's associations and the confessional groups.[68]

Some women's associations in the 'national opposition' ended their traditional links to the DNVP at this time and joined the Nazi movement.[69] This weakened the conservative and military elites' efforts to subordinate Nazism to their own goals. In elections between 1930 and

---

66 Diary of Joseph Goebbels, 29 March 1932, cited in ibid., p. 229.
67 'Grundsätze der NS-Frauenschaft', 20 March 1932, cited in ibid., p. 226.
68 Gehmacher illuminates this process in Austria in 'Völkische Frauenbewegung'.
69 Bridenthal, 'Professional housewives'.

1933 the DNVP lost a great part of its voters to the Nazis while at the same time the *völkisch* milieu faced a dramatic decrease in membership, as for example the Pan German League, which in 1922 had approximately 40,000 members, but had only 8,000 in 1932.

Discontinuities

The original *bündisch* character of Nazism, with its emphasis on the authoritarian principle and male bonding, remained intact despite the massive expansion of Nazi membership. Women had no opportunity to engage in the governing bodies of the party. The female leaders of the *völkisch* women's groups had not expected this. They assumed that the Nazis' attempts to win over women would have practical consequences in the party and later the state. Yet the political field narrowly defined was masculinised under the dictatorship, at the same time as the Nazis engaged in a 'thorough politicisation of all areas of life'.[70] After 1933 the *völkisch* women's associations and their leaders did not oppose the regime because of contradictions in Nazi policies, but because they disliked the disempowerment of women in the political sphere. Guida Diehl once again represented these women.[71] Already in 1926 Elsbeth Zander had pinpointed the central difference between *völkisch* and Nazi goals: the Nazis connected the creation of the *Volksgemeinschaft* with the totalitarian claim of their party.[72] The *völkisch* movement itself opposed parties, because they were believed not to represent the *Volksgemeinschaft*. Protestant women, meanwhile, saw the absolute authoritarian principle as incompatible with the ultimately divine order. Paula Mueller-Otfried, who at seventy years old withdrew from all official offices in 1932 and 1933, openly criticised the exclusion of women from political activity as an 'undervaluing of our sex': 'They speak so much of the German people ... and what they mean is – the German man'.[73] Selma von der Groeben, honorary head of the German-Evangelical Women's Association, criticised the authoritarian principle's religious traits, which she saw as rendering discussion on its meaning impossible.[74] Moreover,

70 Sigmund Neumann, *Die Parteien der Weimarer Republik* (Stuttgart, Kohlhammer, [1932] 1986), p. 73.
71 For more detailed information, particularly about Lydia Gottschewski's criticism of 'Männerbund', see Wagner, *Nationalsozialistische Frauenansichten*, pp. 120–39.
72 E. Zander, 'Nationalsozialistische Frauenaufgaben', cited in ibid., p. 25.
73 Mueller-Otfried, 'Rückblick', cited in Koonz, *Mütter*, p. 276.
74 S. von der Groeben, 'Zeitenwende und Frauenbewegung', *Evangelische Frauenzeitung*, 35 (August 1932), cited in Arendt, *Nationalsozialistische Frauenansichten*, p. 260.

Magdalene von Tiling, head of the United Evangelical Women's Federations and long-time provincial diet and Reichstag member for the DNVP, complained about the disempowerment of women's associations and opposed the absolute claim of the party: 'Neither state, nor people, nor race, nor blood are of the utmost, but rather the Lord is the first and last who has set us in the midst of this fight (for freedom and honour, for *Volkstum* and nation)'.[75]

The *völkisch* men's groups fared exactly like their female counterparts: they were systematically disempowered by 1936. In the following period the NSDAP set out a totalitarian and racist policy which had been co-operatively drafted and supported by the *völkische* and conservatives, men and women. The thought, images, language and political ideas of *völkisch* groups built a foundation which the Nazis strengthened through the assimilation and co-ordination of the extreme right-wing groups. The break lay in the radicalised implementation of *völkisch* programmes in state policy and in the exclusion of women from political leadership bodies, coupled with intense politicisation of all social areas.[76] Difference and equality, public and private lost out to the primacy of the racial policy. The Nazi social order systematically excluded a large part of Germany's population from society and legitimised the persecution and killing of men, women and children. For 'German' women and men, a specific gender order was created against this background, in which the equality of 'Germans' was combined with differences between men and women.

---

75 M. von Tiling, 'Die Verantwortung der evangelischen Frau im politischen Leben gegenüber der nationalen Bewegung', in Hasselblatt, *Wir Frauen*, p. 23.
76 L. Pine, *Nazi Family Policy, 1933–1945* (Oxford, Berg, 1997); K. Lacey, 'Driving the message home: Nazi propaganda in the private sphere', in L. Abrams and E. Harvey (eds), *Gender Relations in German History: Power, Agency and Experience from the Sixteenth to the Twentieth Century* (London, UCL Press, 1996), pp. 189–210.

4

Romania

Maria Bucur

One of the most striking visual artefacts of the short-lived alliance between the fascist Iron Guard (Garda de Fier) and the military dictator Ion Antonescu (September 1940–January 1941) is a documentary film from the regime's first mass meeting to celebrate the new Legionary state (so-called after the Iron Guard's precursor, the Legion of the Archangel Michael (Legiunea Arhanghelul Mihai)). In addition to close-ups of the regime's leaders, the film shows a multitude of shots of the crowd, counting in the tens if not hundreds of thousands. A sea of people is shown at several points, suggesting the Iron Guard truly had a solid mass following. Some of the closer group shots show large numbers of women in traditional peasant garb listening attentively and giving the fascist salute. It was one of the most shocking images I came across in my early investigation of the Romanian extreme right. Who were these women and where had they come from? Did they represent a veridical image of the Legionary movement's support by women, or was this an expensive propaganda forgery? The contrast between these powerful images and the absence of any discussion of the gender dimension of the radical right movements in inter-war Romania suggests that this issue deserves more scholarly attention.

It has become a widely accepted view that the development of Romanian politics in the 1930s was greatly tributary to the extreme-right movements that flourished in Europe during the same period. Although the country was a winner in the Great War, Romanian politicians found it difficult from the very beginning to manage the challenges of unifying and ruling over the newly acquired territories.[1]

---

1 Vlad Georgescu, *The Romanians* (Columbus, University of Ohio Press, 1985); Keith Hitchins, *Rumania, 1867–1947* (Oxford, Clarendon Press, 1994); Armin

The National Liberal Party (Partidul Naţional-Liberal) dominated the
political scene with an iron fist, while its strongest opponent, the
National Peasant Party (Partidul Naţional-Ţărănesc), tried to have a
middle-of-the-road role by combining programmes for economic
modernisation with protection of peasant interests, playing a somewhat populist political game among the rural population, and even
becoming the strongest advocate of women's enfranchisement. In
parallel to, and to some extent as a result of, the political struggles
and corruption increasingly evident among the political elite of the
two parties, the radical right came in as an alternative to 'politician-
ism' – 'politicism'.

Historians have analysed thus far the causes of the popularity and
veritable grassroots growth of the radical right in Romania, especially of
the Legion of the Archangel Michael (later the Iron Guard) from a
largely political and ideological perspective.[2] Cultural and social factors
have been secondary in these analyses.[3] This chapter explores an important aspect of the right-wing movements in Romania during the inter-war
period – the gender dimension of their appeal and limitations. Attention
will be paid to the gendered rhetoric of the rightist ideology and the
gender-specific measures that were central to these movements. Why did
the Iron Guard attract men overwhelmingly, in spite of the familiar
maternalist rhetoric it used to attract women? How central were women
to the fascist rhetoric and in the movement itself?

Heinen, *Die Legion 'Erzengel Michael' in Rumänien: Soziale Bewegung und
Politische Organisation* (Munich, R. Oldenbourg Verlag, 1986) (following citations
come from the Romanian translation, *Legiunea 'Arhangelul Mihail': o contribuţie
la problema fascismului internaţional*, Bucharest, Humanitas, 1999).

2 Heinen, *Legiunea*; Francisco Veiga, *Istoria gărzii de fier, 1919–1941: mistica
ultranaţionalismului* (Bucharest, Humanitas, 1993); Radu Ioanid, *The Sword of the
Archangel: Fascist Ideology in Romania* (Boulder, East European Monographs;
New York, Distributed by Columbia University Press, 1990); Ewald Hibbeln,
Codreanu und die Eiserne Garde (Siegen, J. G. Herder, 1984); Bela Vago, *The
Shadow of the Swastika: The Rise of Fascism and Anti-Semitism in the Danube
Basin, 1936–1939* (Farnborough, Saxon House, 1975); Nicholas M. Nagy-
Talavera, *The Green Shirts and the Others: A History of Fascism in Hungary and
Romania* (Stanford, Hoover Institute, 1970); Martin Broszat, 'Die Eiserne Garde
und das Dritte Reich', *Politische Studien*, 9 (1958); Florea Nedelcu, *De la
restauraţie la dictatura regală* (Cluj-Napoca, n.p., 1981).

3 Heinen is an exception. He devotes an important part of his study to looking at the
social make-up of the Legionary movement. Sorin Alexandrescu asks questions
about the cultural elements of the extreme-right movements in *Paradoxul român*
(Bucharest, Ed. Univers, 1998) and *Privind înapoi, modernitatea* (Bucharest, Ed.
Univers, 1999).

My argument is that frustrations fostered by the shifting, blurry definitions of gender roles during the inter-war years were important in both the ideology of the extreme right and the (limited) appeal of right-wing movements. Thus, for the men from especially the post-war generation, the Legion offered avenues for empowerment along familiar notions of masculinity. Although a gendered rhetoric also attempted to attract women, the appeal of the Legion was less power-ful for them than that of other maternalist nationalist movements. In the case of the Romanian right, it was not pro- or anti-feminism that played a role in this limited appeal for women, for feminism was still finding a voice in women's organisations and politics. Extreme-right movements were competing with other better-known and less radical organisations which offered women avenues for public activism along maternalist lines.

A brief definition of the 'extreme right' must precede the analysis of these developments. Historians generally identify the rise of the extreme right in the inter-war period as both a reaction to the outcome of the Great War and the culmination of certain political developments (e.g. the emergence of mass parties, universal male suffrage), social processes (e.g. the growth and fragmentation of the middle classes, the expansion of the working class), and cultural and intellectual trends (e.g. the development of organicist philosophies, the reaction to the modernist 'decadent' avant-garde) that preceded the war.[4] This 'new' right is also identified by contrast with the nineteenth-century conservative parties, through its more dynamic development as a mass movement, the more radical forms of exclusionary rhetoric it employed (especially the racialising of anti-Semitism), its ambitions to destroy parliamentary politics, its emphasis on movement and action, rather than institution and stability, and its corollary celebration of violence as both necessary and positive as a form of expression and tool for political action.

In inter-war Romania, not all parties and movements that identified themselves as part of a new right were actually radical and novel in line with the definition above.[5] Nor were all 'traditional' right-wing

---

4 See, for instance, Stanely G. Payne, *A History of Fascism, 1914–1945* (Madison, WI, University of Madison Press, 1995); Peter Fritzsche, *Germans into Nazis* (Cambridge, MA, Harvard University Press, 1998); George L. Mosse, 'Introduction, towards a general theory of fascism', in George L . Mosse (ed.), *International Fascism: New Thoughts and New Approaches* (London and Beverly Hills, Sage Publications, 1979).

5 Heinen, *Legiunea*.

parties without elements of radicalism. In fact, one constant trait ran through all political parties and movements: an intense ethno-nationalism, which took exclusionary forms even among self-defined tolerant democratic parties, such as the National Peasant Party.[6] In fact, there was no significant force on the left wing of the political spectrum. Therefore, what stood in a centrist position in the Romanian political landscape of the inter-war years would easily qualify as a rightist position in the larger European context. For the purposes of this analysis, I will focus primarily on parties and movements that either identified themselves with the new right, or were, by virtue of their actions and rhetoric, on the extreme right of the Romanian political spectrum. Of these, the fascist movement the Legion of the Archangel Michael (later the Iron Guard) will be the main focus.[7] Some reference will be made, however, to the gender dimensions of the rhetoric and especially the social programmes of other parties and movements with a less clear identification with the extreme right, such as the eugenic movement.[8]

In 1919 Romania emerged as one of the great victors of the First World War: its size and population nearly doubled, its borders stretching beyond the most ardent nationalists' wildest dreams. However, the challenges of the newly created Greater Romania were tremendous: its ethnic make-up became much more heterogeneous, the administrative structure of the new provinces had to be aligned with those of the Romanian state, and the vast numbers of peasants who had fought in the war had to be turned into loyal citizens, as the threat of Bolshevik revolution seemed to loom at the borders from both Russia and Hungary.

Indeed, the experience of the war had been devastating for many people, who were left after 1918 hoping in vain for retribution or recognition in light of the outcome of the Paris Peace Conference. Peasants hoped for land and a more important voice in public life,

6 See the development of Alexandru Vaida-Voevod's populist and nationalist faction of the National Peasant Party. See Heinen, *Legiunea*, pp. 225–6.

7 There were significant transformations inside this movement from its formation in 1927 until 1941, when it was officially disbanded. The change in denomination in part reflected these transformations (see Heinen, *Legiunea*). Yet, such transformations were more important from a political/institutional perspective, than with regard to construction of gender roles or appeal to followers. Therefore, I will use the term 'Legion' to refer to this fascist movement for the entire inter-war period and 'Legionaries' to refer to its followers.

8 Maria Bucur, *Eugenics and Modernization in Interwar Romania* (Pittsburgh, PA, Pittsburgh University Press, 2002).

as they had been the main fighting force. Ethnic Romanians hoped for a reversal of power relations in economic life and public offices *vis-à-vis* other nationalities, be they Hungarians and Germans in Transylvania, or Jews in the Old Kingdom and Bukovina. By the 1930s, many of these people had become disappointed and thirsty for direct action to right the wrongs of the first post-war decade. The new right found fuel among those disenchanted by the discrepancy between their initial expectations after the war and the actual changes in the 1920s. But such expectations were also based on developments preceding the war.

Most important among these was an intense ethno-nationalism that dominated all political factions in both the Romanian Kingdom and among Romanians who lived in the provinces of the Austro-Hungarian Empire (the Banat, Bukovina and Transylvania). There were only small left-wing parties in any of these Romanian-inhabited territories, in which ethnic Romanians participated. Even the socialist movement in Transylvania was divided along ethnic lines. The National Liberal Party in Romania favoured nationalist policies to encourage the development of industry and infrastructure. It was the leader of the National Liberal Party, Ion I. C. Brătianu, who waited to plunge Romania into the Great War until 1916, in order to enable it to side with the Entente powers, which had promised the Austro-Hungarian provinces to the Romanians.

Before 1918, the nationalist discourse in the Romanian Kingdom had been primarily ethno-linguistic, based on a cultural rather than bio-racial definition of ethnicity.[9] However, there were already critics who wanted to draw the line more clearly, especially between Romanians and Jews. A. C. Cuza, a rabid anti-Semite and follower of Alexandre de Gobineau's ideas, was one of the most outspoken proponents of this minority position.[10] In Transylvania and the other

---

9 See, for instance, Lucian Boia, *Istorie și mit în conștiința românească* (Bucharest, Humanitas, 1997); Peter Sugar and Ivo Lederer (eds), *Nationalism in Eastern Europe* (Seattle, University of Washington Press, 1971); Mirela Murgescu, *Între 'bunul creștin' și 'bravul român': rolul școlii primare în construirea identității naționale românești (1831–1878)* (Iași, Ed. A'92, 1999); John Campbell, 'French influence and the rise of Roumanian nationalism: the generation of 1846, 1830–1857', Ph.D. thesis, Harvard University, 1940.

10 See Leon Volovici, *Nationalist Ideology and Antisemitism: The Case of Romanian Intellectuals in the 1930s* (Oxford and New York, Pergamon Press, 1991). For a discussion of anti-Semitism before 1918, see also William Oldson, *A Providential Anti-Semitism: Nationalism and Polity in Nineteenth Century Romania* (Philadelphia, American Philosophical Society, 1991).

Habsburg-held areas, nationalism was tied more closely to notions of historical precedent. For instance, in Transylvania Romanian nationalists argued in favour of gaining rights on the basis of being the oldest inhabitants of the land (an ethno-linguistic argument), while Hungarian nationalists argued about their right to control this territory on the basis of treaties and military victories (a legalistic argument).[11]

After the creation of Greater Romania, the ethno-linguistic arguments about national identity became more radical. Though the Constitution of 1923 defined citizenship regardless of ethno-religious differences, politicians and other important participants in public debates about the nation (especially in the education sector) made few attempts to construct the nation on the basis of the new fundamental laws.[12] In the first decade, the Liberals remained open to an enlarged Jewish constituency and the National Peasant Party remained largely ethnically Romanian, though not exclusively Orthodox and in principle open to ethnic minorities. By the 1930s, it was becoming clear that such leniency towards minorities was not welcome by the radically nationalist journalists, politicians and their constituencies. In fact, national identity was starting to be identified more closely in exclusionary terms on the basis of ethnicity and religion, and with an added biologising edge about the need to cleanse the nation.

One of the new voices in the nationalist discourse was the eugenic movement. Yet, even though eugenicists held 'hereditary characteristics' to be central to defining the nation and its future 'human capital', they were not unified in how they defined the hereditary traits. Some in this eugenicist group leaned clearly towards a racist exclusionary definition and became supporters of the Iron Guard (e.g. Iordache Făcăoaru and Traian Herseni). Others shied away from such radical definitions and solutions (such as sterilisation), focusing instead on educating the middle classes and peasantry about their responsibilities towards the future generations of the nation (e.g. Iuliu Moldovan and Emil Hațiegan, who were both National Peasant Party members).[13]

---

11 Sorin Mitu, *National Identity of Romanians in Transylvania* (Budapest, Central University Press, 2001); Keith Hitchins, *A Nation Discovered: Romanian Intellectuals in Transylvania and the Idea of Nation, 1700–1848* (Bucharest, Ed. Enciclopedică, 1999); Ildikó Lipcsey, *Erdélyi autonómiak: történeti tanulmányok* (Budapest, n.p., 1990); Zoltán Tóth, *Az erdélyi román nacionalizmus els o százada, 1697–1792* (Budapest, Atheneum, 1946).

12 See especially Irina Livezeanu, *Cultural Politics in Greater Romania: Regionalism, Nation Building and Ethnic Struggle, 1918–1930* (Ithaca, NY, Cornell University Press, 1995).

13 Bucur, *Eugenics*.

A corollary of the intense ethno-nationalism in Romania was the anti-Semitism already present in the mainstream discourse of many ethnic Romanian politicians and intellectuals. In addition to A. C. Cuza, the lawyer already notorious for his almost pathological anti-Semitism, many other public figures, from Vasile Conta to A. D. Xenopol and Mihai Eminescu, expressed negative views regarding the Jewish population, ranging from economic to racist anti-Semitism.[14]

Finally, another important trait of the pre-war political and cultural discourse in Romania for the present discussion was the absence of a unified women's movement. There were several women's organisations that fought for empowerment in the public sphere, but hardly a strong suffragist faction. The issue of women's voting was presented before the Parliament several times before and once during the First World War, but with very little response among politicians. Only after the war did more parties and women's groups embrace a pro-suffragist position, though one that could not be defined as resolutely pro-feminist.[15]

Romanian women were active, however, in other types of organisations. In the Romanian Kingdom, the broad-based Orthodox National Society of Romanian Women (Societatea Naţională Ortodoxă a Femeilor Române, SONFR) was founded in 1910 as a philanthropic organisation that would promote women's interests in the public sphere in two areas. First, the organisation promoted women's assertiveness to protect and strengthen the well-being of the Romanian nation. Secondly, SONFR adhered closely to the religious norms and the principles of the Orthodox Church and offered women the possibility of implementing the ideals of the Church by playing a more prominent role in their communities. The organisation aspired, thus, to translate important components of Orthodox theology and customs in the language of nationalism and promote aspirations of women, especially from the rising middling strata, to play a more prominent role in the public life of the country. Starting from philanthropic endeavours such as helping poor women with hot meals and opening an orphanage, the organisation moved to opening a nursing school and a girls' school (primary and secondary) right before the First World War.[16] During the war SONFR maintained steady activity through several soup kitchens and other types of aid for the civilian popula-

14 Volovici, *Nationalist.*

15 Paraschiva Câncea, *Mişcarea pentru emanciparea femeii în România* (Bucharest, Ed. Politică, 1976).

16 Arhivele Naţionale, filiala Bucureşti, fond SONFR, dos. 381, fos 56–61.

tion and Romanian soldiers. Its most political activity before 1918 was the help given to wounded Romanian prisoners in their efforts to escape from occupied Bucharest into the free zone of Moldavia.[17]

Overall, SONFR was based on the values of Orthodox Christianity and reinforced women's traditional roles as mothers and wives. Still, its programmes supported some women's ambitions for public action. The organisation had a collective leadership, composed of educated women of the middle and upper classes. Some of them were also active in other women's associations, such as the National Committee for Women (Comitetul Naţional de Femei), a loose umbrella group that connected feminist suffragist groups with more conservative women's organisations.[18] Some outspoken feminists, such as Calypso Botez, were on the board of SONFR. After the war Botez wrote on many occasions on behalf of women's voting rights and was one of the first women to be elected to the city council in Bucharest.[19] The President of SONFR, Alexandrina Cantacuzino, was also a self-proclaimed feminist, although her views were less clearly situated in the suffragist camp of equal rights in which Botez stood. It is more likely that Cantacuzino embraced feminism as a statement of her desire for self-empowerment.

There were a few other important women's organisations with roots in the pre-1918 period. The Reunion of Romanian Women (Reuniunea Femeilor Române) was similar to SONFR in actions, values and goals. Astra, a nationalist organisation founded in Transylvania in 1861, had encouraged women to participate in its activities even before 1918, though it did not have a separate women's section until after the war. However, under the impulses of a new President, Iuliu Moldovan, who had broad eugenic ambitions, a Feminine and Biopolitical Subsection was created in 1926. This was to become one of the most active women's organisations in Transylvania for the rest of the inter-war period.[20]

Although new and in many ways radical, the eugenic direction in Astra's development after 1918 articulated a pro-natalist and maternalist language familiar to Romanian women and enabled them to

17 Ibid., dos. 21, fos 1–102.

18 *România Ilustrată*, June 1925, p. 7.

19 See Calypso Botez, 'Drepturile femeii în constituţia viitoare', in Institutul Social Român (comp.), *Constituţia din 1923 în dezbaterile contemporanilor* (Bucharest, Humanitas, [1923] 1990) and 'Problema feminismului – o sistematizare a elementelor ei', *Arhiva pentru Stiinţa şi Reforma Socială*, 2:1–3 (1920), 25–84.

20 Bucur, *Eugenics*.

imagine new important roles in the public sphere without greatly transforming what was already understood as women's social roles. In the first few years of the Feminine Subsection, Moldovan, the leader of the eugenic movement, spoke out on several occasions on behalf of women's enfranchisement.[21] However, both he and Maria Baiulescu, who led the Feminine Subsection, were categorical opponents of the feminist movement. In fact, a lively debate occurred in 1927–28 in the pages of *Buletin Eugenic şi Biopolitic*, Astra's eugenics periodical, clearly delineating the position of Astra's women's organisation as favouring women's greater involvement in public life by expanding their role as mothers and nurturers, while rejecting the notion of simply allowing women to compete freely in the public sphere for the same economic, political and social opportunities opened to men.[22]

In the 1930s, even the rhetoric of pro-enfranchisement disappeared from the Feminine Subsection. Instead, the organisation focused more on reinforcing women's place in the home, educating them to take better care of their infant babies, keep the house in good order, and raise good sons to ensure the future health of the country. Also, the fear Romanians especially in Transylvania harboured in relation to Hungarian revisionism had important effects for the gender rhetoric of Astra's eugenics. Several articles in the same *Buletin* showed a desire to prevent any miscegenation between Romanians and Hungarians. The villains of such marriages were always women. The authors represented Romanian women as weak and traitorous if they married Hungarian men, and Hungarian women as devious and malicious if they married Romanian men.[23] The articles had nothing to say about the men themselves as active in these marriages, depicting them in effect as victims of such unions.

SONFR in Wallachia and Moldavia and Astra's Feminine Subsection remained two of the most active women's organisations during the inter-war period. They attracted large numbers from a broad spectrum of classes, educational backgrounds and political affiliation. However, neither of them expressed overt support or even

---

21 Iuliu Moldovan, *Biopolitica* (Cluj, n.p., 1925).

22 Veturia Manuilă, 'Femenismul şi familia', *Buletin Eugenic şi Biopolitic*, 2:3 (1928), 92–6. Veturia Manuilă, 'Rolul femeilor în asistenţa socială a familiei', *Buletin Eugenic şi Biopolitic*, 1:1 (1927), 24–6; Izabela Sadoveanu, 'Feminismul şi familia', *Buletin Eugenic şi Biopolitic*, 2:5 (1928), 150–5; Izabela Sadoveanu, 'Rolul social al femeii', *Buletin Eugenic şi Biopolitic*, 2:7–8 (1928), 220–31.

23 Bucur, *Eugenics*.

sympathy for the extreme-right political movements, such as the League for Christian National Defence (Liga pentru Apărarea Naţional-Creştină, LANC) or the Legion of the Archangel Michael. For most women interested in public activism along traditional Orthodox Christian lines and in accordance with their self-perception as moral guardians of the hearth and nurturers of their offspring, SONFR, Astra, and a few other similar organisations without ties to the radical right offered a rich array of choices.

What place did women occupy in the ideology of the new right and how did these new political movements attempt to attract women? These questions cannot be answered without looking at the gender dimension of rightist ideology at large. One should first note, however, that Romanian grammar makes gender analysis of ideological texts challenging. The main reason is that the generic plural of most nouns that have both a masculine and a feminine form, such as 'Romanian', 'youth', or 'member', all used very frequently in Legionary and other rightist writings, is masculine. In those cases, it is difficult to make a clear case that these writings were imagining a male-only audience. This grammatical particularity has made it difficult for historians even to begin asking questions about gender roles in the fascist movements. On the one hand, the sociological data about these movements is sketchy and impressionistic at best. On the other hand, the naturalised masculinist bent of the Romanian language has allowed most scholars to remain gender-blind as well in their studies.[24]

In fact, one can easily see how women would consider themselves included as potential followers of the movement, in spite of the overt usage of masculine nouns, precisely because they also read such language as generic. A careful reading of Legionary propaganda in terms of gendered language does offer, however, more help in disentangling the questions of who was the imagined audience of these writings and how would men interpret these texts differently from women.

My analysis focuses on the writings of Corneliu Zelea-Codreanu and two other important propaganda writers for the Iron Guard, Vasile Marin and Alexandru Cantacuzino. The 'new man' played a central role in the depiction of the Legionary movement. Codreanu described this creature as 'a type of hero, in the warring sense, a social hero, [and] a hero of work'.[25] Some writings suggested that the

24 Armin Heinen is an important exception.
25 Corneliu Zelea-Codreanu, *Cărticica şefului de cuib* (n.p., [1937]).

Legionary women's unit, the Fortresses, also aimed to create a new woman, 'a seasoned and decisive soldier like the [new] man'.[26] Yet the description of the Fortresses' actual activities showed that women in fact engaged in very traditional activities, such as sewing and embroidery.

Although the language used by Codreanu could easily be interpreted as referring to 'individuals' rather than 'men', other writings make clearer the masculinist assumptions of Codreanu's ideology. In a call for such 'supermen', Vasile Marin, another prominent Legionary leader, who died in the Spanish Civil War, wrote: 'Legionarism is the fight against the contemporary illness of pure reason', and on behalf of virility.[27] He continued by stressing that 'the primacy of action' was the basis of Legionary morality[28] and called his audiences to join the Legion, 'if there is a bit of strength left in the manhood of your arms'.[29] In Romanian, the last phrase, '*bărbăţia braţului vostru*', can be understood in two ways. *Bărbăţie* can mean 'manhood' in the gender-specific sense, but also 'strength' in a more generic sense. Either way, the choice of this word is not without significance, especially in the broader context of Marin's writings, which contain other strong gender-specific references to the Legionary values. There are other passages that make it even clearer that the 'new man' imagined by Codreanu and Marin was indeed male. In describing the goals of the future Legionary member, Marin writes: 'He is the man of cardinal virtues: hero, priest ... soldier'.[30] All three options were opened only to men.

Alexandru Cantacuzino, who wrote many tracts on behalf of the Legionary movement, spoke even more directly to men and the perceived sense of disempowerment shared by many of his contemporaries. His writings focused on past humiliations suffered by Romanian men, against servility, and on behalf of activism and vengeance. His discussion of disempowerment verged on portraying the Romanian man as emasculated, for Cantacuzino directly spoke of sterility as 'the plague of the present'.[31] Although in English 'sterility' is not gender-specific, in Romanian it refers overwhelmingly to

26 Mihail Stelescu, 'Frăţiile de cruce şi cetăţuile Legiunii', *Pământul Strămoşesc*, 7:3 (1933), 9.
27 Vasile Marin, *Crez de generaţie* (Bucharest, Tip. Bucovina, 1937), p. 149.
28 Ibid., p. 150.
29 Ibid., p. 51.
30 Ibid., p. 146.
31 Alexandru Cantacuzino, *Românul de mâine: Românismul nostru* ([Bucharest], 1937).

men. A woman unable to conceive would be called '*stearpă*'. Cantacuzino's and other Legionary leaders' demand for action were barely veiled calls for violence and revenge, justified by the parallel image of Romanian men as despondent and in need of demonstrating or displaying their masculinity.

Other elements of the Legionary rhetoric and action further reinforce this conclusion. Codreanu's role model was Stephen the Great, a medieval Romanian *voivode* (ruler), widely celebrated in both historical accounts and folklore for both his military victories and his masculine prowess.[32] Stephen the Great was thought to have fathered more children than could be counted among Romanian women of all social strata, something that was never held against him, but rather used anecdotally as evidence of his greatness.

The organisation of the Legion also reflected its masculinist orientation. Armin Heinen, author of the most comprehensive historical analysis of the Legion, writes:

> The Statues of the Legion had four fundamental subdivisions, but as such, it was conceived as an organisation for the *male youth*, to which all other units were subordinated. Thus, in the second section men of any age who wanted to support the [male] youth were to meet, while the third unit had the same goal with regard to women. Romanians from across the border were going to be in the fourth section.[33]

Though Heinen does not pay much attention to the organisation of the Legion from a gender perspective, it is clear from this description that he considers it a masculinist movement, in which women were to play the role of supporters rather than full participants. He notes: 'the [Iron] Guard did not focus on the entire "young generation", but rather on young men ... The woman's mission was reduced, according to these concepts, to biological and social reproduction of the family, a role endangered, it was pointed out, by the "masculinisation" of women.'[34]

The Fortress bore out this maternalist and essentialist view of women as secondary in the Legionary movement. The name of this structure illustrates the very ambivalence about the desire to mobilise and yet preserve as secondary female followers of the Legion. In Romanian the word '*cetăţuie*' is a diminutive of '*cetate*'. This specific form of the word suggests that women's groups were considered

32 Heinen, *Legiunea*, p. 127.
33 Ibid., p. 132 (my italics).
34 Ibid., p. 273.

'small fortresses', most likely with regard to the size of the groups, but also alluding to their significance in the movement. The Fortresses had an autonomous organisation internally, but overall were subordinated in action and goals to the leadership of the Legion. In a document from 1933, Mihail Stelescu listed the goals of the fortresses as follows:

a) Self-education among members of the Fortress in all areas
b) Helping the Legion through all available means
c) To create and spread works that would uplift women's morale
d) To develop and maintain alive the ancient Christian traditions, the national consciousness and solidarity of all Romanian women
e) To give new Romania a new woman, an experienced and decisive soldier like the [new] man.

Stelescu continued by defining the virtues of the ideal female supporter of the Legion: 'the Legionary sister has to be a brave soldier and yet represent a new ideal. Her home has to be an altar, her soul a pure ray of sun.'[35] Although the word 'soldier' appears twice in this text, suggesting a gender-inclusive concept of fighting, heroism and sacrifice, it is little more than inflammatory rhetoric. The Legion was not committed to training women and including them in any way in its central terrorist and political activities. In fact, women like Nicoleta Niculescu, who wanted to become more fully involved in such paramilitary and sabotage activities, had to do so as exceptions to the general role assigned for women, outside of the Fortresses.[36]

The Legionary work camps had a strong masculinist bent as well. They aimed to bring together sympathisers and members for activities that were both to help the financial status of the Legion and to demonstrate its commitment to social activism on behalf of Christian values and the national interest, and against the Jewish threat. The Carmen Sylva camp, though named after a woman, the first Queen of Romania, was made up overwhelmingly of men. Likewise, its most important activities engaged mostly men. One of the main activities was brick-making, deemed a male dominion exclusively.[37] Another activity was the vegetable garden, in which some women also partic-

---

35 Stelescu, 'Frățiile', p. 9.
36 Heinen, *Legiunea*, p. 273.
37 See 'Dare de seamă rezumativă asupra mersului Legiunii dela Iulie 1927 până la Octombrie 1928', *Pământul Strămoșesc*, 2:21 (1928), 1–5.

ipated. Finally, other important activities aimed to subvert Jewish commerce by opening stores operated and supplied only by ethnic Romanians. Women were not an important force in these activities. The only type of female activism the Legion openly acknowledged and encouraged was to make various household items, such as pillows, embroideries, tablecloths, handkerchiefs, bookmarks and paintings, which could be sold to raise funds for the Legion.[38] In contrast with other women's fascist organisations at that time, the women's Fortresses did not emphasise social welfare work as an important goal. The welfare of the Legion in a much narrower sense (mostly financial and as a very informal means of providing safe homes for Legionary activists) was the main focus of the Fortresses.

It was not surprising that the Legion's ideological focus, recruiting efforts and rhetoric were male-oriented. In fact, Codreanu's own experiences of frustration with the outcome of the war and with university life in Iaşi were more common among men than women. Though many women did experience disappointment with the post-war settlement, they had not participated in combat and were therefore unable to articulate the same sense of frustrated entitlement as many young soldiers.[39] There were also far fewer women in the faculties of law and medicine at the University of Iaşi, where Codreanu's movement exploded in the late 1920s, and women generally did not harbour the same feeling that their rights were being violated by the policies of the university. While male students viewed their access to education as a requirement for their future livelihood as breadwinners and a guarantee by the state, most women were simply grateful for having more access to university education in any field. Therefore, when Codreanu began his propaganda and violent activities focusing on the Jewish threat to Romanian students and businesses and on the state's failure to live up to people's expectations after the war, his language resonated more with men than with women. In fact, women's support for the Legionary movement was a secondary, subsidiary issue in the larger quest for attracting a young Romanian male following. This, of course, was a feature common to other fascist movements in Europe.

Codreanu's writings reflect a dismissively tolerant attitude towards women followers. The Legion seemed disposed to accept them as followers, but was unwilling to expand its organisation towards incorporating women's groups and issues in much of its propaganda. In two

---

38 'Surorile Legiunii', *Pământul Strămoşesc*, 7:2 (1933), 14.
39 Heinen, *Legiunea*, pp. 94–5.

volumes published by Codreanu, both fundamental texts of the Legionary movement, there is very little discussion of women's role in the Legion. In the *Booklet of the Nest Chief*, only two paragraphs out of 123 pages focus on women's Fortresses.[40] The pamphlet delineated briefly the normative role for Legionary women: mothers and tools for Legionary propaganda at home. Codreanu's suggestions for discussion topics in the Fortresses did open up the possibility for imagining more lively roles for the female members: 'the Legionary sister as mother; the Legionary sister as wife; the Legionary sister as fighter; the rights and the duties of the Legionary woman'. But most other topics leave no doubt that motherhood and wifehood were the main roles for Legionary women: 'the nourishing meal for the family; the art of cooking; the cleanliness of the house and child-care; how to make all clothing at home; raising children; at church'.[41] In fact, such topics were the focus of most women's organisations in inter-war Romania, from SONFR to Astra. Some of the issues to be discussed in the Fortresses did have radical political undertones, such as the notion that by making clothes at home, one avoided spending money at the tailor shops, which the Lgionaries considered to be a Jewish-dominated business. This rhetoric suggests a politicisation of the home. Yet the *Booklet* did not provide any indication of how to engage the above-mentioned topics, leaving their political implications as mere possibilities, rather than normative, clear directions for the Legionary women.

Other texts, such as the right-wing daily papers (*Cuvântul, Porunca Vremii, Axa*), would provide the materials to fill in these blanks. But very little was published in these papers about women's duties or women's actions as Legionaries aside from basic reformulations of maternalist positions. After a dribble of brief articles about newly gained political powers in the first few issues of *Porunca Vremii* (in 1928 women had obtained a limited right to vote and be elected in communal elections), the right-wing newspaper abandoned any reference to women's public roles until 1937, when it began calling women to assume responsibly their role of mothers.[42] One headline in January read: 'Romanian women! Raise your children in the spirit of the old beliefs and of love for the Nation!'[43] Articles

40 Codreanu, *Cărticica*, pp. 12 and 25.
41 Ibid., p. 12.
42 This lack of focus on gender issues was not typical of the extreme-right movement in general. *Pământul Strămoşesc*, for instance, continued to publish articles on women's roles throughout the 1930s.
43 *Porunca Vremii*, 6:627 (1937), 1.

oscillated between fervent calls to nurturing patriotism and harsh criticisms of women's public roles: 'Today's "intellectual" woman is an element utterly sterile [*sterp*] for society'. The same article concluded, 'We plead for marriage, the only *natural destiny* for woman'.[44] The resurgence in the intensity and prevalence of maternalist propaganda and the critical view of women's political rights were typical of many other mainstream publications.[45] It is unclear why this trend became so pronounced. Most likely, it was a combination of different factors: a response to the greater, albeit still marginal involvement of women in public life; a reaction against the international feminist press; and an echo of the maternalist propaganda in Italy and Germany. This resurgence of maternalist propaganda may also represent an attempt to prepare the nation for war, by reaffirming gender typologies that reinforced the identification of men with heroic virile public roles and that of women with less aggressive and more feminine roles. Yet more research needs to be done on this topic before coming to solid conclusions.[46]

After Antonescu's *coup d'état* on 6 September 1940 and the beginning of his coalition with the Iron Guard, the tone and frequency of articles addressing women's issues and directly women as members of the Legionary movement changed dramatically. An 'Appeal to the Romanian woman' defined the challenges faced by women in the Legionary state as follows: 'the woman of Legionary Romania must fight for re-christening the Romanian nation, de-christened by the chaotic and dissolving tendency of the "emancipation" spirit, imported unknowingly, latently, along with the dogma of democratic materialism'.[47] Feminists were identified as anti-Christian and funda-

---

44 N. Crevedia, 'Să schimbăm mentalitatea femeii', *Porunca Vremii*, 6:667 (1937), 1 [my italics].

45 See, for instance, N. Batzaria, 'Femeia în politică', *Adevărul*, 42:14091 (1929), 3; M. Negru, 'Femeile în Partidele Politice', *Universul*, 47:280 (1929), 1. *Adevărul* was the most popular left-wing paper in inter-war Romania, while *Universul* was the most widely read newspaper during the same period, with mostly nationalist-liberal leanings.

46 The information available to me was inconsistent and anecdotal. Therefore, these claims are merely speculations about possible explanations. However, it is clear in the case of the eugenics movement, for instance, that a turn towards emphasising women's maternalist responsibilities in restrictive terms did take place in the mid 1930s. See Maria Bucur, 'In praise of wellborn mothers: on eugenics and gender roles in interwar Romania', *East European Politics and Societies*, 9:1 (1995), 123–42.

47 Mircea Mateescu, 'Apelul către femeia română', *Porunca Vremii*, 9:1762 (1940), 1.

mentally deviant from the normative roles for Legionary women, while women were allowed to imagine an important positive role in society as a spiritual, 'christening' leader for the Romanian nation at large, and not just their own children and homes.

During the short-lived Legionary dictatorship, these images continued to figure prominently in Legionary propaganda, placing women in a much more central role among the movement's preoccupations than ever before. But a similar rhetoric, minus references to the Legionary state, continued after the official disbanding of the Legionary movement. In June 1941, two articles in *Porunca Vremii* repeatedly defined women as potentially spiritual beings, but decried the feminist movement as a perversion of women's nature and an anti-Christian movement. The author, a priest, went so far as to suggest that, aside from motherhood, any public activity by women was a form of prostitution, and by extension, depraved.[48] In fact, it is difficult to differentiate the rhetoric of the radical right publications from that found in most wartime periodicals with respect to their view of women's normative social roles and the fears they express about women's participation in the workforce. The one significant difference was the references made to boycotting Jewish goods, but such calls were not frequent.[49]

If the issue of women's role in politics and society played a marginal role in Legionary ideology, the attention given to activities undertaken by female members or sympathisers was marginally greater. *For Legionaries*, a 1936 book tracing the early history of the movement, gives some information about women's role in fundraising and support for the Legion's first publication, *Pământul Strămoşesc*. Yet, although women made up roughly 10 per cent of these early supporters, the large volume did not name one woman as an important figure in the activities of the Legion during its first decade.[50]

There were a few exceptions to the overwhelming anonymity of women supporters of the Legionary movement. The wives and mothers of major leaders, such as Codreanu's wife, Elena Corneliu Codreanu, were the object of some attention in the extreme-right press and Legionary actions. The Codreanu wedding, which took place in June

---

48 Gh. Butnariu, 'Meditaţii pentru femeile de astăzi', *Porunca Vremii*, 10:1946 (1941), 1 and 3; and Gh. Butnariu, 'Avertisment pentru femeile de astăzi', *Porunca Vremii*, 10:1961 (1941), 1 and 3. The reference to prostitution was in the second article.

49 *Pământul Strămoşesc*, 2:21 (1928), 5.

50 Corneliu Zelea-Codreanu, *Pentru legionari* (Sibiu, Ed. Totul Pentru Ţară, 1936), pp. 326–7. The book was almost 500 pages long.

1925 in Focşani, became an important moment in the pre-history of the Legion. It drew a great deal of attention from the authorities, and from a very large audience,[51] and became represented as one of the first mass meetings of the movement. Heinen does not pay much attention to this event. A sympathiser of the Legion writes, however, that the wedding had a propaganda dimension, demonstrating the positive values of Codreanu's movement. He continues by claiming that so many people came to see it because they loved grandiose spectacles and had not had a chance to see a national wedding because the heir to the crown, Carol II, had eloped with a commoner woman during the First World War.[52] This interpretation does suggest that Codreanu's wedding ceremony was, indeed, a symbolic gesture in which the *Căpitan* displayed his public persona in a fashion familiar to many people, as a pillar of tradition and stability. His wife, thus, became an accessory to this performance, serving as proof of Codreanu's own 'settled' masculinity. Instead of the Romantic, charismatic, intense image he had up to that point, the *Căpitan* now became a *pater familias*. With his wedding, Codreanu hoped to allay any worries about the social radicalism of his movement. His was a struggle for upholding Christian traditions in the home, not a destabilising force, in spite of his frequent calls to violence and declarations of war.

After 1925, Elena Corneliu Codreanu re-entered anonymity, as publicity around the movement focused solely on the *Căpitan* and other male leaders. She re-emerged as a public figure only after her husband's death, now as a revered widow and mother of Codreanu's child. Again, she was not the object of public attention, but rather served as a symbol for Codreanu's image as a martyr and, by extension, of the Legion's Christian values and goals. Her fate was paralleled with that of the Virgin's flight to Egypt.[53] Thus, even the few women who captured the attention of the extreme-right press and movement were not intended to be role models for other women, but

---

51 According to Heinen, 'tens of thousands of people' watched the wedding. Another
    account, by a sympahiser of the Legion, Grigore Traian Pop, puts the total number
    at 80,000 to 100,000. While the latter may be exaggerating, the number of people
    who came to witness the wedding was clearly extraordinary by comparison with any
    previous wedding that was not royalty. Grigore Traian Pop, *Garda, Căpitanul şi
    arhangelul din cer: o istorie obiectivă a mişcării legionare*, Vol. 2 (Bucharest, Ed.
    Eurasia, 1996), pp. 114–15.

52 Pop, *Garda*, p. 114.

53 Lucrezzia Kar, 'Legenda aurită a creatorului Legiunii: Inteviu cu Elena Corneliu
    Codreanu' and I. P. Prundeni, 'Spovedania unei mari dureri: Elena Corneliu
    Codreanu', both *Porunca Vremii*, 9:1776 (1940), 1.

rather to encourage their support for the Legion, and to demonstrate the commitment of the Legionary movement to its women followers. Instead, such female figures became symbols of the movement's commitment to traditional gender roles, to alleviate any questions both supporters, especially men, and opponents may have had about the Legion's radical social goals.

Other women were present in the Legionary movement from the start. Codreanu's sister became a prominent spokeswoman on his behalf from the mid 1920s. Starting in 1927, when the Legion was created, the organisation's publication, *Pământul Strămoşesc*, sometimes published letters from female admirers or followers of the Legion. One such letter, published in 1928, came from Indiana Harbor, in the United States:

> Three weeks ago I received . . . a red poster: The Call of Our Ancestral Soil. What a beautiful name . . . With the help of my modest knowledge, as a poor but loving Romanian . . . without begging, doing only my moral duty as a Romanian, I believed . . . I thought it would be good to spread the word to our brothers . . . As a result, please Mr Codreanu, do me the honour of receiving 8500 lei . . . Wishing you much success in the ploughed soil and rich harvests for *Pământul Strămoşesc*, which you defend so selflessly, worthy of the gratitude and admiration those from over the Ocean feel, with greetings of a Romanian-sister from the village of Axente Sever, I remain Yours sincerely, Anuţa Lupan.

This letter represents well the deferential attitude many women held towards the Legion and especially its *Căpitan*. Although clearly enthusiastic in supporting *Pământul Strămoşesc*, Lupan, not unlike other Romanian women, was uncomfortable expressing her nationalist feelings in a direct and forceful language. She responded quickly and with joy to Codreanu's call to violent action, but did not herself articulate a similar attitude. She seemed ready to become a follower, but not necessarily a full participant.

Other women were attracted, like some of the male followers, by Codreanu's personal charisma. However, there were certainly gender differences in the specific attributes followers found attractive. One woman wrote: 'the Captain came from a world of the Good, a Prince of the lights . . . a medieval knight, a martyr, and a hero'.[54] The image of Codreanu as a medieval knight suggests a

---

54 Ovidiu Guleş, *Cum am cunoscut Legiunea Arhangelul Mihail* (Timişoara, Ed. Gordian, 1992). The book contains a collection of different essays and a brief memoir by Iulia Maria Cojorean, a follower of the Legion.

very different motivation, of a more romantic, personal nature, rather than political, for this woman's decision to become a participant in the movement.

A recently published collection of memoirs written by women followers of the Legion, *Lacrima prigoanei: din lupta legionarelor românce*, shows some of the important elements that attracted women to the movement. Most of the authors were the first generation in their family to attend secondary schools, coming from rural areas. In the Fortresses they found a 'home away from home'. They spoke highly of the warm, informal atmosphere of these groups, which were at the same time suffused with Christian ideals. Since the leaders often wore traditional garb, they appeared as a familiar and comfortable presence in a unfamiliar world:

> Often [Titi] took me to the [female] students meeting, where she liked to wear a white blouse with a national embroidery on the chest, in a 'U'. That's what Nicoleta [the deceased leader of the Fortresses] had worn. These meetings, though solemn, were also intimate. Our hearts opened up in her [Titi's] presence.[55]

Thus, even though the activities of the Fortresses were secondary to the movement overall, they presented an attractive environment for the female followers and sympathisers. There is no evidence thus far to suggest how women joining the Fortresses saw their role in the Legion other than as faithful followers. In particular, there is little indication that women with ambitions for gender empowerment were attracted to the Legion with this goal in mind.

Finally, there were some women who joined the Legionaries because of sheer opportunism and/or because they hoped to carve out a leading, powerful role in such a dynamic movement. Alexandrina Cantacuzino, the President of SONFR and a self-proclaimed feminist, became an open and avid supporter of the Legion during its short-lived regime. What drove this woman, who had not expressed publicly any sympathies for the Legionary movement and had not facilitated any friendly relations between SONFR and the Legion, to such a change can only be attributed to her desire for self-empowerment and opportunism. Some fear of the regime's violent reactions to non-compliance with its new radical directions may have played a role in Cantacuzino's change of heart. But that could not have led her to

---

55 *Lacrima prigoanei: Din lupta legionarelor românce* (Timişoara, Ed. Gordian, 1994), p. 23.

give interviews about women's role in the Legionary state in the official paper.[56]

There were other women involved in radical rightist movements. Elena Bacaloglu, a journalist who became familiar with the new right after the war, when she was living in Italy, came back to Romania ready to found a Romanian fascist movement in alliance with Mussolini's Fasci di Combattimento. As Heinen rightly comments, she was driven to these efforts by her 'enormous ambition'.[57] Her attempts were thwarted by the police in 1925, but the German scholar suggests that it was destined to fail anyway, as Bacaloglu found only a hundred followers for her movement. Women like her were few and far between. Most other ambitious women searched avenues for empowerment in women's organisations that were less overtly political and more mainstream in the Romanian political spectrum.

Overall women did not rush to join the Legion in significant numbers. Although the sources for a comprehensive sociological analysis of the Legionary movement are missing, the few documents that speak to this question suggest that women made up a small fraction of the followers and sympathisers. A report from 1933 places the total number of women members at 8 per cent. Another statistic from the Carmen Sylva work camp suggests that women made up 11.5 per cent by comparison with men.[58] The infrastructure of the Legion indicates that gender was an important element in the organisation's make-up, with the women's Fortresses constituting a separate element from the 'Cross Brotherhoods' and 'Nests'. Yet the Fortresses never played a prominent role in either the internal reports of the Legion or the propaganda used to attract other followers. Although the Fortresses may have been very active, they were certainly not considered important to the goals, propaganda or self-representation of the Legion. Unlike the British Union of Fascists, the German Nazi Party, or even the Italian Fasci Femminili, the most important fascist movement and party in Romania did not place the participation of women and women's issues in a prominent position in either ideology or institutional development. Without a clear platform and offer of activism with regard to women's issues, the Legion was unable to attract

56 *Porunca Vremii*, 9:1779 (1940), 1–2 (interview with Lucrezzia Kar).
57 Heinen, *Legiunea*, p. 107.
58 There were 82 women, 710 men and 50 children. Ibid., p. 369. However, of the 82 women, only 12 were full Legionaries, 38 were members, and 32 were sympathisers. By contrast, of the 710 men only 78 were sympathisers and 2 were guests. So the percentage of actual members is far greater for men than for women.

women who were already involved in public action in other organisations, such as SONFR or Astra.

The Legion was more successful among the younger generation, partly because its activities and language emphasised the qualities of youth and played on youthful romantic ideas of activism. The Legion also attracted women who shared strong anti-Semitic attitudes and could not find other movements that had the same blend of Christian rhetoric and radical anti-Semitism. One follower justified her support for this important aspect of the Legionary movement as 'justice towards Jews', rejecting the notion that the Legion harboured racist anti-Semitic ideas: 'We received a moral, religious education, and not one to hate the Jews'.[59]

Gender was central to the ideology of the Legion. However, overall the Iron Guard remained a movement initiated and controlled by men and with goals that focused more prominently on re-establishing social, economic and political authority for them, than on engaging women in similar activism. Although not entirely absent from the movement, women were at best a marginal presence, and served to reinforce familiar masculinist notions of the separation between public and private roles and to reassure both followers and opponents of the traditional Christian morality of the Legion in the realm of family and gender roles. With other organisations offering the same and, in some cases, more possibilities for participation in the area of maternalist action, women of different class, political and educational background saw in the Legion an alternative that in many ways did not compete with longer-established organisations. The Legion's 'competitive edge' was more in the area of its activism among students (where women were a minority anyway) and among anti-Semites. But this did not lead to a great influx of women in the ranks of the Legion.

59 Guleş, *Cum am cunoscut*, p. 353. The words are those of Iulia Maria Cojorean.

5

Hungary

Mária M. Kovács

When compared to many other countries of Central Europe the peculiarity of Hungary's inter-war history is that the extreme right was never really able to establish itself as a ruling force other than for relatively short, if crucial episodes, the last of which ended with the conclusion of the Second World War.[1] But in general, extremist populism was alien from Hungary's mainstream conservative establishment, which dreaded rather than supported mass mobilisation and made repeatedly successful efforts to preserve Hungarian politics in a more traditional framework. Movements of the Hungarian extreme right never really merged into a single, fascist-type, dictatorial and ideology-driven mass party which would have developed its own discourse on women's issues comparable to those developed, for instance, by Italian Fascism or German Nazism. The only sustained experiment in inter-war Hungary to establish a mass party of the right, that by Gyula Gömbös after his coming to power in 1932, exhausted itself in two to three years without success.[2]

Therefore, any attempt to describe the discourse of the Hungarian extreme right regarding women and gender would have to rely on the thoughts of a few rather marginal ideologues, mostly on lonely imitators of foreign fascists with very narrow impact within Hungary itself. To the extent that Hungary witnessed a turn to new perceptions of

1 The extreme right was a predominant force between 1920 and 1922, then later during the Depression, and finally after the German occupation of Hungary in 1944.
2 On the aborted attempts to organise a women's section in the Party of National Unity (Nemzeti Egységpárt) by Gömbös, see József Vonyó, 'Nöi szerepek a Nemzeti Egység Pártjában (1932–1939)', in Beáta Nagy and Margit S. Sárdi (eds), *Szerep és alkotás, Nöi szerepek a társadalomban és az alkotómüvészetben* (Csokonai Kiadó, Debrecen, 1997).

female roles, whether in the family, on the labour market, or in public life during the inter-war period, this turn had at least as much to do with forces of mainstream conservatives, or liberals, or the left, as with those of the extreme right.

But this is not to say that the extreme right did not have a very powerful influence in Hungary. The main and lasting input of the extreme right in shaping the country's inter-war history was to have introduced political anti-Semitism to mainstream politics by incorporating the concept of ethno-religious quotas in the legal system. In 1920 the extreme right was able to push through Parliament the notorious *numerus clausus* legislation which put a 6 per cent ceiling on the enrolment of Jewish students in the universities. A thriving and influential community before the war, Hungarian Jews were now subject to discriminatory legislation severely limiting their access to higher learning and, by consequence, the academic professions. From then on until 1945, political anti-Semitism may have periodically subsided or gained in intensity, but it remained a central topic of competitive politics and resulted, by 1938, in the extension of the anti-Semitic quota system from education into the economy and the professions.

As the twist of fate for Hungarian women would have it, it was precisely in this general context of growing ethno-religious fragmentation and illiberal transformation that some of the most important steps towards women's emancipation were taken in the country, including the historic step of granting women the right to vote. This paradoxical timing in turn shaped the politics of emancipation in a deeply ambiguous fashion. So what I propose to do in this chapter is to look at some of these ambiguities, focusing on the interplay between cleavages of ethnicity and gender in the inter-war period.

But before doing that, I would remark that in Hungary, this may have been the first, but certainly was not the last time that major steps towards the emancipation of women would happen simultaneously with the de-emancipation of some other groups. After 1948 Stalinist communism opened up extraordinary opportunities for women, but it also introduced cruel limitations of employment and education opportunities for whole classes of people lumped together in what was, at the time, called category 'X'. Individuals born into families of the former so-called 'ruling classes' were now lumped into this clumsy and crude, but operative social category, which, for all intents and purposes, included those not born into working-class or peasant families. Thus again, as in the inter-war period, the growing inclusion of women went hand in hand with the exclusion of other social groups, including the exclusion of women unfortunate enough to be born into the wrong social category. Thus, for the better part of the twentieth century, Hungarian women, along with men, were involved in mechanisms of selective inclusion and exclusion, whether as beneficiaries or victims, whether along ethnic or class lines, or both. This at least partly explains the difficulties feminists face even today in mobilising a constituency within Hungarian society around a common vision founded on the concept of gender.

Electoral reform and the inclusion of women

In Hungary's multi-ethnic society, cleavages of ethnicity affected Hungarian feminism almost from the very beginnings. It was at the turn of the century that the first major debates on the full legal emancipation of women took place, bringing the problem of women's vote into the focus of public attention. At this time, male suffrage was still limited by both property and educational qualifications, with enfranchised males not exceeding 8.6 per cent of the total population. But by the early 1900s, Hungary's limited electoral system came under heavy attacks both internally, from the social democrats, and externally, from the Habsburg establishment which presided over the quasi-federal structure of the Austro-Hungarian monarchy established with the *Ausgleich* of 1867. Strangely enough it was in the issue of electoral reform that Francis Joseph broke with his general pattern of non-intervention in Hungarian affairs and put pressure on the Hungarian government to broaden the franchise to larger sections of society. The old Kaiser's motives had to do, as always, with trying to stem the tide of Hungarian nationalism. Extending the franchise would have meant the inclusion into the political process of important groups of the Kaiser's tactical allies against Hungarian nationalists, namely the non-Hungarian minority populations residing in the territory of the Hungarian state on the one hand, and a substantial social democratic working-class constituency on the other.

Under such pressures, electoral reform would obviously be an extremely sore point of Hungarian politics. Hungary's feminists wanted to avoid the strategic mistake of allowing the issue of women's vote to be manipulated in the conflict between the monarchy and Hungarian nationalists. They argued that the problem of the female vote was independent of the larger national and ethnic issues at stake in the electoral debate. Or so it seemed at first sight.

True enough, at least as far as the Hungarian feminist movement itself was concerned, in the first decade of the twentieth century ethnicity or religion did not play a divisive role within the movement. At the turn of the century Hungarian feminists were a conglomerate of women activists with diverse roots in liberal, Christian socialist, social democratic and even conservative circles. The first signs of division within this feminist conglomerate only appeared when the prospect of extending the vote to women began to look serious. Indeed, the first split within the turn-of-the-century feminist conglomerate was not caused by conflicts of ethnicity, but by the need to make strategic alliances among Hungary's major political forces in campaigning for the vote for women. The majority of feminist leaders decided to reject the offer of alliance by the social democrats, who tried to win these women over to their campaign for universal suffrage.[3] Instead, in their search for powerful supporters, they opted for the liberal party of Vilmos Vázsonyi, which advocated urgent, but limited electoral reform.

There was a breakthrough for Hungarian feminists in 1917 as Vilmos Vázsonyi was appointed cabinet minister with the task of developing an electoral reform. For the first time in Hungarian history, Vázsonyi's bill included the extension of electoral rights to women, even if the female vote was to be restricted by so-called cultural qualifications promising only to enfranchise women with middle-school education.

But the public response to Vázsonyi's proposal was far more disappointing for feminists than anything they could have anticipated. What was especially shocking was that the main opposition came not from the traditionalist adversaries, but from forces whom feminists had long considered their secure allies in the Christian socialist movement. Christian socialists were, in general, not at all adverse to the idea of the female vote. Their opposition was only directed against

---

3 This decision isolated feminists from social democrats, as the rejection of the social democratic offer elicited a bitter response. 'The feminism of the middle classes is set on a road which leads in other directions than the movement of the working class. A middle-class woman must fight for opening up higher positions for women, because this is all she is interested in. But we, proletarian women cannot share in these aims. For a century, we have been working together with proletarian men in the factories from the morning to the evening. Thus, for us, there is no women's movement, there is no separate movement of any kind, but the one movement that belongs to the working class, that of socialism. A middle-class woman aims at equality with man. And most likely, this is what she will become. And soon as she achieves this equality, she will abandon the rest of us, the women of the working class.' László Rudas, 'Polgári és proletár nőmozgalom', *Nőmunkás*, 24 April 1906.

one particular aspect of Vázsonyi's proposal, namely that the female vote be restricted by educational qualifications.

As soon as Vázsonyi's bill was made public, Christian socialists came up with a startling analysis of census data. An astonishing 40 per cent of all women (260,000) to be enfranchised by the bill belonged to minority populations: 26 per cent of them were of the Jewish faith, 14 per cent were of German mother tongue. This came at a time when Jews and Germans, taken together, only made up a tenth of the country's population. This meant that nearly half of the female electorate to be enfranchised under Vázsonyi's bill would have come from the urban minorities which, again, would have multiplied the electoral strength of minority constituencies.

Not surprisingly, the controversy therefore came to centre on the conjunction between ethnicity and gender. It now turned out how naive liberal feminists had been to assume that they could avoid touching ethnic sensitivities when pushing ahead with their concern for the enfranchisement of women. It became amply evident that in Hungary's multi-ethnic society the issue of female suffrage was no less independent of the sensitive ethnic issues than any other area of electoral reform. If indeed universal suffrage would have enfranchised the masses of non-Hungarian (Slovakian and Romanian) agrarian populations and would have had wide ramifications on Hungary's national policies, a female suffrage restricted by educational qualifications would also have triggered a potential change in the ethnic balance of the electorate by giving disproportionate advantage to the urban minority elements, the Jews and the Germans. At the same time, for nationalist opponents of the bill, the public debate drove home the unhappy realisation that minority groups within Hungary's urban middle classes were conspicuously ahead of the majority society in providing for the formal education of their women. As Géza Polónyi succinctly put it in Parliament: 'The unfortunate reality is that the higher the educational standards are set, the more disproportionate advantage we give to the Jews'.[4]

Stealing a page from the liberals' book, Christian socialists therefore contested Vázsonyi's plan on the ground that it was incompatible with the universalist and democratic intent of liberals, because it would only deepen ethnic cleavages in Hungarian society. A restricted female suffrage, they argued, would sharpen the ethnic division of political power and disadvantage the majority. As Edith Farkas, chair of the Christian Socialist Association

4 *A Nő,* 15 March 1918.

of Women (Kevesztényszocialista Nőegyesület), put it:

> Vázsonyi's concept of a restricted franchise based on educational qualifications is fatally flawed because it favours those noisy mademoiselles (who, in our society, are typically not Christian) over our true Hungarian women. We must admit that it is a shame that Christian society has been too lazy and idle to provide better formal education for its daughters who are, in reality by no means less cultured, but as long as this is the case, we must not allow the noisy middle school element in female society to put itself in the forefront. We demand that there either be no female vote, or if it is to be introduced, our Christian women with their sober mentality be included.[5]

The outline of future conflicts now began to take shape. The rift between liberal feminists and Christian socialist women's groups was opened up, never to be bridged again. Feminists within the Christian socialist movement began distancing themselves from liberal feminism. They now began to put the emphasis on what separated liberal feminists from a wider female constituency, labelling them as ethnically and religiously different, as a minority whose norms and concerns were alien from the sober mentality of majority women.[6] The claim of liberal feminists to represent any kind of common vision for women came to be contested by Christian socialists as a false extrapolation based on the experience only of minority women. Partly as a result of the electoral debate, and partly as a result of the growing political polarisation of the country during the war, by 1918 Christian socialist women's groups broke ranks with liberal feminists and joined the newly established nationalist, right-wing women's organisation, the National Association of Hungarian Women (Magyar Asszonyok Nemzeti Szövetsége, MANSZ). The passions whipped up during the debate of the 1917 bill survived into the post-war period and set the context for the bitter confrontations that followed.

As for the female franchise, its formal introduction was now only a matter of months away. In November 1918 the left-liberal, pacifist government of Mihály Károlyi declared secession from the Habsburg Empire and introduced universal suffrage together with female suffrage in the newly sovereign Hungarian Republic. However, Károlyi's pacifist republic collapsed under the tremendous pressure put on the country by the military offensive from Romania and Czechoslovakia, aggravated by the policies of hostile Entente powers.

5 *Keresztény Nő*, July 1918.

6 Expressions of Ida Bobula, a prominent leader of the conservative women's movement in the inter-war period.

After the five-month episode of Béla Kun's Bolshevik Revolution, women were finally able to exercise their right to vote for the first time in 1920.

The female franchise introduced in 1920 was wider than anything imagined before. The concept of cultural qualifications did not disappear totally, but it was reduced to a mere requirement of literacy without any proof of formal schooling. Other than that, women came to enjoy identical voting rights with men: all citizens with six years of citizenship, over the age of twenty-four and with permanent residence for at least six months, were enfranchised.[7]

However, defying earlier expectations, the first exercise of women's vote did not lead to the development of a powerful women's lobby in Hungarian politics, nor did it provide any kind of support for those political groups which had historically fought for the extension of the vote to women. On the contrary, with the experience of war and two leftist revolutions behind their backs, in 1920 the majority of women voted for the forces of the right, bringing the extremist Christian National Party (Keresztény Nemzeti Párt) into power. Time had come to confront the bitter reality that the majority of women had no affinity to either liberals or the liberal feminists who had earlier put up a fight for bringing women into the political process. 'Everywhere, in the beginning the introduction of female suffrage brings support for forces of the reaction', concluded Anna Kéthly, the prominent women leader of the Social Democratic Party (Szociáldemokrata Párt), one of the three women politicians to become Members of Parliament during the inter-war period.[8] Liberal feminists were equally disillusioned, although they also felt sadly justified for having stopped short of supporting universal suffrage in favour of more restricted voting rights:

> Many among the old fighters for the democratic cause are today disillusioned and have become pessimists. They feel that the concept of a wide suffrage for women brings clericalism in practice and therefore

---

7 According to figures given by Ignác Romsics, the electoral decree of the Friedrich government in 1920 enfranchised 74.6 per cent of the population over the age of twenty-four. In 1922 new legislation initiated by the Bethlen government introduced an educational restriction of four years of elementary education for males and six years for females. A further restriction was introduced in the case of females by raising the voting age to thirty years. A total of 750,000 persons were disenfranchised by these restrictions, out of whom 550,000 were females. Cf. his *Ellenforradalom és konszolidáció*, (Budapest, Gondolat, 1982).

8 Anna Kéthly, 'Előszó a harmadik kiadáshoz', in Ágost Bebel, *A nő és a szocializmus* (Budapest, Népszava Kiadó, 1928), p. 10.

many among them do not feel that women are mature enough to exercise their vote.[9]

This explains why neither feminists, nor liberals, nor social democrats were particularly upset when, in 1922, Prime Minister Bethlen
reinstated some amount of cultural restrictions on voting rights, and
set them selectively higher for women than for men, resulting, in the
next elections, in a marked decrease in support for the extreme right.

The *numerus clausus*: conjunction between anti-feminism and anti-Semitism

The electoral advances of the extreme right in 1920 put feminists
under new pressures and, above all, triggered a further division
among them along ethno-religious lines. During the same year
Parliament began debating the *numerus clausus* bill that eventually
ended up restricting the admission of Jewish students to universities.

One of the reasons why the debate around the *numerus clausus* is
so interesting for students of women's history is that this bill was, in
its original version, intended to restrict only the rights of women, and
not at all those of Jews. Anti-Semitism was not the original motivation behind the bill. Initially, the restrictions were not intended to
apply to groups defined by ethnicity or religion, but only by gender.
Women of all ethnic and religious affiliations were to be banned from
admission to make way for the male war cohorts and refugee students
from the territories detached from Hungary by the peace treaty. In its
original version, the bill did not even mention ethnicity, or religion,
but only women.[10] The universities took the passing of the bill for
granted, so that in anticipation of the bill, they simply banned women
from enrolling.

But in Parliament, debate about the proposal dragged on for a year. It
was during this year that the extreme right managed to shift the focus of

9 *A Nő*, 20 March 1922.
10 By 1917 the proportion of female students at the medical faculty was 29 per cent,
  as opposed to a mere 5 per cent in 1913, and other faculties, except law, experienced a similar growth in the number of women students. Twenty-four of the
  eighty-four professors newly appointed at the medical faculty under the communist
  revolution of 1919 were women. The rapid rise in the number of women students
  was, of course, due to the war, so that as the war cohorts began returning to school,
  all universities faced the problem of overcrowding, exacerbated by the presence of
  refugee students from the detached Hungarian territories of Romania and Slovakia.
  Katalin N. Szegvári, *Numerus Clausus rendelkezesek az ellenforradalmi Magyar-
  országon* (Budapest, Akadémiai Kiadó, 1988).

the political debate away from women and refocus it on the Jews. By the end of the year, all talk about restricting the access of women was completely abandoned. In the end, the restrictions only applied to Jews. The law set a 6 per cent ceiling on the proportion of Jewish students – men and women – and banned those above the ceiling from enrolling. The law made no specific mention of women. So, at least as far as the legal system was concerned, the danger of discrimination against women, as women, was averted. This is how, as if by default, women became the indirect beneficiaries of the efforts of the extreme right to bring anti-Semitism onto the centre stage of political debate, and thus turn ethnic identity into the only politically relevant identity.

Conflicting loyalties

But the outcome of the struggle over the *numerus clausus* did not restore peace among women's organisations. What it did, instead, was to deepen further the ethnic cleavage among them. Given the fact that universities maintained the unofficial ban on women's admissions, naturally, all women's groups continued to lobby the government for lifting the ban. But while liberal feminists framed their protest in an overall rejection of the restrictions, including their application to Jews, the National Association of Hungarian Women adopted a different strategy. While they protested against discrimination against women, they explicitly approved the limitations on Jews. In 1925 they demanded that the anti-Semitic restrictions not be lifted even after the League of Nations threatened to introduce sanctions against Hungary for violating the anti-discrimination clause of the Minority Treaties.[11] To quote the chair of the National Association, Cecile Tormay:

> We demand the enforcing of the *numerus clausus* law not in order to oppress the alien race, but in order to promote our own race, because we think it would be insane and suicidal on the part of the nation not to want to recruit its intelligentsia from among its own, native race.[12]

11 In 1925, 80 out of 528 local branches of the association sent petitions to the speaker of the house voicing their support of the numerus clausus. *MANSZ*, May–July 1925, p. 16.

12 Cecile Tormay, *MANSZ*, May–July 1925, p. 16. What gives these words a particularly curious colouring is the fact that Tormay herself came not from a Hungarian family, but from a family of long-time German settlers, and made the problems and traditions of German minority existence in Hungary the subject of many of her respectable literary pieces. Her usage of the term 'native' as against the 'alien' race is symptomatic of the kind of assimilationist zealotry so common to minority intellectuals in a nationalist culture.

Such explicit approval of anti-Semitic discrimination by the National Association clearly served the purpose of trying to salvage the cause of women from the damaging reputation it had historically acquired through the close connection of liberal feminism with Jewish women.[13] In an effort to remedy this public image, the National Association adopted a consistently anti-Semitic posture. Membership in the association was not open to Jews. Admission was conditional on presenting proof of non-Jewish origins. From 1920 onwards, members of the association were requested only to vote for 'Hungarian Christian' candidates put forward by parties representing the 'Christian national cause'.[14]

All in all, the *numerus clausus* law presented the women in the National Association with the dilemma of having to opt between conflicting loyalties: that of women irrespective of ethnicity on the one hand, and that of their own ethno-religious affiliation irrespective of gender on the other. What the extreme right succeeded in doing in 1920 was to pit these two choices against each other and establish the precedence of ethno-religious identity over gender. To the extent that it ever existed, the group identity of Hungarian feminists was shattered along ethno-religious lines.

Eventually, the National Association was able to score important successes. Upon its lobbying efforts, most faculties in Hungarian universities were again reopened for women in 1925. In 1926 the stubborn opposition of the medical faculties to readmission of women was suppressed by the personal intervention of the Minister of Education, Count Klebelsberg, a close friend of the chair of the association, Cecile Tormay. With this, the threat of institutionalised anti-women discrimination at the universities and in the professions was finally put to an end.[15]

13 Tormay formulated their position as follows: 'Our organisation has nothing in common with international feminism. The world abounds in thousands of feminist organisations that are both international and interconfessional. But the idea that Christian women should form a national association belongs to Hungary, it is ours, and other nations will learn it from us. Our association is not an outgrowth of a foreign movement ... It sprang from the Hungarian soil, it is as native as Hungarian wheat and this is why it represents the vitality of our nation.' *MANSZ*, May–June 1925, p. 4. The problems of women at universities were closely associated with the Jewish problem: for example, in 1917, 68 per cent of women enrolled in the medical faculty and 48 per cent of women enrolled in the humanities were Jewish.

14 Andrea Pető, 'Minden tekintetben derék nő', in Beáta Nagy and Margit S. Sárdi (eds), *Szerep és alkotás*, Cskonai Kiadó, Budapest, 1977, p. 277.

15 From the late 1920s, the proportion of women in the student body of the universities was a steady 10–15 per cent.

By the 1930s, the image of the educated professional woman came to be accepted by ever larger segments of Hungarian society, especially after the Great Depression destroyed the remnants of the illusion that men, by themselves, could safely be counted on to provide financial security for middle-class families. Even if some areas of the legal profession still remained closed for women, on balance, from the 1930s, the right of women to work in an ever-growing circle of highly qualified occupations was no longer seriously questioned.

As for reaching beyond the educated classes, the National Association put the emphasis on philanthropy in rural communities where it attempted to build a rural base for the association. The nominal membership of the association was rather high for the inter-war period: in the 1930s it had close to half a million members out of a population of eight million.[16] Under Gömbös, the extreme right made repeated efforts to mobilise the constituency of the association for a mass party, but without much success. In 1939 the suggestion to turn the association into a national party of women also ended in failure.[17]

But while the political mass mobilisation of women never really took off during the inter-war period, in the late 1930s the dilemma of conflicting loyalties among women's activists re-emerged once more in a sharp form. In 1938 a new debate on electoral reform was opened up. The National Association, together with other women's organisations, including liberal feminists and social democratic women's groups, campaigned for the elimination of selective restrictions on women.[18]

At the same time, Parliament began debating the first so-called Jewish law, which imposed new limitations on Jews, barring them from access into the legal, medical and engineering professions and a few other areas. Again, as in the 1920s, the National Association took an active role in popularising the anti-Semitic measure which effec-

16 Pető, 'Minden tekintetben derék', p. 271.
17 *Magyar Női Szemle*, 1929.
18 In the end, the law did not lift the restrictions on women. Paradoxically, it still made women 'more' equal to men by imposing on men those restrictions that had so far only applied to women, leading to an overall decrease in eligibility. According to the new law adopted in 1938 women were still eligible if they had six years of elementary schooling, but the law raised schooling requirements from four to six years in the case of men, too. The age of eligibility remained thirty for women and twenty-four for men. Gyorgy Ránki (ed.), *Magyarország története*, Vol. 8 (Budapest, Akadémiai Kiadó, 1976), p. 941.

tively cancelled the legal equality of Jews, including Jewish women, in Hungary.

In conclusion, I would like to make two remarks. First, I would like to suggest that the story of Hungarian feminism during the interwar period may serve as a cautionary tale about the methodological pitfalls of constructing a narrowly focused dual image of history in which women's history can be removed from the general trend of evolution and be artificially made into a source of nostalgia for a sense of lost unity.

Secondly, I believe that the story leaves us with a disturbing lesson with regard to processes of emancipation under illiberal, authoritarian or even dictatorial conditions. It demonstrates how processes of emancipation may well remain central under such conditions, but at the price of breaking up multiple and overlapping identities into competitive or irreconcilable fragments.

6

Serbia, Croatia and Yugoslavia

Carol S. Lilly and Melissa Bokovoy

The inter-war Kingdom of Yugoslavia, originally titled the Kingdom of Serbs, Croats and Slovenes, came into being at the end of the Great War. A conglomerate of multiple ethnic groups, languages, religions and cultures, it rested on shaky foundations from the outset due to conflicting national and political visions among the ruling elite. In particular, the incessant and often violent quarrels between Serb and Croat political parties paralysed the fledgling democratic regime. On 6 January 1929, determined to end the political infighting, King Alexander Karadjordjević, heir to the pre-war Serbian dynasty, disbanded Parliament and declared a dictatorship. Unsurprisingly, this attempt to create unity by means of force failed. Instead, the polarisation of Yugoslav society increased, and within five years Alexander himself was assassinated by a member of the fascist Croatian Ustaša with the aid and support of extreme-right organisations in Italy, Hungary and Macedonia.

As the Second World War approached, Prince Paul, acting as Regent for Alexander's underage son Peter, made some moves aimed at reconciling Serbs and Croats within Yugoslavia. These moves were, however, both too little and too late, and when the war reached the Balkans in the spring of 1941, Yugoslavia dissolved into a bloody fratricidal conflict. Fascist Italy and Nazi Germany invited the Ustaša to preside over a new Independent State of Croatia. Serbia, meanwhile, came under German occupation realised with the co-operation of Dmitrije Ljotić's proto-fascist *Zbor*. This history of inter-war Yugoslavia's descent into occupation, partition, fascism and civil war is well documented. However, there are large gaps in this historiography as few if any historians have turned their attention to the role that women were assigned or played in the nationalist, extreme-right or fascist organisations of the first Yugoslavia.

Elsewhere, the relationship between women and the extreme-right has generated considerable interest in recent years. The general ideals associated with the extreme right include nationalism, authoritarianism, collectivism, opposition to democracy, anti-modernism, and an obsession with youth and masculinity. Women have mainly been seen by extreme-right organisations as reproducers of the nation and preservers of national culture and tradition. Hence, such organisations have generally sought to restrict women's activities to the private sphere of child bearing and rearing, while excluding them from the public sphere and especially from politics.

The gendered policies of extreme-right organisations in Croatia and Serbia during the inter-war period and the Second World War closely mirrored those promoted by fascists in Germany and Italy. It must be noted, however, that the impact of those organisations was, for the most part, quite small. Yugoslavia's most significant extreme-right organisation was the Croatian Ustaša movement, which was illegal until it took power in Croatia in April 1941. Some inter-war organisations in Serbia may be described as proto-fascist, but they were small and even though one of them, Dmitrije Ljotić's Zbor, attained a degree of power and influence in the early 1940s, wartime Serbia could not really be described as a collaborationist regime. Its status was somewhere between that of the occupied Czech lands and quisling Croatia. Importantly, it had no army of its own during the war and a German governor supervised and censored all activities of the Serbian leaders. Moreover, those few extreme-right organisations acting in Serbia paid almost no attention to women before the war, and very little afterward.[1] During the war, the Croatian Ustaša did increase its attention toward women. In both Serbia and Croatia, however, the main effect of the extreme right's gendered policies was to enhance certain trends already evident in the inter-war period and, importantly, to eliminate the expression of any alternative views.

Women in Serbia and Croatia had actively participated in inter-war civil society and helped shape Yugoslav political culture. That activity itself was, of course, framed and shaped by the historical and political context. To begin with, women were clearly subordinate to men in both regions. Although an all-Yugoslav women's suffrage movement existed, as we shall see, it achieved little in its efforts to secure political equality

---

1 This is not to say, of course, that their programmes were not gendered. But since they tended to focus their programmes and propaganda on fairly narrow political issues during this period, their views on issues concerning women and the family were unfamiliar to the general public.

for women in the inter-war Kingdom. Indeed, the vast majority of women in this heavily agrarian country, where peasants still comprised 70 per cent of the population, were raised in a traditional, patriarchal and conservative political milieu. They also were acting in an era of nation and state building. The small middle classes had spent the nineteenth and early twentieth centuries embroiled in struggles for national independence in which the destiny of their communities had rested on the skills and virtues of men. Women, meanwhile, had been expected to provide the nurturing home and well-tended hearth. Finally women's roles and positions in the new South Slav state also depended heavily on the political atmosphere and discourse within each individual nation. Specifically, in inter-war Yugoslavia, the nationalisms of the two largest groups, Serbs and Croats, often overpowered any discussions of women's participation as individuals in a liberal state, stimulating instead debate about their roles as members of a particular nation.

The status of women in inter-war Yugoslavia was based on nineteenth-century statutes and was quite unfavourable in European terms. Although women had been promised the vote in a unified Yugoslavia, they did not receive it and were thus entirely excluded from political life. Women's political views were, therefore, often either unknown or invisible. Certainly, some women's organisations held clear and public political opinions, but many other groups and most individual women still considered politics outside their sphere of influence and tended to address it in only the vaguest terms.[2] Hence, women's responses to political movements like democracy, socialism, authoritarianism or fascism remain largely undocumented.

Although the precise statutes varied in different regions of the newly created country, women's legal status was also one of inequality and subordination to men. Married women's legal rights over property were severely limited or excluded, as was their right to guardianship over their children. Antiquated inheritance laws based on the largely defunct communal organisation, the *zadruga*, almost completely excluded wives. Illegitimate children had no rights and paternity investigations were not permitted.[3]

---

2 Jovanka Kecman, *Žene Jugoslavije u radničkom pokretu i ženskim organizacijama 1918–1941* (Belgrade, Narodna knjiga, 1978), p. 169.
3 Neda Božinović, *Žensko pitanje u Srbiji u XIX i XX veku* (Belgrade, Dvadesetčetvrta, 1996), p. 100; Thomas Emmert, 'Ženski pokret: the feminist movement in Serbia in the 1920s', in Sabrina Ramet (ed.), *Gender Politics in the Western Balkans* (University Park, Pennsylvania State University Press, 1999), pp. 33–7; Kecman, *Žene Jugoslavije*, pp. 56–63.

In terms of education, the first women's schools had been opened in most parts of the future Yugoslavia in the 1870s and in some cases earlier. Nonetheless, Yugoslavia's overall illiteracy rate remained very high (45 per cent in 1931) and women's higher yet (56 per cent).[4] The percentage of literate women could not have increased radically in the following years, since by 1938/39, still only 33 per cent of girls between seven and fifteen attended school.[5]

At the time of South Slavic unification, a substantial number of women already worked outside the home. According to incomplete statistics, women made up some 20 per cent of the non-agricultural workforce in 1922 and 28 per cent by 1940. They did so, of course, for substantially less pay than men and with several legal restrictions. Women were not permitted to work in industry, mining, or jobs that might be harmful to their health. After 1922, female workers were theoretically entitled to four months of paid maternity leave, but the law was very weakly enforced. In any case, most women were employed in agriculture or as domestic servants and were unprotected by any laws.[6]

As in America and other European countries, women's organisations developed partially in response to such inequalities. As we will see, however, the majority of women's groups in inter-war Yugoslavia considered women's emancipation at best a secondary goal. In fact, the women's movement in inter-war Yugoslavia was extremely varied, reflecting the diversity of the many regions making up the state. The oldest women's organisation was formed in 1864 in Novi Sad, with others following toward the end of the nineteenth and into the early twentieth century, usually in urban areas. In September 1919 at the initiative of the Serbian National Women's Union (Srpski Navodni Ženski Savez), representatives of fifty women's organisations in the newly created country attended a meeting in Belgrade to form a Yugoslav women's union. After some disagreement concerning its name, the National Women's Union of Serbs, Croats and Slovenes (Narodni Ženski: Savez Srba, Hrvata, i Slovenaca) was formed with the goal of developing women's humanitarian, ethical,

---

4 Ljubodrag Dimić, *Kulturna politika Kraljevina Jugoslavije 1918–1941*, Vol. 2 (Belgrade, Stubovi kulture, 1997), p. 192. Again those percentages differed widely in different parts of the country. In Slovenia, for example, in 1931 94.2 per cent of women were literate, while in Macedonia the figure was only 18.3 per cent. Kecman, *Žene Jugoslavije*, p. 25.

5 Kecman, *Žene Jugoslavije*, p. 25.

6 Božinović, *Žensko pitanje u Srbiji*, pp. 100–1; Kecman, *Žene Jugoslavije*, pp. 26, 33, 41, 46.

cultural, feminist, social and national activities and representing Yugoslav women in international women's organisations. This was later renamed the Yugoslav Women's Union (YWU, Jugoslovenski Ženski Savez). By 1921, the Union included 205 organisations representing 50,000 women from all over the country.[7]

Even from the beginning, however, the YWU did not encompass all women's organisations in the country. In fact, according to Jovanka Kecman, one-third of all women's organisations did not belong to the YWU in 1921 and over time that fragmentation only increased.[8] To begin with, those women's groups with an explicitly religious orientation generally chose not to join the YWU, nor did the largest women's organisation in Croatia, Croatian Woman (Hrvatska Žena). Then in 1926, ten Belgrade societies left to form their own association, the National Women's Union, apparently out of dissatisfaction with the YWU's leadership. Three years earlier, the more feminist-oriented groups, while not leaving the YWU, had also formed their own organisation, the Alliance of the Women's Movement (Alijanse Ženskih Pokreta.)[9]

Even those organisations remaining within the YWU exhibited tremendous diversity in their goals, values, ideals and activities. Essentially, these organisations fell into four categories depending on the primary nature of their activity: humanitarian, social welfare, feminist (pro-suffragist) and professional. By far the majority of organisations focused on humanitarian and social work, a fact recognised by the government, which offered them considerable material support for their activities.[10] While some of the organisations that dealt mainly with humanitarian and social work also supported women's full equality with men, not all of them did. And even those that did generally put very little effort into such 'feminist' activities as agitating for women's suffrage or equal rights in the workplace. The majority of that work was carried out by the few explicitly feminist organisations and by some (though not all) of the women's professional societies.

---

7 Božinović, *Žensko pitanje u Srbiji*, pp. 104–5; Emmert, 'Ženski pokret', pp. 35–6; Kecman, *Žene Jugoslavije*, pp. 163–7.

8 Kecman, *Žene Jugaslavije*, p. 170.

9 Ibid., pp. 175–82. Communist scholars of the women's movement have always differentiated between the bourgeois feminist women's movement and the socialist workers' women's movement. While it is true that most inter-war women's organisations were largely made up of middle-class urban women, they were by no means all feminist, whereas those female activists associated with socialist, workers' and communist organisations usually did support classic feminist goals like suffrage and equality in women's employment and legal status.

10 Ibid., p. 171.

The following two chapters examine women's activities in relation to the extreme right under the very different circumstances of inter-war and wartime Serbia and Croatia. The chapter on Serbia examines how women's organisations and journals in inter-war Serbia influenced the forging of national and gender identities during the inter-war period and into the Second World War. The chapter on Croatia also reviews the relationship between inter-war women's organisations and the extreme right, but then focuses on how the fascist Ustaša used gender within its ideological discourse. Taken together, the two chapters both reveal the diversity of women's experiences within inter-war and wartime Yugoslavia, and point to some interesting commonalities. Both show the predominance of nationalist views among women's as well as men's organisations in inter-war Yugoslavia, suggesting that that aspect, at least, of fascist ideology was already completely consistent with the extant political culture. Moreover, and perhaps more important, both show that while extreme-right organisations sought to restrict women to the private sphere, women were in fact able to participate in Yugoslavia's civil society and were not merely passive recipients of their fate. Many Serbian and Croatian women, though not necessarily pro-fascist, did support and promote fascist policies toward women.

7

Serbia

Carol S. Lilly

While all women in inter-war Yugoslavia were raised in a traditional and conservative political milieu, women in inter-war Serbia seem to have been particularly well prepared for the policies of the extreme right by their inter-war women's organisations and women's journals.[1] As we have seen in the previous chapter, the vast majority of women's groups throughout Yugoslavia focused on humanitarian and social work. That emphasis was especially evident among Serbian women's organisations, most of which, even if they remained within the Yugoslav Women's Union (YWU, Jugoslovenski Ženski Savez), were quite traditional in their views. Likewise the women's media was largely traditional in its approach. Most women's journals focused strictly on those topics considered to be appropriate for and of greatest interest to women, including fashion, cosmetics and romance, but also housekeeping tips, recipes and national handicrafts. Some slightly more didactic women's magazines also offered women cultural materials such as literature, poetry and the arts. Only a very

Research for this chapter was made possible by grants from the Wilson Center for International Politics, the International Research and Exchanges Board, the American Council of Learned Societies, and the Research Services Council of the University of Nebraska at Kearney. I am also extremely grateful for the research assistance provided by Dr Momèilo Pavlović at the Institut za savremenu istoriju in Belgrade and the technical aid provided by Giuseppe Cimmino. Jill Irvine's comments on an earlier draft were also much appreciated.
1 Nearly all women's organisations and journals in inter-war Serbia were clearly intended for and directed at the small population of urban middle-class women. Unfortunately, information about the interests and attitudes of the vast majority of peasant women is extremely scarce. Therefore, the conclusions drawn about Serbian women in this chapter should be understood to refer only to that small group of literate women residing in urban environments.

few were openly feminist. Those few explicitly encouraged women to
see themselves as equals of men and to expand their activities beyond
the household and charitable work. Most, however, denied having
either feminist views or often any ideological perspective whatsoever.

Essentialism

Perhaps the most important common characteristic linking women in
inter-war Serbia to the extreme-right ideology was essentialism – the
belief that differences between people (whether men and women, Jews
and Germans, or Serbs and Croats) were natural and inherent rather
than cultural or socially constructed. Serbian women, whether they
considered themselves feminists or not, seemed to accept quite
happily the notion that women were not only inherently different but
indeed more moral and virtuous than men. Among feminists, this
belief was closely tied to a view of women as the most reliable proponents of the peace movement and disarmament. However, Serbian
women's essentialist beliefs also meant that they believed women to
be naturally better suited to some kinds of activities than others. Such
views could then be used to argue that women should stay out of politics and the public sphere altogether, focusing on those domestic and
nurturing activities for which they were 'naturally' intended.

Indeed, it was precisely that view of women's natural abilities that
most influenced the activities of women's organisations in the inter-
war era. Of the 106 women's organisations that sent in reports to the
YWU in 1925, ninety-five or almost 90 per cent of them dealt primarily with humanitarian or welfare activities, while only five were
feminist organisations which focused primarily on securing women's
suffrage and six were professional bodies concerned with women in
certain (usually-gender segregated) vocations. Serbian organisations
focused even more heavily on humanitarian activities: 66 per cent of
all humanitarian or welfare organisations were Serbian, while only 20
and 30 per cent of the feminist and professional ones were.[2] In most
cases, the humanitarian organisations tended to focus on meeting the
needs of female children and youth or poor mothers. Many, however,
directed their charitable activities to all needy persons, including
orphans, war invalids and refugees. Clearly, the leaders of these
organisations saw it as natural that women should take an active role

---

2 'Izveštaj o radu Saveznih društava u 1924–1925', Belgrade, 1925, Arhiv Jugoslavije, Belgrade (hereafter AJ), PSII–101.

in such nurturing activities. In fact, the YWU argued to the Yugoslav government that, because social work was so inherent to women's nature, they should always be included in all discussions of new laws on social reform and, indeed, must have the right to vote, at least at the district level where such activities typically took place.[3]

Moreover, even in those cases where organisations' charitable activities focused exclusively on women's needs and interests, they tended to see those interests as falling within certain fairly limited and domestic boundaries. Several such organisations, for example, catered specifically to the health and educational needs of pregnant women, new mothers and newborns.[4] Meanwhile, those organisations that focused on the educational needs of young girls often saw their future in very traditional (and, as we will see below, national) terms. For example, the Circle of Serbian Sisters (Kola Srpskih Sestava, KSS) of Banja Luka said its school for girls would work to raise good mothers who would be able to prepare good sons for the fatherland. Likewise, the KSS school for girls in Belgrade sought to implant elevated ideas in girls so that they could 'develop a sense of sisterly love and learn to sacrifice for their families and their nation'.[5]

Even more than the women's organisations, women's non-feminist journals in Serbia stressed women's roles as wives, mothers and housekeepers. Numerous articles in such journals as *Domaćica, Žena i svet* and *Ženski svet* published articles which unequivocally described women's tasks as primarily domestic. In one of the clearest examples of essentialism, an anonymous author harshly criticised those women who tried to be too much like men:

> Today's real woman ... knows that she cannot be the same as a man and have the same characteristics, because their paths are different, they can never be the same and one can never replace the other. Each has its own special rights and obligations. They don't overlap but complement one another. Every woman striving toward 'real progress' must understand this.[6]

3 Milena Atanacković, 'Izveštaj o radu NŽS u 1925–1926 g.', and 'Rezolucija', Bled, 26–28 October 1926, in *Kongres Narodnog Ženskog Saveza,* Belgrade, 1926, AJ, 2311. This approach toward seeking the right to vote may have represented a clever compromise between those feminists in the YWU who wanted to focus on suffrage and the more conservative women who felt the organisations should concentrate mainly on charitable activities.

4 'Pravila Društva "Srpska Majka"', 21 April 1929, AJ, 14–61–182.

5 Letter from Council of KSS of Banja Luka to Queen Marija, 15 January, 1927, AJ, 74–418–618; 'Izveštaj Glavnog odbora KSS', in *Izveštaji Kola Srpskih Sestara za 1927 godinu,* Belgrade, 1928, AJ, II 7875.

6 'Žena u varoši', *Domaćica,* 46:1–2 (1931), 1–2.

Many other articles specified exactly what those 'special rights and obligations' were. For example, an article in *Domaćica* in 1931 said that a 'real woman' would continue to run the house, maintain order, clean, cook, and most important, raise children, while her 'companion in life' struggled to feed the family.[7] Of course, motherhood was considered a woman's most important duty to herself, her family and her nation. Indeed, many of those who wrote in women's journals connected a woman's role as mother to national health and survival.[8] As one article in a women's journal explained, 'When bearing children is in question, there is no problem for the woman worker, she wants to be a mother and wants to strengthen the state with her fertility and therefore she bears children'. 'Motherhood before all and above all' should be women's main slogan, the article continued, and every woman who is not ill should have at least two children, 'because every woman who does not bear at least one child is not a good patriot and does not wish her fatherland well'.[9] Another urged women to leave their jobs and create the next generation as in the pre-war era, 'when we had no governesses or nursemaids but did have a healthy race and high moral values'.[10]

One of the strongest articles in this vein came only three months before the German invasion. Published in the February 1941 issue of *Žena i svet*, it was the winning entry in an essay competition on the theme 'Our duties'. The author, from Skopje, insisted that women must return to the path followed by Serb women and mothers when they had defended freedom and built the fatherland. A woman must be first and foremost a housekeeper and mother, for, she asked, could

7 Ibid.
8 On birth control see Dr Jelica Vučetić, 'Nekoliko reći o ograničenju porodu', *Jugoslovenska žena*, 2:8 (27 February 1932), 2; J. Maricka, 'Za slobodu u ograničenju poroda', *Jugoslovenska žena*, 2:13 (7 May 1932), 2; Dr Julka Chlapec-Djordjević, 'Hrišćanska crkva i birth control', *Jugoslovenska žena*, 3:26 (7 January 1933), 1 and 3:27 (21 January 1933), 1.
9 Polekcija D. Dimitrijević-Stošić, 'Materinstvo je najglavniji poziv svake žene', *Žena i svet*, 8:10 (1932), 1–2. Evidence that such views were held not only by the editors of such journals but also their readers may be gleaned from one journal which asked its readers their favourite occupation for women and also what occupation they thought most women would choose. Of the eight printed responses, three said home-maker and another three some version of teacher. More relevant yet, all eight agreed that most women would choose homemaker as their favourite occupation. 'Naša anketa za konkurs: O ženi radilici', *Žena i svet*, 1 (1928), 10.
10 Jovanka Nikolić, 'Majke činovnice ili samo dobre majke', *Žena i svet*, 8:9 (1932), 5. See also J. Zr., 'Majka i njeno dete', *Ženski svet*, 5:8 (1934), 3–4; Anka Raketić, 'Žena i njene dužnosti', *Ženska misao*, 1:6 (15 June 1935), 1–2.

anything be more elevated or noble than educating children, and teaching them respect, honour, and love for freedom, their people and fatherland? Family, as the basis of all social life, she continued, must be at the centre of every woman's work. 'Daughters, sisters, wives, mothers', she concluded, 'let us get to work and pass through the storm and chaos and the attacks on culture, religion, people and mankind.'[11] It is unclear from this essay whether the author supported or opposed Nazi Germany's plan to reshape the world according to the fascist ideology. What is clear, however, is that her message to women was the same as Hitler's: return to the home, raise children, support the family, and be prepared to sacrifice for the fatherland.[12]

Anti-modernism

Because modern women were often seen as rejecting the 'natural' differences between men and women, anti-modernist views were also common among many Serbian women. As with the emphasis on motherhood, this phenomenon was particularly evident in non-feminist women's journals and again enormous diversity was present. Not all articles were anti-modernist: several pointed out that modern women were not really that bad and could be as good, or even better, at parenting than their foremothers.[13] What is interesting about these articles, however, is their defensive posture, which suggested that negative stereotypes of the 'modern woman' were pervasive and could only be refuted with caution.

Indeed, many more articles harshly criticised the attributes of modernity in women. Specifically, women were reprimanded for falling prey to the sins of alcohol, tobacco, fashion, luxuries,

11 Vera Kostić, 'Naše dužnosti', *Žena i svet,* 17:2 (1941), 1–2.
12 To be fair, however, even those relatively conservative charitable women's organisations also often had a broader and more realistic notion of women's roles in society. Thus the Motherhood Society (Materinsko udruženje) announced its decision to open a seasonal day-care centre, available from spring through fall, since peasant women often had to help bring in crops leaving their children alone. Moreover, in the spring of 1940 when various women's organisations began preparing lists of women who had volunteered to help in case of war, those lists included women with such traditional skills as nurses, cooks, seamstresses and child-care providers, but also administrative workers, chauffers, telephone workers, doctors and architects. See Letter from Materinsko udruženje to Queen Marija, no date, 1938?, AJ, 74–106; List provided to Queen Marija, 9 March 1940, AJ, 74–138; Letter to Queen Marija, 20 April 1940, AJ, 74–138.
13 'Naša anketa o današnjoj majci i o današnjoj deci', *Žena i svet,* 12 (1928), 10; Dr Marija Ilić, 'Težnje moderne žene', *Žena i svet,* 6:1 (1930), 2–3.

gambling, indolence and (more rarely) sex.[14] One article graphically described the post-war woman as holding a cigarette in twisted lips, with one hand in her pocket while the other held a cocktail. Such women, it stated sadly, are nothing but 'lost sheep'.[15] Another vividly detailed the differences between old and new mothers. In the past, as now, the author explained, women had gone to parties or social gatherings, but unlike then, no current mother would race home to check on her children. Old mothers, she continued, were tireless, never had their hands folded in their laps, and never went a minute without working. They could talk as they worked, although, she added, back then they listened more. But where women in the past took handicrafts with them to a party, now, she complained, they take make-up, cigarettes and cards.[16] The same essay that won the contest on 'Our duties' began by stating that in these difficult times Serbian women must first awaken themselves from the selfishness into which they had fallen as a result of post-war modernism.[17]

While some of these articles tried to adopt a balanced view, condemning some characteristics of the modern woman while supporting her new education and independence, many also clearly associated feminism and women's aspirations toward equality in politics and the workplace with all other sins of modernism. The true Serb mother, they argued, was the soul of unselfishness who gave all of herself to the family, seeking nothing for herself. She sought no satisfaction outside the home, took only what was left over, and was happy to stay home when others went out.[18]

Ultimately, however, many of these anti-modernist articles did not so much criticise modern women as bemoan their fate. They spoke with great concern about the double burden being inflicted on working women, suggesting that their new equality and freedom did them more harm than good. Several female authors thus referred to working women as 'slaves' or 'martyrs'.[19] Interestingly, an article written by

---

14 See 'Žene koje piju', *Ženski svet,* 4 (1930), 20; S. M., 'Savremena žena i njena individualna sloboda', *Žena i svet,* 7:8 (1931), 5; J. Zr., 'Žena i piće', *Ženski svet,* 4:2 (1933), 3–4; 'Samo sam ranije . . .', *Žena i dom,* 1:3 (September 1933), 58; 'Problem današnjice – vaspitanje devojaka', *Ženska misao,* 1:3 (1 April 1935), 1; Raketić, 'Žena i njene dužnosti'.

15 Žena u varoši'.

16 Stanka S. Lozanić, 'Naša zena – nekad i sad', *Domaćica,* 46:6–9 (1931), 32–6.

17 Kostić, 'Naše dužnosti'.

18 'Gdja Mirjam odgovara nam', *Žena i svet,* 12 (1928), 11; Lepa A. Joviềić, 'O domaćem životu u Srbiji', *Ženski svet,* 10 (1930), 14–15.

19 See for example, Kostić, 'Naše dužnosti'; Raketić, 'Žena i njene dužnosti'.

a man stated this argument most clearly. In it, he stated that it was obvious that modern working women carried a double burden, and that while some called this situation emancipation, he considered it the exact opposite. 'I would not give women more rights, but more privileges. I would build them a house in which they are free.' Women in offices and factories, he argued, in fact suffered from tyranny. This author's solution was to renovate the family, and free it of the cynicism and meanness of the era of trade.[20]

More often, however, these articles simply urged a return to the past. One article on women and work thus began: 'Will we ever return to the old ways: women in the house and men at work? Millions of women hope so because men have become used to women bearing a double burden.'[21] The most extreme case sneered at feminist women's organisations for demanding that women be saved from the marital yoke where the woman is only a 'machine for making babies' and a slave to her husband. To free women from marriage, she argued, meant throwing them out on the street into an unequal struggle with men and leaving them without defence. It was under those circumstances, she insisted, that they were really slaves. According to the laws of nature, she continued, women create and educate the new generation while men worry about economic security and make a more comfortable life for their wives and children. The mother is really the pillar of the house and family who instils in children the first ideas about life, God, duties, love, respect, morality and patriotism. Therefore, she explained, it is false to say that women are slaves to their husbands and the family, 'because women are given equality only in the family, where they have an even more elevated and important role than do men'. Were women given the right to vote, she argued, they would not gain equality but would only lose what worthiness they already had and it would destroy their last hope for an improved life and the creation of a better, more ideal humankind.[22] Here again one can see a confluence between the messages promoted by traditional inter-war women's journals and the extreme right. Both not only directed women to stay at home, but also sought to convince them that in so doing they would really be serving their own best interests as well as their nation's.

---

20 U. S., 'Ropstvo moderne žene', *Žena i svet,* 6:11 (1930), 2.
21 Meg., 'Oèajnice ili pokojnice', *Ženski svet,* 3:2 (1932), 14–15.
22 Olga Aksentijević, 'Pitanje oslobodjena žena', *Žena i svet,* 17:2 (1941), 6.

Nationalism

Perhaps the strongest similarity between the extreme-right ideology and Serbia's women in the inter-war period concerned their attention to the needs of the nation over those of any individual. Serbian women's organisations bore a strong national component. Many had been formed shortly before the Balkan Wars or the First World War and had applied their humanitarian mission first and foremost to aiding wounded soldiers, the families of fallen soldiers, war orphans and refugees. Consequently, they clearly associated their work with Serbia's national survival. Many still considered giving homage to Serbia's fallen soldiers one of their main tasks. Thus, women's organisations regularly held requiem masses for and built monuments to various Serbian military heroes.

For similar reasons, most Serbian women's organisations and journals also exhibited a strong attachment to Yugoslavia's royal family, the Serbian Karadjordjević dynasty. Several organisations were, in fact, named after various members of that royal family, including the Society of Princess Zorka (Društva Knjeginja Zorka) and the Society of Princess Ljubica (Društva Knjeginja Ljubica). To some extent, of course, the attention paid and constant gratitude expressed to the royal family was simply politically and financially astute. After all, these organisations were constantly asking the Karadjordjevićs and especially King Alexander's wife, Queen Marija, and Prince Paul's wife, Princess Olga, for financial support. Yet it is also clear that in many cases the affection expressed by Serbian women's organisations and journals for the ruling family was deep-seated and entirely sincere. Women's journals were filled with pictures of the royal family and one organisation even stated that it was its 'holy duty' to educate youth in a spirit of honest love and loyalty to the ruling house of the Karadjordjevićs.[23] Given such dynastic loyalty, King Alexander's assassination in October 1934 inevitably drew strong expressions of sorrow from women's organisations and journals throughout Yugoslavia. Many Serbian women's organisations soon undertook pilgrimages to the King's grave and the Main Council of KSS erected a monument in Brnjačka Banja to 'King Alexander the Unifier', as he was often called. The unveiling ceremony was attended by some 20,000 people.[24]

23 Letter from KSS Prijedor to the King, 9 August 1930, AJ, 74-354-530.
24 'Godišnji izveštaj: Rada Dobrotvorne Zadruge Srpkinje u 1935 g.', 12 February 1936, AJ, 74-138; 'Godišnji izveštaj o radu Glavnog odbora KSS u Beogradu', in *Vardar*, XXVII, Kalendar Kola Srpskih Sestara za prostu 1940 godinu, Belgrade, 1940, AJ.

Many Serbian women's organisations were also closely connected to the Serbian Orthodox Church. The Church frequently supported the charitable activities of Serbian women's organisations. In addition, Serbian women's organisations often expressed their nationalist views in religious terms. For example, the KSS in Banja Luka justified its request for funds to build a Serbian girls' boarding school by explaining that the Roman Catholic Church already had four boarding schools in the region and that, because people in the area were so poor, even Serbs often sent their children to the Catholic schools where they had to learn Catholic prayers, attend Catholic Mass, and were 'educated in a way foreign to our faith'. The organisation further confirmed its national credentials by pointing out that in 1906 it had built the first Serbian day-care centre to protect Serbian children from the influence of the Roman Catholic Church.[25]

It is characteristic that the most extreme forms of Serbian nationalism were expressed by those Serbian women's organisations outside of Serbia proper, especially in areas that had been under foreign occupation until after the First World War. For example, in its letter to the King, the Women's Society of Southern Serbia (Žensko Društvo Južne Srbije) said its goal was to work on tasks humanitarian, cultural and above all national:

> The heavy wounds remaining on the souls of our people after 500 years of the Ottoman yoke and the traces on our spirits and our language from various foreign influences before liberation require long and serious healing. Our association ... heals the old wounds and errors and prepares women for their future as wives and mothers, giving them a Serbian education and a useful craft.[26]

Among the most nationalistic of the women's organisations was the Charitable Community of Serbian Women (Dobrotvorna Zadruga Srpkinja) in Sarajevo. At its yearly meeting in 1936, one leading activist, Jovanka Šiljak, said that they were creating a spiritual national body with faith in God and great love for the nation, and that the organisation's current task was to call all – men, women, old, young, rich, and poor – to work for the nation and wipe out the enemies:

25 Letter from Council of KSS of Banja Luka to Queen Marija, 15 January 1927, AJ, 74-418–618; 'Kolo Srpskih Sestara u Banja Luci, Izveštaj', 15 January 1927, AJ, 74-418–618.
26 Letter to the King from Žensko društvo Južne Srbije, 15 March 1926, AJ, 74–106.

We can all tell that our state foundations are wobbly; will we wait
and see our children enslaved again? No. We women Serbs raise our
voices against all those, of whatever tribe or religion, who are
consciously or not rocking our state's foundations for which so many
of our best children gave their lives ... Long Live Undivided
Yugoslavia![27]

Three years later at a memorial requiem for Vojvoda Stepi Stepan-
ović, the President of that society gave an even more inflammatory
speech. She described the great services and sacrifices of

Little Serbia, the Piedmont of Serbdom and Yugoslavism for the liberation of Bosnia-Hercegovina and our fatherland. She sacrificed
hundreds of thousands of her best sons, gave up her name, flag, existence, and eventually the blood of her king. But still they aren't
satisfied and want more, they want to kill her spirit, rip out her heart,
wipe out every trace of her, but this will never be! Mother Serbia will
give more sacrifices, take more blows for the good of the King and our
fatherland Yugoslavia, but she will endure.[28]

For the most part, however, exclusivist nationalism was not typical
of Serbian women's organisations. Some were indeed quite deliberately non-nationalistic, while still clearly national. For example,
several important organisations, including the KSS, regularly asserted
that they treated all needy people alike, regardless of ethnicity or religion. In contrast to those societies in Bosnia-Hercegovina that were
concerned mainly with the education of Serbian Orthodox children,
these central organisations often stressed that non-Serbs and non-
Orthodox children were also welcome and were included among those
housed and educated in their boarding schools.[29] Several KSS reports
also referred to the importance of developing toleration and mutual
trust among women from the different nationalities in Yugoslavia.
Their attitude was fully consistent with the mission of the YWU,
which claimed that one of its main tasks was 'to lead one part of our
nation – women – through all the political, ethnic, and religious
disagreements which tear at our strength and prevent wide application
of our power and to imbue them instead with correct concepts of

27 'Zapisnik godišnje skupštine Dobrotvorne Zadruge Srpkinja', 12 February 1936,
   AJ, 74–138.
28 Letter from Èedomir K. Jovanović, Kragujevac, 2 June 1939, AJ, 74–253–379.
29 'Izveštaj Glavnog odbora KSS', in *Izveštaji Kola Srpskih Sestara za 1924–1925
   godinu,* Belgrade, 1926, AJ, II 7875; 'Spomenica Društva Knjeginja Zorka –
   1924–1934', AJ; Request to King and Queen for money from Društva Majke
   Jevrosime, 3 January 1933, AJ, 74–495.

national unity'.[30] Of course, the very existence of such statements emphasising the importance of mutual tolerance and respect might also imply its absence.

Nonetheless, there is no doubt that most Serbian women's organisations were strongly pro-Yugoslav in orientation. Unfortunately, the nature of inter-war Yugoslavia, which was ruled by the Serbian dynasty and has been described as typified by Serbian hegemony, makes it difficult to ascertain exactly how a pro-Yugoslav stance differed from a pro-Serbian one. After all, most Serbian women's organisations and journals took their cue from the King and promoted integral Yugoslavism. That is, they treated the Serbs, Croats and Slovenes as three tribes of a common nation. Therefore, when these organisations and journals presented themselves as nationalist organisations and described their efforts to educate students in a national spirit and preserve national traditions and values, it is not always clear whether they were referring to Yugoslav national values or Serbian ones, or whether, indeed, they recognised any distinction between them.

An example of how Yugoslav and Serbian nationalism could easily be conflated was provided by the Charitable Community of Serbian Women in Veliki Beèkerek (in Vojvodina). In a request to the King for financial support, this society first established its Serbian national credentials by explaining that in 1884 it had opened a day-care centre for Serbs in their national language so as to educate them in a national spirit. It then continued that during the last two years it had held free courses in the state language (Serbo-Croatian), which were attended by about 100 women of national minorities. 'In this way we spread the Yugoslav spirit and bring our national minorities together.'[31]

Serbia during the Second World War

Following the German invasion of Serbia in April 1941, the collaborationist regime, led by Milan Nedić and supported by Dmitriji Ljotić's Zbor, adopted and promoted policies that further accentuated those typical of the pre-war era. Women were completely excluded from politics, discouraged (at least in theory) from working outside

30 'Izveštaj Glavnog odbora KSS', in *Izveštaji Kola Srpskih Sestara za 1926 godinu*, Belgrade, 1927, AJ, II 7875; 'Izveštaj o radu Saveznih društava u 1924–1925', Belgrade, 1925, AJ, PSII-101.
31 Request from DZS Vel. Beèkerek to the King for money, 28 June 1934, AJ, 74–495.

the home, and urged to focus on the primary tasks of bearing children
(especially sons) for the nation and raising them in a 'national spirit'.
Thus, in the first issue of a wartime women's journal published in
Serbia, the male author argued that if women wanted internal happiness 'they must return from the offices, cafes, and streets to their
homes, become wives, and in beautifying the days of their husbands,
beautify their own lives, they must bear children and, educating them,
become the foundation of the family, society, and state'. Women's
duties, the author continued, were determined by sex:

> Nature has had her say and who are we to run from it? Could there be
> greater happiness for a woman than waiting for her husband in the early
> evening on the threshold of the family nest? Or than giving to her
> husband a child of their mixed blood to continue their lives? Or offer-
> ing to her husband love that is only for him? Or teaching a child the
> first lines of love to the family and fatherland? Or knowing that she is
> an inspiration to her husband to build a great bridge, write a great
> novel, finish an important job, or compose an opera, and thus improve
> society? These characteristics take nothing away from her femininity.
> We Serbs need such women who will regenerate our tormented
> nation.[32]

As we have seen, however, Serbian women during the inter-war
period had been well prepared for such messages by their non-feminist women's organisations and journals. Most apparently accepted
the idea that women's natural roles lay in housekeeping, motherhood
and, to a lesser degree, education and charity work. In addition, many
were apparently either unconvinced by or disillusioned with the
concept of women's rights. They rejected many, if not all, attributes
of the 'modern woman', seeing her as either degenerate and selfish or
overburdened and enslaved by work. Finally, they were quite strongly
national, if not always nationalistic. They already connected their
maternal and nurturing roles with Serbia's survival and hence had a
strong sense of their value and contribution to the national mission.
One may surmise, then, that Serbian women were generally open to,
if not always enthusiastic about, the extreme right's call for women
to remain in the home where they would play a supporting, but
nonetheless crucial role to their menfolk's struggle for economic and
national survival.

What they were probably less prepared for was the exclusivity of
that call. For while the content of the extreme right's gendered

---

32 B. M., 'Današnja žena', *Naša žena,* 1:1 (June 1942), 2.

message had been common fare during the inter-war period, especially in non-feminist women's journals, that message had been surrounded by many other articles describing women's achievements outside the home (especially in foreign countries) and an almost universal agreement that while women perhaps should not try to do everything that men did, they were, in fact, intellectually and often physically capable of it. While women were most often portrayed in these journals as mothers, wives and sisters, they were also depicted in articles, photographs and advertisements as athletes, office workers, artists, writers, musicians, social activists and, in foreign countries, even politicians.

Articles in women's journals under the Nedić regime included no such images. Moreover, such articles were now written almost exclusively by men and they described women in much more demeaning ways. True, they revered women as mothers, wives and objects of male adoration, but one, for example, also stated bluntly that women, with all their efforts, had not created even one-quarter of what men had and that women's 'intellectual abilities, *inasmuch as they have them*' could reach their fullest expression within the home.[33] Another similarly explained that while men daily opened new pages in the history of the world, 'women now as in the past cook, put on bedding, wash, and encourage and inspire men'.[34]

German occupation also meant the immediate dispersal of all independent organisations, including those formed and run by women. By 1942, the Nedić government was gradually permitting the re-creation of some, but only those with an agenda acceptable to the new regime and only under strict supervision. Thus, the lead article in the first issue of the new wartime women's journal explained that while it supported the co-operation of women in organisations whose goal was the progress of the nation, women should never put their efforts into trying to get the same rights that men have.[35] Ultimately, then, whatever the similarities, there was also a clear boundary between the essentialism, anti-modernism and nationalism of inter-war women's organisations and the much more misogynistic policies of the extreme right.

I do not, therefore, mean to suggest that women in inter-war Serbia were proto-fascist or likely to accept the policies of the wartime

33 Ibid. (emphasis added).
34 M. K., 'Srpska žena i njena uloga u obnovi Srbiji', *Naša žena,* 1:3 (September 1942), 4–5.
35 B. M., 'Današnja žena'.

fascist regime with enthusiasm. Nonetheless, they had clearly played an active role in creating a political culture that prioritised many values consistent with those promoted by the extreme right. Hence, it seems likely that when fascist regimes like Ljotić's Zbor increased their degree of political influence, they did not always need to impose their views upon women by force.

8

Croatia

Melissa Bokovoy

In 1919 the Croatian writer and journalist Zagorka, the pen-name for Marija Jurić, travelled to Belgrade to observe the proceedings of the first congress of the National Women's Union of Serbs, Croats and Slovenes (Navodni Ženski Savez Srba Hrvata, i Slovenaca). Called on the initiative of the Serbian National Women's Union, the Congress, according to Zagorka, was dominated by Serbian women, who were in the majority. Zagorka worried about the tendency of the older generation of Serbian suffragettes to use the suffering and experiences of Serbian women during the war to elevate them to a position of privilege in the new organisation and wondered whether this organisation would truly represent the interests of Croatia and Croatian women. While admiring their sacrifice and patriotism under the most difficult of circumstances during the First World War, Zagorka asserted:

> They understand Yugoslavism [*Jugoslavenstvo*] as a territorial concept, and not as a national idea and a banner of unity [*jedinstvo*]. What one can discern in their eyes and in their words is an iron grip around Serbian patriotism that one must remember is a tribal patriotism that accepts sacrifice, which as of now, they can't overcome. Following this logic, they demand primacy in the Women's Union.[1]

Zagorka identified the major tension existing within the first Yugoslavia – the fear of Serbian dominance or hegemony over all other national groups, whether it be in the formal political arena or in such organisations as the National Women's Union of Serbs, Croats and Slovenes.

Indeed, Croatian politics and political culture during the inter-war

---

1 Zagorka, 'Snimke iz Beograda', *Jutarnji list*, 10 October 1919, p. 3.

period were dominated by the Croatian question. All inter-war Croat parties sought to modify, rewrite or destroy the unitary constitution of the Kingdom of Serbs, Croats and Slovenes. The largest of the Croatian parties, the Croatian Peasant Party (CPP, Hrvatska Seljačka Stranka), adopted a confrontational stance from the very beginning of the Kingdom and demanded greater autonomy within Croatia. In this sense the CPP can be seen as a party representing the rights of Croats, both urban and rural. It cannot be portrayed as a conservative party because the founders of the party, Stepjan and Ante Radić, were committed agrarian socialists. Nonetheless, throughout the inter-war period, the CPP was both anti-modernist and thoroughly nationalist. As the conflict over the structure of the state came to overshadow all else, Croatian political elites were increasingly committed to reviving Croatian history, literature and the arts, as a way to bolster their claims for greater autonomy and in some cases independence. Croatian nationalism became the currency of political discourse.

Many Croatian women's organisations were instrumental in building the foundations for the revival and celebration of Croatian culture and the activities surrounding the re-emergence of the Croatian people onto the world stage. The largest of the Croatian inter-war women's organisations, Croatian Woman (Hrvatska Žena), engaged in both social welfare and cultural activities. The cultural activities concentrated mainly on promoting Croatian literature, art, music and history throughout the state. They sponsored everything from poetry readings of the Croatian 'greats', to a fund drive for the creation of the stations of the cross depicting the tragedies of Croatia through time, to discussions about the lack of economic opportunities for women in the Croatian villages. In each town or city at least one such organisation busied itself with nation-building activities and in doing so placed women squarely in the role of preservers, promoters or creators of Croatianness. Hence, even though women were excluded from the formal political system, Croatian Woman and organisations like the women's section of the Society of Zagreb Men (Društvo Zagrebčana), as well as honorary female members in the Brothers of the Croatian Dragon (Družba Brače Hrvatskog Maja) and volunteers for the Croatian Theatre, were socialised and socialised others to fulfil their duty to the Croatian nation.

Croatian women's journals also promoted the national mission. Despite her attendance at the first meeting of the National Women's Union of Serbs, Croats and Slovenes, Zagorka soon forsook this organisation and by 1925 focused her attention on creating a periodi-

cal for Croatian women, *Ženski list,* for the promotion and bettering
of Croatian culture and society. This periodical, typical of women's
journals, offered articles and advice on fashion, entertaining and the
household. The journal also had a deeper political agenda. While
denying that it promoted a feminist point of view, the journal also
contained articles about women's rights in other countries, often
featuring Tomáš Masaryk's writings on women's suffrage and the
advancement of women in the public sphere. It also featured articles
on police women, aviators, doctors, and other professional women
outside of Croatia. At times it was almost a *National Geographic* for
women with information about other places in the world as well as
those in Croatia.

Another women's weekly, *Naša žena: Tjednik za Ženski svijet,*
founded in 1935 and edited by Dr Zdenka Smrekar, adopted a similar
stance to that of Croatian Woman and *Ženski list.* The first issue articulated clearly its editorial goals: 'In this difficult time in our public
life, we thought a cheap weekly necessary to help Croatian woman to
save, to help her be a good housekeeper, wife and mother and to
inform her about the world, the state, and society and the economic
terrain. [It exists] not to debate, but only to consider women's interests.' Smrekar appeared to be a good choice for the editorship of *Naša
žena.* She was a well-respected educator, writer and lecturer, member
of the Zagreb chapter of Croatian Woman, and dedicated to women's
education and economic advancement. In 1937, when Croatian
Woman decided to widen its scope to educational and economic
opportunities for girls and women, Smrekar was appointed to lead the
'social-feminist' section created to carry out the new charge.

By the late 1930s, as the royal dictatorship began to show signs of
negotiating with the Croats for revision of the Vidovdan constitution,
mainstream Croatian women's organisations and their leaders saw an
opportunity to intensify their participation in the civic and economic
activities of Croatia. Not only did Croatian Woman add a 'social' and
'feminist' section to its organisation, but a group of leading Zagreb
women pushed for the creation of the women's section of the Society
for Zagreb Men in 1937. The founding members of the association,
which included not only many of the wives of the Zagrebčani, but
secretaries, bank workers, a pharmacist, a journalist (Zagorka), a
composer and a professor of music, articulated a clear plan of action.
It was Zagorka who 'tossed out some ideas of how we can concretely
develop our organisation'. She suggested that the members gather
stories and legends about Zagreb and talk with the older residents

'who are carrying with them to their graves the most beautiful little vignettes of Zagreb life'; sponsor lectures about and organise excursions around the city in order for women to get to know the city; and create reproductions of famous paintings by Croatian artists who painted landscapes of their country, price them reasonably and sell them to women for their homes. One of Zagorka's favourite projects for improving the economic fortunes of peasant women made it to the list. Zagorka wanted to put rural women to work moulding, casting and painting porcelain figurines of Croatian greats and well-known monuments or sculptures for consumption by urban women. 'With good advertising and aggressive propaganda throughout society, there would come a time when every house [in Zagreb] would have one of these ornaments.'[2]

Through commemoration, public displays, lectures and education, Zagorka, *Naša žena*'s Zdenak Smrekar, members of Croatian Woman, and Zagreb's other cultural and civic associations sought to nationalise Croatian women by teaching them their civic obligations, collective virtues and the personal values required for members of a revised Croatian state. During the late nineteenth and early twentieth centuries, 'nationalising' the population had largely focused upon Croatian men, and many civic organisations, like the Brothers of the Croatian Dragons or the Society of Zagreb Men, continued this nationalising process during the inter-war years. After 1918, however, some women clearly believed that it was their duty to do the same but for Croatian women. Thus, when the Croatian Ustaša came to power in 1941, the role of women in the nationalisation process was already a well-established part of the public and private discourse.

There were, however, important differences between the national or even nationalist orientation of inter-war Croat women and men, and the ideals promoted by Croatia's wartime fascists. The Ustaša concept of nation was racialised, its political tactics violent and brutal, and its leadership unsophisticated compared to the gentile and refined cultural and political sensibilities of Zagreb's elite. Moreover, the process of nationalising Croatian women, while essentialising them and at times rejecting some of the social and political advances brought by modernity, had in fact occurred within a pluralistic society and there had remained a distinction between the public and private.

2 Državni arhiv (Opatička Ulica), Fund 791: Društvo Zagrebčana, Signatura 35: Upravni odbor, 'Zapisnik sastavljen na I sastanku Gospojinske sekcije Društva zagrepčana dne 28.IX. 1937'.

Fascism immediately sought to destroy this distinction and, as we shall see, few of the women leaders from the inter-war mainstream political organisations joined Ustaša women's organisations.

Fascism in Croatia

On 10 April 1941, when the Croatian Peasant Party refused to co-operate with Italy and Germany in dismantling the Yugoslav state, the Axis powers invited the politically insignificant fascist Ustaša to proclaim an independent Croatian state and preside over its development. The Ustaša, which had operated predominately from Italy during the 1930s and whose membership and ideology were not known to most Croats, numbered fewer than 2,000 and its leader, Ante Pavelić, had to be summoned from Italy to take the helm of the new state. Ustaša ideology was a hybrid of two political currents, one domestic and one foreign. From several strands of nineteenth- and early-twentieth-century Croatian political thought, the Ustaša sought to establish an independent nationally homogenous Croatian state. It rejected the idea that there could be a lasting union between Croats and Serbs and thus rejected the notion of a South Slav state. It also adopted the racial politics of two Croatian exclusionists, Ante Starčević and Milan Šufflay, who used a demonic concept of Serbs as the cornerstone of their ideologies. To Starčević, the Serb was an inhuman beast, and Šufflay argued that Serbs were racially different. Ustaša leader Ante Pavelić embraced these ideas and called the Serb 'a scheming Byzantine oriental, an alien thorn in Croatia's flesh'. The Ustaša's racialised definition of membership in a Croatian state was codified in Article Twelve of the Principles of the Ustaša Movement of 1933, which stated: 'While the peasantry is the foundation and source of the Croat people, all social strata of the Croat people form one national entity, for as long as their members have Croat blood'. Within these racialised notions of community and belonging, women would play a prominent role in reproducing the nation's citizens.

The other source of the Ustaša ideology was Fascist Italy. Supported by Mussolini during the 1930s, the Ustaša embraced many of the trappings of Italian Fascism. It celebrated Croatia's long and glorious past and claimed that it was upon this tradition, heritage and history that a new and better future would be based. The Ustaša also spoke of Croatia's divine mission and its importance in the struggle against the two evils of the modern world, capitalism and communism. Mile Budak, the Ustaša's main ideologue and Minister of

Religion and Education in the new state, wrote extensively on the degenerative effects of these two systems. In 1938 he asserted: 'Communism and Capitalism are two opposing world outlooks, two opposite systems, two opposite forms of slavery of the human soul, liberty, pride and dignity. Both are equally alien to the soul of the Croat people.' Budak and the other Ustaša leaders believed the only way to preserve the Croatian way of life and culture was to turn to the village, the land and the extended patriarchal family of the countryside, the *zadruga*. Budak continued:

> It is in the nature of every man, especially of every Croat, to have his own home . . . Both communism and capitalism seek to take that away from him, each in its own way, and so to enslave him . . . Our old *zadruga* offered a better, happier and richer life than today's households . . . [In the future Croat state] the owner of the land is the *zadruga*, all who belong to the same hearth.

Here, Budak was expressing sentiments found in many parts of interwar Europe, balancing the demands and changes brought by modernity and maintaining traditional values and authority. The Ustaša drew upon the patriarchal brand of collectivism practised in its home regions, the Dinaric villages of Lika and the hinterlands of Bosnia-Hercegovina and Dalmatia, to articulate its view of Croatia to its new citizens, what it meant to be Croatian, where each individual stood within the Croatian nation, and what the future state would look like. Each individual man or woman would be required to serve the Independent State of Croatia in explicitly gendered ways. In the case of women, the Ustaša regime stood for returning women to home and hearth, restoring patriarchal authority, and confining female destiny to bearing future Croats and teaching them how to be Croatian. In this discussion, women were to reproduce the citizens, soldiers and mothers of the body politic. The Ustaša's racialisation of Croatianness also supported the contention that women were responsible for the boundaries of the national group (through restrictions or non-restriction on sexual or marital relations).[3]

The Ustaša, however, did expect women to serve the state in others

---

3 For a discussion of the conflation of the body and nation as well as family and nation see Anne McClintock, 'Family feuds: gender, nationalism and the family', *Feminist Review: Nationalisms and National Identities*, 44 (Summer 1993), 61–80; Nira Yuval-Davis and Floya Anthias (eds), *Woman, Nation, State* (Basingstoke, Macmillan, 1989), p. 7; Katherine Verdery, 'From parent state to family patriarchs: gender and nation in contemporary Eastern Europe,' *East European Politics and Society*, 8:2 (1994), 223–55.

way as well: to form voluntary organisations, to perform gender-specific roles such as attending to the wounded, and caring for war widows and orphans, and to supply labour when the state needed it, especially agricultural labour. Upon taking control of the state, the Ustaša hurriedly created a women's branch of the organisation. It also established an official newspaper for this organisation, *Ustaškinja*, and an Ustaša youth association for girls and young women. Some of the women who headed or staffed these organisations were the daughters, sisters or wives of leading Ustaša members or Croatian nationalists, like Irene Javor, whose father was the Croatian revolutionary and martyr Stipe Javor and whose brother, Ivan, was an early member of the movement. Vlasta Arnold, who became a leading member of the women's branch, was the daughter of the Croatian writer, philosopher and pedagogue Đure Arnold. Some, like Silva Radej, editor of *Ustaškinja,* came into the movement because of their commitment to the ideology of the Ustaša. Others came to the movement to continue the work that they had begun with Catholic organisations. A few women, like Zdenka Smrekar or Marica Stanković, may have believed that their services represented a continuation of their inter-war activities. In June 1941 Smrekar was named the division head for women's education in the Ministry of Religion and Education by the new fascist government of the Independent State of Croatia. A month earlier, she had established the organisation of Ustaša Women's Education. Smrekar, however, fell into disfavour by 1943. Stanković, who was initially attracted to the explicit Catholicism of the Independent State of Croatia, stubbornly resisted attempts by the state to politicise her organisation, the Great Crusading Sisterhood (Veliko Križavsko Sestrinstvo).

The national hero, not heroine

The idea of struggle and sacrifice had been a major current running through Croatian nationalism for two centuries or more. It was claimed that each generation of Croats, since their 'enslavement' by the Hungarians in 1102, had suffered injustices. Yet whether suffering at the hands of Hungarians, Austrians, Turks or Serbs, the Croats always continued to fight for the establishment of a Croatian state, and many willingly sacrificed their lives for this end. This motif, a common one among the South Slavs, was immediately introduced into the Ustaša state when Ante Pavelić made his first speech in May 1941:

Brother Ustashi, the Croatian people have survived their great and celebrated resurrection. Yet, everyone knows that this resurrection did not
come overnight. It was over a long series of decades and centuries of
preparation for this Croatian, national, and state resurrection. Through
the centuries of slavery, in times of truncated freedom, the Croatian
people gave from their hearts their sons, who were pioneers, who
worked and struggle their whole lives for this which we have today.
And especially in the last twenty years, the Croatian people give of
themselves to these fighters, gave their sons, who readied the final
paths, who committed the last act, the final part of this liberation of the
Croatian people.

We thank the sons of the Croatian people, we genuflect to all those
geniuses, to all those names we know and to all those we do not know,
who through the centuries and through the last decades gave their lives
in the foundation of the Independent State of Croatia. From Petar
Svačić, from beg Gradaščevic, to Zrinski, and Frankopan, to Ante
Starčević, and Eugen Kvaternik, from Stepjan Radić, to Stipe Javor,
and those who at this very hour of freedom give their blood, their life
for the freedom of the Croatian people and the Croatian state. We bow
to them, we bow to their great memory, to their ghosts, and shout: We
celebrate you![4]

In this speech, Pavelić and the Ustaša, while not firing a single shot
to create the Independent State of Croatia, laid claim to 'a centuries-
old tradition' of resistance, sacrifice and struggle, and they did so by
gendering the images of struggle and sacrifice. In addition, this
speech had a strong preoccupation with death and immortality, as well
as invoking the religious imagery of resurrection. Like religious
thought, Ustaša nationalist ideology transformed fatality into continuity through acts of struggle and war, and these practices of war and
policing were largely the preserve of men.[5] Pavelić consoled future
soldiers with a comforting myth of continuity – their death, as the
death of their ancestral brothers, would be transformed into life, the
life of the nation. In the act of death comes life, and men gained the
procreative potential.

As the war progressed, the Ustaša was more explicit about the
connection between fatality and continuity. A year later, the Ustaša
journal on society, culture and politics, *Hrvatska Smotra* claimed:

---

4 *Ustaša*, 22 May 1941 quoted in Fikreta Jelić-Butić, *Ustaša i Nezavisna Država
Hrvatska, 1941–1945* (Zagreb, Liber, 1978), p. 137.
5 Benedict Anderson, *Imagined Communities: Reflections on the Origin and Spread
of Nationalism* (New York, Verso, 1991), p. 11 does not draw the conclusion that
immortality through struggle and war is largely the preserve of men.

'This bloodshed in the defense of their own hearth, home, and country – this is the most valuable sacrifice ... this is history, this is life, and this, with the powerful imperative of Starčević's spirit and will, has become a principle of Croatian politics'.[6]

In the imagery of both texts, women were absent from the endless sequence of male heroes who 'are strung out one after another, almost like a series of "begats", and producing the impression of the nation and its state as a temporally deep patrilineage'.[7] In these passages, as well as in most of the Ustaša's writings, men were the dynamic, active and heroic agents of the nationalist enterprise, and women's procreative capacity was 'denied and appropriated by men as the ability to give political birth, to be the originators of a new form of social and political order'.[8] Croatian men became the moral and political creators and protectors. Even in the issue of *Ustaškinja* published to celebrate the second anniversary of the state, the editor, Silvia Radej, wrote an anniversary message that completely excluded women, with the exception of mothers who 'give birth, inspire love, and raise children: sons, husbands fight, perish. It has always been this way, through the centuries.'[9] Women in this national struggle were invisible or in the background, and relegated to roles defined by nature.

National community as family

In imagining the common experiences of a nation, nationalists, most often historians, construct a series of myths to which each member of the nation is ancestrally related. As Walter Connor has argued, these myths of common descent, which define the nation, seldom accord with factual history, but what matters is what people perceive. Therefore, those engaged in the nationalist enterprise promote a familiarity with the national mythology and the name of the progenitor which is as important to a sense of belonging as is the knowledge of one's own genealogy.[10] In order to break down social and family

6 *Hrvatska smotra*, 10:2 (1942), pp. 84–6.
7 Verdery, 'From parent state to family patriarchs', pp. 238–9.
8 Carole Pateman, 'The fraternal social contract', in John Keane (ed.), *Civil Society and the State* (London, Verso, 1988), p. 114 quoted in Verdery, 'From parent state to family patriarchs', p. 243.
9 Silva Radej, 'Uz 10. travnja', *Ustaškinja*, 2:1 (1943), 4.
10 Walter Connor, 'The nation and its myth', *International Journal of Comparative Sociology*, 23:1–2 (1992), 48–57.

orders so that individuals will serve the interests and collective needs of the new state, the political leadership promotes ties which give each individual the sense of shared blood, a sense of a national family. As McClintock has posited, 'the family offers a "natural" figure for sanctioning social hierarchy within a putative [supposed, reputed] organic unity of interests'.[11] The image of nation working like a family offered 'an indispensable metaphoric figure by which hierarchical social distinctions could be shaped into a single historical genesis narrative'.[12] Political leaders of the most diverse ideological strains have been mindful of the common blood component of national identity and have not hesitated to appeal to it when seeking popular support. In 1941 the Ustaša used the language of family to produce the impression that a nation operates as a family.

Returning to the two previously quoted speeches, the Ustaša imagined the Croatian nation as an extended patrilineage of 'heroes'. According to Ustaša as well as mainstream Croatian nationalists, the father of all Croats was Ante Starčević, who founded the Party of Croatian Rights in the mid nineteenth century, and who argued that Croatian statehood had never been wholly extinguished. According to the mythology, his entire life was devoted to transforming Croatia into a real sovereign state. In constructing the family history of the Croatian nation, the Ustaša recorded the deeds of sons and fathers who fought and sacrificed themselves for the dream of their progenitor Starčević. Yet, the Ustaša reserved a special place next to the father for itself.

Like many members of the Ustaša, Starčević was born in the Lika region of Croatia. In Ante Pavelić's biography published in the Ustaša publication *Spremnost*, Lika was described as 'the Croatian Sparta, those from Lika are healthy, strong, heroic, and significant'.[13] The biographer continued, 'The father of our homeland, Ante Starčević, carried on him the indelible stamp of his people of the Lika region, the Leader [Pavelić] also carries this in his blood'.[14] The comparison linked Starčević to Pavelić, who was portrayed as Starčević's heir. Other members of the Ustaša were accorded the next privileged places in this family. Like a family, other Croats occupy positions subordinate to Pavelić and the Ustaša.

What is remarkable in this piece is the absence of women. The

---

11 McClintock, 'Family feuds', p. 63.
12 Ibid.
13 Ivan Bogdan, 'Poglavnik', *Spremnost*, 10 April 1942, p. 2.
14 Ibid.

article told of Pavelić's birth into 'an old peasant family' and imme-diately described the Croatian peasants as belonging 'to the forefront of the Croatian nation'. The names or facts about his mother, father, brothers, sisters, wife and children did not matter. He belonged to the Croatian nation; he was 'the collective individual'.[15] His birth and existence were owed to the collective identity of the nation, not to an individual, to parents, or to a mother. As Verdery has observed for Romanian nationalism, 'Women may create life in this world, but more fundamental to the nation's continuity is its eternal life, ensured through culture, heroic deeds, and qualities of spirit: the realm of men'.[16]

Spremnost's use of photographs, etchings and stories presented a Croatian nationalism which George Mosse has characterised as 'a kind of homo-social masculine bonding'.[17] No image describes this phenomenon better than the photograph of two young boys in uniform, shaking hands with Pavelić, also in uniform, with the caption, 'This picture symbolises the future of the Croatian state. The youth [all boys], the *sole* owner of the future of Croatia, see in the Leader, a legendary hero and their teacher'.[18] The ideology of the Ustaša suggested a lineage which was 'to reproduce itself without recourse to females, or even to sex'.[19] The nation's survival and future depended upon men and their male progeny.

Ustaša ideology, like Italian Fascism, argued that the responsibil-ity of each (male) youth 'was to create a family, and a national progeny'.[20] For the Ustaša, the male had to take responsibility for all private relations 'in love and sexuality'.[21] Not to do so would lead the youth down the path to degeneracy. If an 'erotic' act resulted in impregnating a young woman, the father must 'undertake his moral and material responsibilities for all, including the mother with whom he has conceived'.[22] The woman should accept marriage and be spared the humiliation of poverty, misery and illegitimacy for the child, or worse yet, an abortion. To act otherwise would stigmatise

15 Verdery, 'From parent state to family patriarchs', p. 242.
16 Ibid.
17 Ibid.
18 Picture, *Spremnost*, 17 May 1942 (my emphasis).
19 Verdery, 'From parent state to family patriarchs', p. 243.
20 'Značenje i uloga mladosti u nacionalističkim prokretim', *Hrvatska smotra*, May–June 1941, p. 251.
21 Ibid.
22 'Žalosni problem Ljudskog pometnuća', *Hrvatska smotra*, May–June 1941, p. 412.

the child and this child 'would be undervalued and neglected'. Women in the this picture were to be little more than objects, performing a 'natural' act, but not being able to preside over the development of the child without help from the father or the state. Men and the patriarchal state were to protect women from the predations of other men, who were morally degenerative or, worse yet, racially inferior.

The Ustaša connected the discussion of women's role in the nationalist enterprise with the view that the new social order could be based on the 'natural' society of the peasantry. It saw in the urban and modern society of Croatia corruption, degeneracy, immorality, and 'unnatural' forms of political and societal organisation. Its aim was the moral regeneration of the 'way of life' of the unique historical community of Croatia, which was predominately peasant. The Ustaša designated women to resuscitate this way of life.

Juxtaposing the character and values of urban and rural women, the Ustaša imagined 'modern, urban women' as deviations from the 'natural and vital' order. Affluence and the comforts of a consuming society had made them selfish, individualistic and 'noisy'. In comparison, peasant women were imagined as 'true martyrs', self-sacrificing and hard-working. They fought not for individual, liberal rights, but for the 'nation's life and the future'. For the Ustaša, modernity had brought women out of the home and into the public sphere, a place where they did not belong. Yet, it believed that modernity need not be 'a negative factor' on women. Coupled with the 'values' of peasant women, modernity could be a positive force.[23]

The Ustaša envisioned a home and hearth in the village up to the standards of the middle class – 'clean sheets, clean body, and clean surroundings'.[24] If provided with the proper tools of modernity – such as roads and schools – women could keep their families healthy, homes clean, and children schooled. By bringing doctors, medicine and education to the villages, women's sphere would be modernised, yet remain separate. They would be liberated from the misery and poverty of the village, and could then concentrate on providing a secure, healthy and safe home for their husband and children – future Croats. Given the opportunity, women were 'the source of the future, the condition of our existence'.[25] Accordingly, the Ustaša state had to pay greater attention to the 'women-mother'. Why? As Balentović

---

23 Ivo Balentović, 'O teškom životu naše seljačke žene', *Hrvatska smotra*, December 1941, pp. 533–6.
24 Ibid., p. 534.
25 Ibid., p. 535.

pointed out, young women were having too many abortions and the mortality rate among young women was 'frightfully great'. This meant fewer citizens for the Croatian Ustaša state.

Conclusion

In the vacuum of power created by the dissolution of the first Yugoslavia, the Ustaša leadership tried to reinvent the Croatian nation using specific symbols and myths, and it did so with a purpose. Without the trappings of a legitimate state, the Ustaša leaders had to mediate through the nation relations between their followers, non-followers and themselves. In their ideology, they emphasised community over the individual, struggle and sacrifice for the nation, the national community as family, the tradition of the nation embodied in the peasantry, and the significant role women could play in establishing a new 'organic' and 'natural' Croatian state. However, the Ustaša's message promoting order, discipline, authority, homeland, family, race, history and tradition had at its foundation the privileging of men over women and regulating and restricting women's citizenship, sexuality, labour, and civic and social participation. The rhetoric surrounding the establishment of the Independent State of Croatia clearly signalled women's subordinate role in the struggle to achieve national independence.

9

Latvia

Mara I. Lazda

Latvia in the twentieth century was a battleground of several political 'rights' representing varying degrees of extremism, including conservative nationalist movements, extreme-right groups, and, from 1941 to 1945, German Nazism. Despite the different goals and programmes of the political 'rights', gender played a central role for all in disseminating their ideologies and attempting to construct a new nation. This chapter focuses on the conflicts and intersections between political, gendered and national identities in the development of the right and illustrates the ambiguities and dualities inherent in their approaches to gender and the nation that were instrumental in their support.

The late 1920s saw the first strong appearance of the right in inter-war Latvia. After the Great War, the multi-ethnic population of Latvia – like Czechoslovakia, Poland and Yugoslavia – became a nation-state. The independent Republic of Latvia was a parliamentary democracy that funded minority schools and supported the rights of minorities to cultural expression. However, excessive divisiveness in the government and the world-wide economic crisis in the 1920s led to growing support for extreme-right movements and calls for increased protection of the rights of the ethnic Latvian nation. In 1934 the leader of the conservative Agrarian Union (Zemnieku Savienība), Kārlis Ulmanis, carried out a peaceful coup, disbanded all political parties, including his own, and arrested the leaders of the extreme right and left.[1] Despite Ulmanis's support for nationalist policies that

---

1 Andrejs Plakans, *The Latvians: A Short History* (Stanford, Hoover Institution, 1995), pp. 132–3, 141. Plakans notes that Ulmanis's coup government was, overall, well-received and his popularity grew through the 1930s. See also Andrejs Plakans, *Historical Dictionary of Latvia* (Lanham, MD, Scarecrow Press, 1997), pp. 153-4. Georg von Rauch, *The Baltic States: The Years of Independence: Estonia, Latvia,*

promoted the rights of the ethnic Latvian nation, the extreme-right remained highly critical of him. Central to Ulmanis's nationalist rhetoric was the promotion of traditional gender roles and the link between motherhood and the strength of the nation. In contrast, extreme-right groups, especially as they increased their militarism, focused on recruiting Latvians who were 'real men' and stressed their respect for 'masculine courage'.[2] The extreme right maintained a highly contentious relationship with the Latvian state throughout the inter-war period, and none of its organisations successfully built a mass following in the years leading up to the Second World War.

The beginning of the Second World War and the Soviet occupation of Latvia ended Ulmanis's government of national unity and extinguished all expressions of ethnic Latvian nationalism. In 1941 the Nazi occupation replaced the Soviet and tried to gain support by allowing limited expression of Latvian culture and restoring the images of traditional gender roles linked to Latvian national identity destroyed by the Soviets. The Nazi regime's manipulation of gender roles familiar to the Latvians was central to the dissemination of racial ideology and propaganda, for it provided the illusion of Latvian sovereignty while in fact promoting Germanisation. Latvians, in turn, used these gender images sanctioned by the Nazis to resist the fascist occupation regime and to nurture the concept of Latvian independence.

This chapter on the right in Latvia, therefore, offers insight into three aspects of the relationship between the right, gender and nation in twentieth-century Europe: first, the centrality of gender in the formation of new nation-states in inter-war Europe; secondly, the manipulation of gender by fascist regimes such as the Nazi occupation state in Latvia in consolidating their power and popularising racial ideologies; and thirdly, the use of gender images intended to construct ideas of national sovereignty under occupation and to resist Nazism. The history of rightist movements in Latvia from 1918 to 1945 demonstrates the central significance of gender in the programmes of all groups of the right and illuminates the different approaches to gender and nation that determined success or failure. Although individuals – including rightist Latvian politicians, extreme-

---

Lithuania 1917–1940, trans. Gerald Onn, 2nd edn (New York, St Martin's Press, 1995), pp. 146–60.

2 Latvian State History Archive (hereafter LVVA), f. 3235, apr. 3, l. 109, p. 8. Firecross pamphlet, *What is Firecross?*, 1932. Fond 3235 contains Political Police reports, correspondences and investigation materials.

right group members, Nazi occupation officials, and resistance leaders – had different plans for Latvia and Latvians, they all manipulated gender roles in their attempt to create an ideal ethnically based society.[3]

With the establishment of independence in 1918, Latvia's leaders faced questions of defining the nation: first as the 'nation of Latvia' (*Latvijas tauta*), and secondly, as the 'ethnic Latvian nation' (*Latviešu tauta*). Approximately 72–75 per cent of Latvia's population was ethnically Latvian throughout the inter-war period, while significant Russian (7–10 per cent), Jewish (5 per cent) and German (4 per cent) populations also lived in Latvia.[4] In the years immediately after the war, Latvia's politicians constructed a citizenship law based on *jus solis*: all former citizens of the Russian empire who had lived within the borders of what was now the Republic of Latvia had the right to citizenship. Voting rights were given to men and women over the age of twenty-one. Minorities had government representation and elected sixteen to nineteen deputies in the hundred-member parliamentary assembly.[5] The constitution of 1922 guaranteed the equal rights of all members of the nation of Latvia, including the freedom of speech, religion and the press. Additional laws addressed the specific rights of minorities, such as the rights of minority languages. Minority schools – including Russian, German, Jewish, Polish and Lithuanian – received support from the state.[6]

---

3 There are few works on the history of the right in Latvia and almost no information on the role of women and gender. Much research remains to be done, and this chapter serves only as a preliminary study of this subject. For the inter-war period and the right, see, for example, Armands Paeglis, *Pērkonkrusts pār Latviju, 1932–1944* (Riga, Zvaigzne, 1944); Imants Mednis, 'Labējā spārna politiskās partijas Latvijas republikas parlamentārajā periodā (1920–1934)', *Latvijas arhīvi*, 1 (1995), 21–6. See Haralds Biezais for the relationship between the inter-war right and Nazi occupation, e.g. 'Gustava Celmiņa Pērkonkrusts dokumentu gaismā', *Latvijas Zinātņu Akadēmijas Vēstis*, 1–4 (1992), 39–43, 40–3, 43–5, 44–7.

4 Plakans, *The Latvians*, p. 132. Plakans discusses the development of the idea of a Latvian *Volk* or tauta, see pp. 6–7, 43, 84, 90–2, 101–2.

5 Arveds Švābe, *Latvju Enciklopēdija* (Stockholm, Apgāds Trīs Zvaigznes, 1951), vol. 2, pp. 1638, 1883–4.

6 The Constituent Assembly passed the Law of School Autonomy on 8 December 1919, which guaranteed the rights of the minorities to control of schools in their native languages and provided state support for this education. This law remained in effect until 17 July 1934, when Kārlis Ulmanis's government centralised education and limited the number of minority schools supported by the state. The Law of 6 December 1918 permitted the use of German and Russian in courts, in addition to Latvian. Švābe, *Latvju Enciklopēdija*, vol. 2, p. 1638; vol. 1, p. 828.

From the beginning, women representing the political spectrum played a role, albeit a relatively small one, in the founding structure of the new state. Six women, including socialists and independents, were elected to the 150-member Constituent Assembly. Their initial political influence, however, did not translate into significant parliamentary representation, despite attempts by the Latvian Women's Association (Latvju Sieviešu Apvienība) to elect delegates from a women-only candidate list, and women were largely limited to city and local government.[7] Two women who served as leaders of women's organisations throughout the inter-war period did make political gains on the national level: Valerija Seile was appointed Minister of Education in 1921 and Berta Pīpiņa of the Democratic Centre Party (Demokratiskā Centra Partija) was elected in 1931 as the first and only woman parliamentary deputy.[8]

Economic and political tensions in the late 1920s threatened the broadly defined nation of Latvia. Latvia's export-based economy suffered with the world-wide Depression, and unemployment grew. The 'ultra-liberal' election law that allowed any group of a hundred citizens over twenty-one years of age to propose a list of candidates led to great instability; in 1931 twenty-seven parties and groups had parliamentary representatives in a body of a hundred members.[9] Conservative parties and political right organisations increasingly called for the protection of the *ethnic* Latvian nation. Conservatives, led by the Agrarian Union, saw the solution in stronger centralised leadership, and proposed that the constitution be amended to increase the powers of the President. When Parliament did not accept these changes, Ulmanis, backed by members of the army, the National Guard and the Agrarian Union, organised a bloodless coup on 15 May 1934.[10]

Ulmanis sought to establish political control by arresting the leaders of the extreme right and left; other suspected opponents of the government were put under Political Police surveillance. The extreme right accused him of not sufficiently promoting and protecting the rights of ethnic Latvians. According to one of the most extreme right groups, the Thundercross (Pērkonkrusts), during the parliamentary system Ulmanis had ruled with the blessing of Germans, Jews,

---

7 Līlija Brant, *Latviešu sieviete* (Riga, A/S Valters un Rapa, 1931), pp. 193–9.
8 Pārsla Eglīte (ed.) *Latvijas sieviete valsts 75 gados: pētījumi, statistika, atmiņas* (Riga, Zvaigzne, 1994), pp. 190–1.
9 Švābe, *Latvju Enciklopēdija*, vol. 3, p. 1986.
10 Plakans, *The Latvians*, p. 133.

Russians and Poles. Although Thundercross approved of Ulmanis's dismissal of Parliament and arrest of social democrats, it concluded: 'the only way for Latvia to escape its destruction and to be reborn is through the establishment of a Latvian Latvia [and] we know that Ulmanis is not capable of this'.[11] After 1934, the extreme right, driven underground and led by the Thundercross, became more aggressive in its tactics.

The extreme right before 1940

The extreme right in independent Latvia was manifested in many organisations that were banned and reorganised several times throughout the inter-war period and ultimately went underground. Prior to Ulmanis's coup, they had worked with some semblance of legal status, and in the case of Thundercross even sported grey-shirted uniforms, but after May 1934 the extreme-right movement was entirely underground. The best-known groups were the Latvian Nationalist Club (Latvju Nacionālais Klubs), Firecross (Ugunskrusts), Young Latvia (Jaunā Latvija), Fatherland Guard (Tēvijas Sargs) and the Thundercross (Pērkonkrusts).[12] The organisations overlapped,

11 LVVA, f. 3235, apr. 1/22, l. 808, p. 46c; apr. 3, l. 113, p. 91. *Pērkonkrusta ziņojums*, 19 May 1934. An anonymous flyer found by the Political Police declared: 'May 15 was an historic day, when the old, corrupted order collapsed. Everyone breathed a sigh of relief when they discovered that the parties have been liquidated, the open enemies and of the state and destroyers of national morale – socialist leaders – arrested. [But what happened?] How can we believe [the new leaders], when even the store signs are only partially repainted and all economic life is still in the hands of the minorities.' LVVA, f. 3235, apr. 1/22, l. 710, p. 95. Another essay claimed that indeed 15 May happened out of the realisation that Firecross was becoming too powerful. 'May 15 is an expression of frustration constructed by incapable politicians to save their fallen prestige and financial situation.' LVVA, f. 3235, apr 1/22, l. 710, p. 90.

12 The first manifestation of rightist groups was the Latvian Nationalist Club (Latvju Nacionālais Klubs), founded in 1922, liquidated in 1927. The collapse of this organisation spurred many others, including the Latvian Activist National Association (Latvju Aktīvo Nacionālistu Savienība), the Latvian National Movement (Latvju Nacionālā Kustība) and the National Activist Club (Nacionālo Aktīvistu Klubs). Firecross was founded on 19 January 1932 and shut down on 12 April 1933. Thundercross was founded soon after the liquidation of Firecross and worked as a legal society from 23 May 1933 to 30 January 1934. Young Latvia was established on 15 August 1933 and lasted until 17 August 1934. In its later years, Fatherland Guard, according to the Political Police reports, served as the inner military core of Thundercross, which tried to develop its reputation as a respectable political party. Fatherland Guard was founded and reshaped several times, first in 1923, and

both in programme and membership, and there is little to distinguish them, except the degree of their increasing radicalisation and anti-minority and anti-Semitic stance, with the Thundercross as the most extreme. Each of these groups began ostensibly as a social club registered with the Ministry of the Interior; the Thundercross was the only group registered as a political organisation. The number of members varied, from a few dozen to a few thousand. Thundercross claimed that its membership reached 15,000, but the actual number was between 5,000 to 6,000.[13] Time and again, the ministry liquidated these organisations. Usually this was done on the recommendation of the Political Police, who gave similar justification for closing each organisation – essentially that the groups did not confine themselves to the fostering of cultural and sports activities, as the statutes registered with the ministry claimed they would. As the tone of these groups became more aggressive, the Political Police reported that the organisations also 'cultivated hatred against Jewish inhabitants of Latvia'.[14] One ministry official wrote: 'observing the work of Thundercross, it has been made clear, that the said party supports anti-state activities [and] is the continuation of Firecross, with the same goals to use violent means to change the existing governing structure, and to establish in its place a fascist-nationalistic dictatorship'.[15]

Both men and women over the age of eighteen could become members of most extreme-right groups. As was common in other European right movements, women were members of separate 'women's sections'. The statutes of the earlier groups such as Firecross do not stress any nationality or ethnic requirement, as 'any

---

finally liquidated on 30 January 1934. After the liquidation of Thundercross, the leaders of the right quickly decided to go completely underground with their work, after a shortlived attempt at working through Native Land (Dzimtene). LVVA, f. 3235, apr. 1/22, l. 701, pp. 131–3; apr. 1/22, l. 708, pp. 8, 263. Paeglis focuses on the Firecross and Thundercross in *Pērkonkrusts pār Latviju*.

13 Švābe, *Latvju Enciklodija*, vol. 2, p. 1896; von Rauch, *The Baltic States*, p. 153. I have not found a complete membership roster for any organisation – only partial lists, individual regional records, and police reports of individual meetings. Paeglis also comments on this problem in *Pērkonkrusts pār Latviju*, p. 40.

14 LVVA, f. 3235, apr. 3, l. 109, p. 33. Letter from Political Police to Riga Administrative Region, regarding the liquidation of Firecross, 21 March 1933.

15 LVVA, f. 3235, apr. 1/22, l. 708, pp. 1–3. One of the reasons given for liquidating Fatherland Guard was that it had founded sections not outlined in the statutes, e.g. a military section and a women's section. LVVA, f. 3235, apr. 1/22, l. 708, p. 93.

male citizen of Latvia, regardless of [his] profession, skill, or religion, over the age of eighteen' could be a member, and female citizens could be members of the women's section, 'under the supervision of the governing committee'. However, the targeted group – ethnic Latvians – is clear from the stated goals of 'uniting the Latvian nation in a patriotic organisation'.[16] Thundercross statutes in May 1933 clearly limited membership to ethnic Latvians.[17]

Little information is available concerning the specific roles of women's sections and comes primarily from Political Police reports; clearly, the women questioned in these reports downplayed their roles and often claimed that they did not remember anything about the organisational structure or its personnel.[18] In lists of members, women do not number more than ten for every one hundred men and are listed specifically as women's sections members.[19] When questioned, women stated that they were in charge of welfare and dues collecting;[20] however, 'simply' providing aid may indeed have been an effective recruitment tactic. 'Women', according to one report on Firecross activities after its liquidation, 'have proven to be good propagandists and recruiters of new members.'[21] Women had more distinct roles after organisations were forced to go underground. Despite their denial of direct involvement, women's names reappear

16 LVVA, f. 3235, apr. 3, l. 109, p. 1. Firecross statutes.
17 Paeglis, *Pērkonkrusts pār Latviju,* Appendix, p. 28. I found one mention of a woman taking a leading role in organising the extreme right in the group Latvian Nationalist Movement, headed by a Mrs Lazdiņa. According to police reports, however, this organisation's activities were limited to 'drinking tea in Mrs Lazdiņa's apartment and complaining that the middle class is pathetic and that fascists no longer help them'. The dismissive tone of the police report perhaps hid the significance of the group, but I have not yet found other sources of information regarding this group. LVVA, f. 3235, apr 1/22, l. 701, p. 132.
18 See, for example, the reports on H. Vītols, V. Merga and V. Cālītis, which follow the same pattern of denial as Vītols's, 'Whether she filled out an application or not for membership and to whom she may have given it, she does not remember. After she became a member, she once went to the organisation's headquarters.' The Political Police search unearthed posters, but 'she did not distribute any of these'. Vītols also received propaganda literature, 'but she neither read them nor gave them to anyone else to read'. LVVA, f. 3235, apr. 3, l. 116, pp. 74–6. Political Police report.
19 For example see LVVA f. 3235, apr. 3, l. 113, pp. 148–9. I did not find women's names on any list of names of those in leadership positions.
20 LVVA, f. 3235, apr 3, l. 116, p. 75.
21 LVVA, f. 3235, apr. 1/22, l. 701, p. 116. The wife of former leader of Thundercross, G. Celmiņš, in particular, served as a contact person. See police reports of March 1935 in LVVA f. 3235, apr. 3, l. 116, pp. 60–76, 107.

throughout the historical record of all the organisations, an indication that at least some women participated actively. Reports stress that women are still 'active in the underground "Pērkonkrusts" organisation in the women's section, and have participated in this organisation's secret discussions'.[22] Moreover, in a March 1934 meeting of Young Latvia, women far outnumbered men – approximately sixty women attended and a few men.[23]

Despite the visibility of women in these organisations, the programmes and propaganda of the right pay only cursory attention to women. They focus on men and masculinity, especially as the groups became increasingly militaristic, and encourage violence against socialists and Jews.[24] Firecross defined itself as a 'battle organisation' that honoured 'the courage of men, honest speech and work, concord, and persistence'. Firecross despised 'weakness [and] apathy regarding the national question'.[25] The most trustworthy elite of the Thundercross were the 'cadre combat comrades' and each signed a pledge to 'stand and fall for Thundercross, to act like men, and if necessary, to sacrifice their lives'. Each right group developed a military component: shortly after its foundation, Firecross organised 'shock groups' whose duty was to defend Firecross members and leaders; Thundercross members divided into groups of 'battle comrades', including 'battle comrade candidate', 'full battle comrade', 'Young Latvians' for boys between the ages of sixteen and eighteen, and 'Latvian boys' for boys under the age of sixteen.[26] I have found no equivalent 'battle structure' for women or girls.

Extreme-right propaganda assigned few roles to women. Thundercross addressed women only to reassure them of its strength: 'Latvian [men] and Latvian [women], we have prepared widely and carefully against the administrative terror and persecution'.[27] The Nationalist Activist Club appealed only to men to defend their land

22 LVVA, f. 3235, apr 1/22, l. 708, p. 194.
23 LVVA, f. 3235, apr 3, l. 121, p. 233.
24 LVVA, f. 3235, apr. 3, l. 109, p. 4. Police report on Firecross activities, 1932.
25 From the pamphlet *What is Ugunskrusts?* LVVA, f. 3235, apr. 3, l. 109, p. 8.
26 LVVA. f. 3235, apr 1/22, l. 708, pp. 79–81.
27 LVVA, f. 3235, apr. 3, l. 120, p. 138. As Maria Bucur notes in Chapter 4, the gendered nature of the Romanian language complicates the analysis of texts. Latvian also typically uses the masculine plural to address a mixed group. However, in the case of the propaganda addressed in this chapter, it is striking that the authors, as in this example, use both masculine (*latvieši*) and feminine plural (*latvietes*) of Latvians to address their intended audience. It is, therefore, likely that when only the masculine plural is used, the target group is male.

and follow in the footsteps of their brothers and fathers:

> Compatriot! [male] If a Latvian heart beats in your chest, if you are a
> Latvian [male] and love your land, for which your Fathers and Brothers
> have spilled their blood; if you want to see the safe and sunny future
> of the Latvian nation – your place is with the activists! ... [With us]
> you will find manly determination [vīrišķu gribu], [male] friends, trust-
> worthy fellow battle comrades, those who search for new knowledge
> and truth.[28]

The increased militarism of the extreme right – Thundercross defined
itself as a 'battle organisation' – diminished the active role of women.
Thundercross members greeted each other with 'Ready for Battle!'
('Cīņai sveiks!').[29]

Anti-Semitism was related to anti-Marxism, anti-Bolshevism and
anti-internationalism, and played a key role in the propaganda of the
right from the 1920s. According to the 1925 writings of the Latvian
Nationalist Club, 'tomorrow belongs only to internationalism – a
movement that leads to self-destruction and self-murder, so that the
Jews may build their world rule on the ruins of the nation'.[30] The
pamphlet *Thundercross: What does it do? What does it want? How
does it work?*' asked: 'Who does not like [us]?' 'Jews and their associates – Marxists, Foreigners, Leaders of Shopkeeper Parties, and the
Weak-willed [Mazdūšīgie]'.[31] These enemies, in sum, are grouped
together as weaklings in contrast to the strength of true men.

Right groups, especially Thundercross, recruited new members
from the National Guard[32] and university student organisations, especially fraternities.[33] Supporters of the right represented all
generational, educational and professional backgrounds, from university professors and doctors to students, farmers and carpenters.[34]
Extreme-right propaganda was targeted at young ethnic Latvian men
and students. Yet, despite its growing popularity, and the surrounding political and economic instability, the extreme right failed to
become a mass movement.

---

28 LVVA, f. 3235, apr. 1/22, l. 701, p. 306.
29 *Pērkonkrusta rakstu krājums*, nr. 1, p. 7, reprinted in Paeglis, *Pērkonkrusts*,
   Appendix, p. 205.
30 LVVA, f. 3235, apr. 1/22, l. 471, p. 2.
31 *Pērkonkrusta rakstu krājums*, nr. 1, p. 4, reprinted in Paeglis, *Pērkonkrusts*,
   Appendix p. 203.
32 LVVA, f. 3235, apr 1/22, l. 708, p. 8.
33 Aivars Stranga, *Ebreji un diktatūras Baltijā* (Riga, SIA NIMS, 1997), pp. 88–9.
34 LVVA, f. 3235, apr. 3, l. 113, p. 302.

The Ulmanis dictatorship

Despite the claims by the radical right that Ulmanis had neglected the Latvian nation, Ulmanis's national authoritarian government did foster the idea of an *ethnic Latvian* nation. The ethnic Latvian nation took precedence over the nation envisioned in the founding constitution. The state continued to support some minority schools, for Ulmanis preferred conservative leaders of minority communities.[35] However, he also proposed policies to encourage assimilation into ethnic Latvian society: new laws required that children attend a Latvian school if one or both of their parents were Latvian. This brought an end to parents' freedom to choose schools for their children, which had not been linked to nationality; before the policy change Latvian children could and did attend schools where the main language of instruction was German.[36] In addition, Ulmanis sought to stabilise the economy through a policy of state-ownership, corporatism, and prioritisation of the agrarian sector, and the 'nationalisation' of the economy often came at the expense of German, Jewish and Russian owners who had previously dominated the urban economic sector.[37]

The character of Ulmanis's regime has been the subject of much debate, and has been called 'authoritarian nationalism',[38] 'authoritarianism',[39] and 'authoritarian democracy',[40] as well as fascism.[41] Ulmanis's government of 'national unity' was authoritarian and dictatorial; he

35 For example, the Jewish community in Latvia was very diverse, with strong secular and religious groups. After 1934, Ulmanis backed the Orthodox anti-Zionist party, Agudes Israel. Thus, Hebrew schools continued to exist until 1940, but secular Jewish schools were abolished. Z. Michaeli, 'Jewish cultural autonomy and the Jewish school systems', in M. Bobe (ed.), *The Jews in Latvia* (Tel Aviv, D. Ben-Nun Press, 1971), p. 216. For a detailed analysis of Ulmanis and the Jewish community see Stranga, *Ebreji un diktatūras Baltijā*.

36 Švābe, *Latvijas Enciklopēdija*, vol. 1, p. 828.

37 Stranga, *Ebreji un diktatūras Baltijā*, p. 70.

38 Ibid., p. 63.

39 Romuald Misiunas and Rein Taagepera, *The Baltic States: Years of Dependence 1940–1990*, 2nd edn (Berkeley and Los Angeles, University of California Press, 1993), pp. 12–13; Plakans, *The Latvians*, pp. 133–4.

40 von Rauch, *The Baltic States*, p. 154; Martin Blinkhorn, *Fascism and the Right in Europe 1919–1945* (Harlow, Longman, 2000), p. 81.

41 Andrejs Plakans writes that those who call Kārlis Ulmanis's regime 'fascism' have most often been historians in the Soviet period who used this term for periodisation or Soviet propagandists who used the term as a convenient label against those who opposed communism. Plakans, *Historical Dictionary of Latvia*, p. 66. See also Blinkhorn, *Fascism and the Right in Europe*, p. 110.

circumscribed political opposition through arrests, and instituted strict surveillance measures and censorship of the popular press. Nevertheless, it would be inaccurate to label Ulmanis's regime as fascist. Even though Ulmanis's regime shared characteristics with fascist regimes in Europe – including a respect for Italian fascism and corporatism and promotion of Latvian pro-natalist propaganda – Ulmanis also banned the most fascist groups under his regime. Like Benito Mussolini, Adolf Hilter, and other fascist leaders, he fostered the idea of a 'leader cult' and became a symbol of unity, as the '*Vadonis*' or 'Leader' of the Latvian nation. Each year 15 May became known as the 'Celebration of National Unity', which the journal of the National Guard, *Aizsargs*, described in 1935 as 'Celebration of the Vadonis': '[With] big processions and gatherings, songs, praise, and ovations, the united nation praises its leader'.[42] However, unlike Mussolini and Hitler, Ulmanis did not introduce an authoritarian 'national unity party'. Undoubtedly, those of Ulmanis's economic and social policies that implemented increased state control in entrepreneurship and education had the effect of providing preferential treatment for ethnic Latvians, discriminating against private enterprise, and hurting minority communities. Ulmanis cut state support for minority education and extended it only to conservative minority groups. Stricter language laws, especially targeted at German, banned the use of foreign languages on public signs.[43] Even though these policies did reflect a xenophobia present in society and in the concept of 'national unity', Ulmanis advocated the assimilation of minorities into Latvian society and condemned violence against them.[44] Ulmanis's regime is best described as 'national authoritarianism' – he limited free speech and extended state control into various sectors of society, with the ultimate goal of strengthening the ethnic Latvian nation.

Ulmanis saw the roots of a strong Latvia in its rural culture and folkloric ties, and guided this development with the motto 'Your land – yours to till' (*Pašu zemei – pašu arājs*). The city should look to the country for guidance and morality. The organisation of nation-wide events and holidays reinforced this idyllic image of ethnic Latvia. Begun in 1930, 'Forest Days' grew in size and participation, including students, boy and girl scouts, and soldiers.[45]

Significantly, gender roles played a central role in Ulmanis's

---

42 *Aizsargs*, 15 June 1935, pp. 401–2. Cited in A. Šilde, *Latvijas vēsture 1914–1940* (Stockholm, Daugava, 1976), p. 672.
43 von Rauch, *The Baltic States,* p. 169.
44 Plakans, *The Latvians,* p. 135.
45 Šilde, *Latvijas vēsture,* pp. 669–70.

development of a united Latvian nation. In contrast to extreme-right organisations, which focused on Latvian masculinity and militarism, Ulmanis's government directly addressed both women and men, and focused on the moral and cultural virtues of the nation. This accorded with ideas already integral to conservative women's organisations, which saw in national unity a way to promote women's rights.[46] In the 1934 introduction to its newly established periodical *Latvian Woman* (*Latviete*), the Council of Latvian Women's Organisations (Latviešu Sieviešu Organizāciju Padome)[47] called for the equal rights of women and men, but also emphasised its goal to 'strengthen a sense of national consciousness in women', and to 'protect families – [through] the protection of women and children'.[48] In March 1934 Berta Pīpiņa, a women's activist and parliamentary deputy, stressed that 'the family is the cell, from which the entire nation's organism grows and develops'.[49] These largely middle-class Latvian women and women's societies believed that Ulmanis provided women with a central role as 'national unifiers'. Shortly after the coup in May, the President of the Women's Council, Līlija Branta, made a direct connection between motherhood of the family and motherhood of the nation. Men may have laid the foundation for families in terms of broad political and social relationships, wrote Branta, but women were responsible for the daily upbringing of the family, for moral, ethical and patriotic education. Thus, she concluded, 'the family shapes the nation and the state ... Women must not forget that they bear the same responsibility for our nation's and country's fate, as do men.'[50] Women saw their roles as mothers of the nation as active and participatory, in a working relationship with men. Nature, wrote organisation member Elija Kleine, had provided women with deep sources of strength, bestowing on them the honour of becoming

---

46 See Perry Willson's chapter on Italy, in which Italian women pursued a similar strategy in a 'mix of patriotism and feminism'.

47 The Council of Latvian Women's Organisations (Latviešu Sieviešu Organizāciju Padome) was founded by several women's organisations in 1925: Latvian Women's National League (Latvijas Sieviešu Nacionālā līga) est. 1922; Latvian Women's Aid Corps (Latviešu sieviešu palīdzības korpuss) est. 1919; later joined by Young Women's Christian Association (Jauno Sieviešu Kristīgā Apvienība) est. 1928; Association of Educated Women of Latvia (Latvijas Akadēmiski Izglītoto Sieviešu Apvienība), est. 1928, the Theological Association of Latvia (Latvijas Teologu Apvienība), the Association of State [Woman] Workers (Valsts Darbiniece). Ilze Trapenciere (ed.), *Sievietes ceļā* (Riga, Valga, 1992), p. 242.

48 Berta Pīpiņa, 'Ievadam', *Latviete* (January 1934), p. 1.

49 Berta Pīpiņa, 'Ģimene tautu dzīvē', *Latviete* (March 1934), p. 33.

50 Līlija Branta, 'Sieviete kā tautas vienotāja', *Latviete* (May/June 1935), pp. 69–71.

mothers. However, she continued, this does not mean that women are solely defined by motherhood, but rather that women should use their natural strength and become well-rounded, educated individuals in order to contribute to the new society Ulmanis had created.[51] According to the Women's Council's programme, only as responsible citizens with equal rights could women succeed in their duties in the home, and to the Latvian nation.

Ulmanis's plea to Latvians to return to their rural roots and ancient, pure folklore culture was reflected in articles in *Latvian Woman* as they increasingly associated 'Latvianness' and simple beauty, free of foreign influence. Moreover, the Riga women's organisations sought to include women from rural areas in their meetings, for they saw the country as the heart of Latvianness. Articles in *Latvian Woman* repeatedly encourage women to become 'more Latvian'. In 1935 Branta lamented that Latvian women did not yet have their own 'Latvian spiritual face' (*garīgā seja*), for Latvia's history of domination by foreigners had left its marks on Latvian women: 'Strange elements are still visible in the formation of Latvian women's spirit. These have remained from the times when foreign nations (Russians and Germans) shaped our nation's spiritual life.'[52] The solution women proposed was to cleanse women of impurities and to find beauty. Women's Council member Karola Dāle encouraged women to 'Find beauty in daily life! ... You, Latvian mothers and sisters ... search for and find something valuable and beautiful in each day and do not forget to teach this to your children ... Then there will be fewer unhappy families ... fewer suicides ... and the future will shine brightly and be clear.'[53] Pīpiņa concluded that the woman in the new Latvia 'must become physically and spiritually pure and honourable ... because her final goal is to be the nation's mother and guardian ... Excessive concern about appearance and fashion [is unnatural]'.[54] The 'modern Latvian woman', who is interested only in starving herself into slim elegance, who is thus selfish and self-absorbed, must be seen as a negative development and be encouraged to change.[55]

---

51 Elija Kliene, 'Sieviete jaunās dzīves krustceļos', *Latviete* (May/June 1935), pp. 76–80.
52 Līlija Branta, 'Meklēsim dzīves vērtības', *Latviete* (January 1935), p. 2.
53 Karola Dāle, 'Skaistas un ikdiena', *Latviete* (1934), p. 111.
54 Berta Pīpiņa, 'Sievete jaunajā Latvija', *Latviete* (May/June 1934), p. 90.
55 Hildegarde Reinharde, 'Modernā Latvju sieviete', *Latviete* (November 1937), pp. 61–2.

Ulmanis's social policies outlined the duties of all family members in the upbringing of the nation through public celebrations such as Mother's and Family Day. In 1935 the Ministry of Education became responsible for the planning of national Mother's Day and included representatives of women's organisations in the planning committee. Lilija Branta stressed that the meaning of Mother's Day was not only to remind people that they must honour their mothers, but also that 'The concept of the mother holds the key to eternity. As long as the mother survives, so too will humanity.'[56] In 1938 Mother's Day became Family Day, to stress the unity of the nation and more closely tie the fate of the nation to the family. The Ministry of Social Affairs planned an official ceremony in which Ulmanis presented money to poor families.[57] 'Isn't it time', asked the author of a 1938 *Latvian Woman* article, 'that both members of both sexes realised that the future is in their hands?'[58]

The development of the right in Latvia reveals the centrality of gender in the construction of the new nation-states that won their independence after the First World War. Where the extreme right failed to build a broad basis of support and became increasingly militaristic and exclusionary, Ulmanis's regime had, by the late 1930s, gained support or at the very least general acceptance from most Latvians. While Ulmanis's policies of censorship are a partial explanation of the lack of opposition, restrictions were not so severe, nor was Ulmanis's authoritarianism sufficiently repressive to silence opposition completely or to dictate to the press. Ulmanis's national authoritarianism increased in its appeal to both Latvian men and women as the tie between family, gender and nation became stronger and more direct. The beginning of the Second World War in 1939 and the loss of Latvia's independence in 1940 reinforced and strengthened this connection, and in turn the Nazis used these ties to establish control and seek acceptance.

The Nazi occupation

Nazi troops entered Latvia on 26 June 1941 and occupied Riga on 1 July. Latvia became – with Lithuania, Estonia and Belorussia – one of the General Commissariats of the Reich Commissariat for the Ostland, under the supervision of the Ministry for the Territories for

56 Lilija Branta, 'Mātes dienas valstiskā nozīme', *Latviete* (May 1935), p. 82.
57 Berta Pīpiņa, 'Ģimenes dienas svinības', *Latviete* (January 1938), pp. 14–15.
58 Katrīna Draudziņa, 'Pārdomas ģimenes dienā', *Latviete* (May 1938), p. 38.

the Occupied East, based in Berlin.[59] Although the precise details of
what was planned are unknown, it is clear that the goal for Latvians
was colonisation, Germanisation, and dispersal of the Latvians.[60]
However, implementation of cultural Germanisation was gradual and
contributed to Latvians' construction of the illusion of sovereignty
under Nazi occupation. More importantly, the 'status' of Latvians on
the racial scale – not *Untermenschen* but also not Aryan – created an
ambiguity both supporters of and resistors to Nazi rule could exploit.

Latvians' initial acceptance of the Nazis, despite the horrors of the
Shoah,[61] must be considered in the context of gender roles during the
year of Soviet occupation from 1940 to 1941. The appeal of traditional gender images was strengthened after their destruction by the
Soviets. A new class-based, internationalist policy had replaced
Ulmanis's nationalist ideology after the entrance of Soviet troops. The
Soviet regime dissolved all independent Latvia's cultural and social
organisations, including the Boy Scouts, women's organisations and
ethnic cultural groups. The reshaping of the Latvian population was
an important part of the controls imposed by the Soviets. The most
destructive measures of the first year of Soviet occupation were arrest
and execution and mass deportation; approximately 35,000 people
were victims.[62] The Nazi invasion on 26 June interrupted Soviet
deportations, and many Latvians greeted the Germans as liberators
who, they hoped, would restore Latvian independence. This was a
complete reversal of the traditional German–Latvian relationship.
Prior to the Soviet occupation, Latvians viewed the Germans with
hatred and many Latvians had rejoiced at the repatriation to Germany

59 Raphael Lemkin, *Axis Rule in Occupied Europe* (Washington, Carnegie Endowment
for International Peace, 1944), p. 117.
60 Katrin Reichelt discusses the many drafts of *Generalplan Ost* and the General
Settlement Plan that outlined the fates of Eastern Europeans. Dr Lenz of the
Ministry for the Occupied Eastern Territories estimated that 10 per cent of Latvian
blood could be German; others then concluded 30 per cent of Latvians could be
Germanised. Reichelt, 'Latvia and the Latvians in the Nazi race and settlement
policy: theoretical conception and practical implementation', in Commission of the
Historians of Latvia et al. (ed.), *Latvija Otrajā Pasaules Karā: Starptautiskās
konferences materiāli 1999. gada 14.–15. jūnijs, Riga.* (Riga, Latvijas vēstures
institūta apgāds, 2000), pp. 266–74.
61 In 1939, approximately 93,000 Jews lived in Latvia. Of the 70,000 Jews who were
still in Latvia after the first Soviet occupation, only 4,000 survived. Under Soviet
occupation between 1940 and 1941, approximately 5,000 Jews were deported to
Siberia in the mass deportations of June 1941, and approximately 18,000 were
drafted or evacuated. Misiunas and Taagepera, *The Baltic States*, p. 64.
62 Misiunas and Taagepera, *The Baltic States*, p. 42.

of Baltic Germans in 1939 and 1940. A contributor to *Latvian Woman* praised the destruction of the German elite in March 1939 and criticised admiration for them: '[We understood] how thin this culture [of the so-called *Kulturtraeger*] was, how shallow were its roots in our culture . . . when this minority's domination was destroyed'.[63]

Familiar gender roles gave the illusion of Latvian continuity. In fact the Nazis were instituting Germanisation. The Nazi regime constructed women's and men's roles in accord with traditional Latvian images – with reference to Latvian folklore and rural life – but the 'German way' served as the ideal model. However, these same gender roles also became a tool of resistance to the Nazi regime, as resistance movements manipulated gender roles into their rhetoric against the Nazis. The use of traditional gender images that resembled those in the inter-war independence period under Ulmanis's 'national unity' contributed to Latvians' tacit acceptance of the Nazi regime arriving in 1941.

Initial Latvian acceptance of the Nazis was linked also to cultural policies that appeared to allow limited expression of national sovereignty as the Nazis renewed some pre-war organisations liquidated by the Soviets. However, German racial 'superiority' became increasingly apparent. German culture and language were gradually introduced alongside the Latvian equivalents or replaced them. The Nazi regime reopened museums and theatres but erased evidence of their ties to a Latvian *nation*: the Latvian National Opera became the Riga Opera House; the Latvian National Theatre was now the Riga Theatre. Germans and Baltic Germans replaced Latvians in the administrative offices, while the renaming of buildings and streets – Independence Boulevard became Adolf Hitler Boulevard – was a constant reminder of the German dominance.[64]

Gender role construction played a significant role in the Nazi regime's consolidation of power, garnering of support, and dissemination of racial anti-Semitic ideology.[65] At the same time, the familiarity of traditional gender roles contributed to ideas of a Latvian

63 Anna Rūmane, 'Pārdomas vāciem aizbraucot', *Latviete* (March 1939), p. 103. By 1940, 52,000 people had repatriated from Latvia to Germany. Plakans, *The Latvians*, p. 142.

64 Latvian Embassy, *Latvia under German Occupation* (Washington, DC, Press Bureau of the Latvian Legation, 1943), pp. 59, 66.

65 In her study on women in Nazi Germany, Claudia Koonz suggests that traditional gender roles and 'rhetoric about loving women' could have made anti-Semitism more acceptable. Koonz, *Mothers in the Fatherland: Women, the Family, and Nazi Politics* (New York, St Martin's Press, 1987), p. 56.

nation, contrary to Nazi intentions. This is most evident in the official and resistance rhetoric found in the periodical press under Nazi occupation. Analysis of the press reveals how Nazi propaganda used gender to construct an anti-Bolshevist, anti-Semitic nation in Latvia, while Latvians linked traditional gender images to a continuity of the independent Latvian nation.

Initially, the former members of the Thundercross hoped that the Nazi arrival would finally rid Latvia of the evils of communism and help establish a pure and Latvian Latvia. Although a few Thundercross leaders did serve in official positions in the Nazi governing structure, collaboration between these extremists and the Nazis was short-lived. The Thundercross's member base had shrunk considerably during the Soviet occupation, as the Soviets arrested and deported many leaders to Siberia. More significantly, the Nazis did not trust the Latvian fascists, and on 17 August 1941, they closed down Thundercross.[66]

The main daily newspaper published under occupation was the official Nazi-controlled Latvian language newspaper, *Fatherland* (*Tēvija*).[67] The editors and writers of *Fatherland* were Latvian – some had been active in the Thundercross – but worked under the watchful eye of the Nazi government, which distributed confidential 'press instructions' to the top editors of all officially approved papers. These press regulations determined how each 'race' should be depicted: Germans as liberators, Russians and Jews as conspirators and demons, and Latvians as grateful to the Germans.[68] The instructions allowed limited expression of Latvian national identity – 18 November 1918, Latvian independence day, could be privately commemorated. However, noted Nazi officials, the main theme of

---

66 Paeglis, *Pērkonkrusts,* pp. 182–3.
67 E. Flīgere (ed.), *Latviešu periodika: bibliogrāfiskais rādītājs,* vol. 4 (Riga, Latvijas Akadēmiskā Biblioteka, 1995), p. 125. *Fatherland* (*Tēvija*) was the most widely published Latvian language newspaper during occupation and one of the only ones to be published consistently throughout the occupation. Furthermore, perhaps the greatest testament to the significance of *Fatherland* is its availability in antiquarian stores in Riga today. There was conflict between the editors and the Nazi officials. On 5 February 1942 editor Kreišmanis questioned the second-class status of Latvians: 'What are these kind of conditions, in which the gap between Germans and Latvians grows? ... It is my understanding that Latvians received half as many rations (if not even less) than the people of the Reich.' LVVA, f. P–70 apr. 5, l. 3, p. 227.
68 See, for example, 'Vertrauliche Presseinformation Nr. 32', 4 November 1942. LVVA, f. P–74, apr. 1, l. 2, pp. 77–8.

these celebrations should be gratitude to the Germans for liberating Latvians from the Soviets. This day 'marked the beginning of the German–Latvian struggle against Bolshevism'.[69]

The images of women and men found in *Fatherland* illustrate how the Nazi structure sought to control the Latvian nation under occupation without revealing its ultimate plans. Three months after the first issue of *Fatherland*, an article defined the duties of Latvian women and men in rebuilding the nation after Soviet occupation. The author describes the Soviet occupation as a period that had 'wrenched out [a] deep gash into the living flesh of the nation and torn up such wounds in the soul of the nation, that decades [would] pass before these [would] be healed'. Now, women and men each had their roles:

> [W]e should ... take special notice of the responsibility that life and work bestowed on the woman ... Our nation's fate is in a remarkable way placed into the hand of the woman, our future is entrusted to her. She is chosen, to pave the way for rebirth. For what is the honour of fighter and victor for the man, the honour of mother is it for the woman.[70]

This article outlined the roles for women and men: women were mothers of the national body, men were soldiers and protectors. While the author does not ignore the role of men in the survival of the nation, the responsibility for the preservation and indeed the advancement of the nation fell to the woman. The praise of women as mothers, however, could also pose a threat to Nazi power as women began to realise their strength in motherhood. The call for increased births was also consistent with Ulmanis's inter-war pro-natalist policy as well as with the emergency created by the demographic losses during the Soviet occupation and could thus be understood as a call for strengthening the ethnic Latvian nation. The Nazi power in Latvia endeavoured to curb ideas of autonomy by forbidding clear expressions of Latvian independence and increasing its control over motherhood and family.

Fatherland linked the national body to the physical body with prominent articles on fitness and team sports. Sports were a way to shape both the physical and mental health integral to national health and purity. Nazism also linked athleticism to anti-Semitism and anti-Bolshevism. Since women were responsible for the spiritual and

---

69 'Vertrauliche Presseinformation Nr. 52', 15 November 1943. LVVA, f. P-74, apr. 1, l. 4, pp. 47–8.

70 K. Kundziņš, 'Latviešu sieviete', *Tēvija*, 25 October 1941, p. 2.

physical health of the body of the nation, their personal health was crucial and sports had a special purpose for women in preparing them as mothers of the nation. The occupation regime blamed the decline of women's sports on Bolshevism and liberalism. The Soviet occupation had stunted the development of Latvians:

> While in the rest of Europe male and female athletes prided themselves with greater and greater accomplishments, we could only watch, learn, and plan. Often sports' directors were allowed to organize activities only for male athletes. [In Germany] German youth grew up healthy and because of this now, when the fates of states and nations are decided, it is in the right place.[71]

Under the Nazis, Latvian women athletes could finally try to rid themselves of Bolshevism and attain the same level of athleticism and physical health as in Germany: 'Now, also Latvian female athletes, after the year of awful Bolshevik domination, we can again start to think about sport activities'.[72]

These passages illustrate the duality of *Fatherland* images, those of sovereignty and Germanisation. This duality could suggest that an independent Latvia was possible, without explicitly stating such. However, the potential strength of Latvian female athletes remained overshadowed by the superiority of German athletes.

As in Germany, propaganda in Latvia declared that team sports were essential for both women and men to foster *Volksgemeinschaft*, a sense of community.[73] A 1941 *Fatherland* article condemned Bolshevik emphasis on 'socialist competition, which meant not only a senseless pursuit of [new] records, but also the appropriation of the teachings of Marx and Lenin'. In 'Jewish Bolshevism', the beauty of the athletic body was overshadowed by Bolshevist 'barbaric sports methods [for which reason women] appeared more and more rarely on the battlefields'.[74] National Socialism now gave women the opportunity to care for their health (and that of the nation) in athletics. Athletic training for women was preparation for motherhood of the

---

71 M. B., 'Jauni uzdevumi ari mūsu sportistēm', *Tēvija,* 21 November 1941, p. 4.
72 Ibid., p. 4.
73 Gertrud Pfister, 'Conflicting feminities: the discourse on the female body and the physical education of girls in National Socialism', *Sports History Review,* 28 (1997), 93. Pfister also notes that Nazis had to accept competitive sports as a result of the propaganda surrounding the Olympic Games. This, she writes, Nazis did by accepting successful competition as the culmination of the 'National Socialist team spirit' or 'the success of the new national community'.
74 M. B., 'Jauni uzdevumi', p. 4.

nation. Nazi leaders, however, did not specify *which nation*.

Men's athletic bodies, on the other hand, appeared both as athletes and as soldiers. Here, as in Nazi Germany, health was not as great a concern as was preparation for battle.[75] This was particularly clear in the plea of the Director of Latvian Sports, Roberts Plūme, in 1942: 'Latvian [male] athletes! I turn to you with a burning invitation to enlist in the service of our Fatherland ... [T]he time has come when we must prove our athletic, genuinely masculine poise, and with a weapon in our hands we must go into battle against humanity's greatest burden – Bolshevism.'[76]

The definition of fatherland was again left unclear. It was not in the interest of the National Socialist state for athletes to develop a strong team loyalty outside the state. For this reason, the Nazi state repeatedly reminded Latvians they had not yet reached German levels of skill and discipline. Athleticism served the dual purpose of 'healing the national body' destroyed by Bolshevism and defending the nation against future attacks.

Limitation of women to their roles as mothers did not, according to images found in *Fatherland*, necessarily mean that women were subordinate to men. In fact, women, as mothers of the future nation's men, were in some ways more powerful than men, but only if they realised their primary roles as mothers: 'Our woman's quest for intellectual equality with men is out of place [in our society] because she is superior in her comprehension of life and will forever remain superior'.[77] The Bolshevik's so-called emancipation of women, according to this article, had weakened women by forcing them to work outside the home and to surrender the care of their children to mass institutions. The National Socialist return of women to their role of motherhood could be a source of strength for women and for the nation.

The occupation power carefully controlled motherhood and this source of potential strength, however. The founding of the organisation Nation's Aid (Tautas Palīdzība) in November 1941 formalised the relationship between the health of the nation and the woman-mother. Most significantly, it also limited the autonomy of women as mothers of the nation. The family, as a cornerstone of society in wartime, became a public entity, and reports on its activities were found in almost every issue of *Fatherland*. These articles again

75 Pfister, 'Conflicting femininities', p. 97.
76 Roberts Plūme, 'Visi lielajā cīņā!', *Tēvija*, 17 February 1942, p. 2.
77 A. Vilde, 'Mūžīgais uzdevums', *Tēvija*, 5 March 1942, p. 1.

embodied the dual nature of the gender construction under Nazi occupation. While the rhetoric in *Fatherland* emphasised protection of and respect for the family, it also appealed for the involvement of all society in the raising of the national family.

The renewal of the celebration of 'Family Day', introduced by Ulmanis, reinforced the public nature of the family, while also serving as a sign of continuity with inter-war Latvia.[78] Family Day, which was first celebrated under the Nazi occupation for two days on 16 and 17 May 1942, focused on children who had lost their parents in the previous year of Soviet rule. Such a day was necessary, according to Nation's Aid officials, because the Bolsheviks had tried to destroy family life, and those who had lost their parents had now become the children of the entire nation. The first day of Family Day focused on identifying Bolshevism as the murderer of families, and Nation's Aid organised several commemorative ceremonies at memorials to 'victims of Bolshevism'. The second day focused on the family itself and was marked with ceremonies to present gifts to families with many children.[79] In this way, the Nazis eliminated the distinction between public and private motherhood, and women and families became dependent on the state. Nation's Aid might seem to be a source of sovereignty, but it remained under the control of the totalitarian regime.

The duality of Nazi gender images is also evident in pro-natalist propaganda. National Latvian images softened racial rhetoric. Latvian authors of *Fatherland* articles cried for large families in the language of folklore. In a front-page article in February 1942, a story appeared about a family of seven sons. The father was elated at the thought of a country full of his descendents. Unfortunately, in the end the survival of the family depended on one child, who did not understand the importance of his mission and not only sold the family farm, but did not have children:

> Having become an educated man, Austris found a beautiful wife and made himself such a beautiful apartment, that society's elite enjoyed spending its time there and did so often. They did not have children, and when, last year, he also died ... the circle was closed, and Austris became the sunset of his family's name.[80]

In this story, traditional Latvian values – farm life and folklore – were

---

78 'Atklāta skate, "Māte un bērns"', *Tēvija*, 10 May 1943, p. 3.
79 'Tautas Palīdzības darbs vērsās plašumā', *Tēvija*, 22 April 1942, p. 2.
80 V. Lesiņš, 'Tautai un mūžībai', *Tēvija*, 2 February 1942, p. 1.

in direct opposition to the corruption of liberalism and intellectualism. The play on words was also significant: Austris, a Latvian boy's name, contains the root 'aust', which means to dawn. Thus in the conclusion Austris (dawn) became the sunset of the nation.

The resistance

As it became increasingly clear that Nazis had not come to liberate Latvia, resistance movements grew. Some were rooted in groups founded in 1940 to resist the Soviets. Others, however, were tied to inter-war right groups and even to those who had for a time collaborated with the Nazis. Women were active in the resistance and some organisations, such as the Latvian Nationalist Union (Latviešu Nacionālistu Savienība), had separate 'ladies' committees'. The Latvian National Council (Latviešu Nacionālā Padome), an organisation based in the Jelgava Pedagogical Institute, worked to establish contacts with the Jelgava Girls' *Gymnasium*.[81]

Although the approach and membership of organisations differed, many defined national resistance in terms of gender. These resistance groups used gender roles similar to those seen in Nazi propaganda to resist the Nazis and to create the idea of an independent, sovereign Latvia. Underground publications assigned Latvian women a special role in the liberation of Latvia from the Nazis.[82] A 'war of weapons' was not possible for the Latvians, but a 'war of the spirit' (*gara cīņa*) was. The article continued: 'The woman is the one who must again raise in honour the purity of the soul and virtue'.[83] The author noted, however, that some Latvian women had failed in this duty, and these women's actions are a 'crime against our nation's soul and our nation's flesh [*miesa*]'. The author argued, 'what can we expect from

---

81 The main organisations were Latvian Nationalist Union (Latviešu Nacionālistu Savienība); Latvian National Council (Latviešu Nacionālā Padome); Latvia's Guard (Latvijas Sargi), Jaunpulki, Free Latvia (Brīvā Latvija); Daugava's Hawks of Free Latvia (Nacionālās Latvijas Daugavas Vanagi). Uldis Neiburgs, 'Nacionālās pretošanas kustības organizācijas Latvijā padomju un vācu okupācijas laikā (1940–1945)', in *Latvijas Otrajā pasaules karā*, p. 163. Neiburgs, 'Latviešu pretošanas kustības preses izdevumi Latvijā Nacistiskās Vācijas okupācijas Laika (1941–1945)', unpublished M.A. thesis, University of Latvia, 1998, p. 21.

82 Few underground publications survived, and those that did are in poor condition. One of the main publications (though it had less than ten issues) was *Tautas Balss* (Voice of the Nation). See Neiburgs, 'Latviešu pretošanas kustības preses izdevumi'.

83 'Sieviete un audzināšana', *Tautas Balss*, n.d. 1942.

a woman, what can this woman contribute to the nation, who easily succumbs [*sevi vienkārši atdod*] to the first person who comes along – a stranger – for a pair of silk stockings, theatre tickets, or a can of face powder? Our nation's morale is especially threatened now, when we are in conflict with a foreign power's military.'[84]

Resistance publications also raised fears that 'thoughtless' women might contaminate the ethnic nation. They used their own racial arguments against the Nazis. *Voice of the Nation* condemned 'mixed marriages' between Latvian women and Germans as 'treason':

> It is perfectly clear to anyone that the descendants from such a marriage are lost to the Latvian nation, but Latvian woman must be aware that she received her blood from her nation and her only and greatest duty is to give it back ... If the Germans have written laws to protect their nation's blood and honour, then we must also have the same demands.[85]

Resistance movements also turned to traditional rural roots that had been central to nation-building under Ulmanis and urged Latvians to return to the country. 'The Latvian land, which our ancestors tilled for centuries, calls for a Latvian farmer ... For this reason our duty is to donate our strength to our land and not leave in search of fame and fortune.'[86] Traditional images tied to the Latvian independence period, especially the period of 'national unity', appeared throughout resistance propaganda.

Conclusion

The history of right movements in Latvia in the first half of the twentieth century – including extreme-right groups and conservative nationalists, as well as the National Socialist occupation regime – may not be understood without an analysis of each movement's approach to gender and nation. Extreme-right movements such as Thundercross failed to build a mass movement because of their exclusionary and militaristic strategy, which neither included women nor appealed to men at large. Ulmanis's government of national unity, on the other hand, tied gender identity and the family closely to the strength of the nation. The National Socialist occupation regime manipulated the gender roles associated with inter-war Latvia in order to build support

84 Ibid.

85 'Oficiālā prese un mēs', *Tautas Balss*, 30 March 1942, Also see *Tautas Balss*, 15 April 1942.

86 'Lauki aicina', *Tautas Balss*, 30 March 1942.

and hide its goals of Germanisation. However, these images associated with Nazism were also co-opted by those who resisted the extreme right. Although each movement differed in its extremism and goals and its plan for an ideal society, gender was a central tool for all in constructing the Latvian nation. The history of the extreme right's struggle for control of the ethnic nation through gender roles in Latvia reveals not only the tensions in the development of the new European nation-states in the inter-war period but also the conflicts in Nazism as it sought to apply its ideology outside the core.

10

Poland

Dobrochna Kałwa

Before equality: women under the partitions

Women's history is quite a new discipline in Poland, where it has been researched only since the end of the 1980s. It is no surprise, therefore, that historians have so far expressed little interest in the gender aspects of nationalism. Paradoxically, one can find quite a large number of publications devoted to women's role in the history of the Polish nation, especially in the nineteenth century. This is not a surprise, for the period is crucial to any attempt to depict or explain aspects of the twentieth-century history of Poland and Polish women's history. The one and a quarter centuries of the Time of the Partitions deeply influenced the Polish nation and patterns of political, cultural and social activity of its members, both men and women. In 1795 the Polish state broke down, and its territory was incorporated into the states of Russia, Prussia and Austria. Although the Polish state had collapsed, the nation survived. However, it changed under new political circumstances. First of all a new meaning of the nation was born. In the Republic of Poland-Lithuania, the pre-partition state, the nation was considered as a citizen-community participating in political life by electing a king, passing laws, and deciding on a budget or a foreign policy. Only members of the aristocracy enjoyed the privilege of participating in national politics; townspeople and peasants were excluded from this national-political community. Although noble women had no political rights, they became members of the nation, partly because of their activity during the Partitions. In 1795 Polish nobles lost their political rights and thereby the basis of their national identity. Their exclusion from political life in Russia, Prussia and Austria resulted in a redefinition of the nation, which became not a political, but an ethnic and cultural community. The nation grew from a small group of privileged nobles to a national mass society. The process of broadening the Polish non-state nation created new roles and duties for its members. One aim determined the national activity of that time – the rebirth, or, using nineteenth-century patriotic language, the 'resurrection' of an independent Poland. Different ways of reaching it were envisaged, from political underground and military uprisings to legality and compromises with state authorities. Paradoxically, in spite of the complexity and variety of national movements, the woman's place in national society was still exemplified by the figure of the Mother Pole.

Her image turned out to be so powerful that Polish historians describing women's situation in the nineteenth century still use a construction of an 'archetypal' figure of the Polish Woman, who has always been posited as a patriotic and steadfast icon of the Polish fight for the independent nation and/or state. She was – historians, like nineteenth-century national activists, have repeated this – to protect the nation from moral decay, guard the nation's posterity against Germanisation and Russification, and, last but not least, play an important role in clandestine political movements for the independence of Poland. In this context, historians have accepted a national myth created under the Partitions – the myth of the Mother Pole, a new, national, female icon. She became a sort of a role model for women, delineating/dictating the woman's place in the nation not only in the nineteenth century, but also in the inter-war period. This powerful image has also influenced the way in which Polish women involved in the national struggle for freedom have been seen up until now.

What kind of ideas concerning women were fundamental to the creation of the Mother Pole? According to Nira Yuval-Davis, concepts of women's role in nationalism are related to three aspects of the nation, considered as a state, cultural or ethnic community. In terms of the nation-state, woman is represented as a member of a civic community.[1] The idea of a cultural nation involves woman as a transmitter of cultural values and constructor of national identity. The last concept – the ethnic nation – reduces women to biological reproducers (of the nation). The analysis of the Mother Pole figure reveals that all three concepts complement one another. She was a transmitter of

1 In German historiography this concept of the nation is known as *Staatnation*, *Kulturnation*, *Volksnation*. See Nira Yuval-Davis, 'Gender and nation', in Nick Wilford and Robert L. Miller (eds), *Women, Ethnicity and Nationalism: The Politics of Transition* (London and New York, Routledge 1998), pp. 23–5.

the national tradition, culture, customs and language (as the person responsible for the education of the children), she was a biological reproducer, and she was a participant in the political struggle for the nation, often punished for her anti-regime/underground/clandestine activity just like a man.[2]

In the analysis of the Mother Pole figure the influence of Catholicism should also be mentioned. In Eastern Europe, as in some Western countries in the nineteenth century, especially in the case of non-state nations, religion determined nationality. Polish nationalism was Catholic. In the nineteenth century Polish nationalist ideologists created pairs of concepts which were the basis for the building of a modern national identity. Such figures as the Catholic Pole, the Protestant German, the Uniate Ukrainian or the Orthodox Russian became an inseparable part of a system of national identity. The religious policy of Russia (discrimination against Catholics and the privileged position of the Orthodox Church) and of Germany (where in the *Kulturkampf* the state sought to subordinate the Catholic Church) consolidated belief in the sacred dimension of nationality. Even in the Catholic Austro-Hungarian Empire, where Poles were not discriminated against on religious grounds, national identity was connected with Catholicism, and this differentiated them from Ukrainians, who were members of the Uniate Church.

The influence of Christianity on the figure of the Mother Pole was especially evident in the idea of women's sacrifice. Two aspects were especially important: the figure of the Holy Mother and the Romantic idea of the Polish nation as the Messiah of Nations. Poland was (and still is) personified as a woman. Like the Virgin Mary, Mother Pole had to sacrifice her son(s), and as a Pole she should be ready for self-sacrifice.

This idea of self-sacrifice is not a Polish phenomenon but concerns almost all nations influenced by the Catholic Church. Gender aspects of national sacrifice in modern Ireland, described by Mary Condern, provide an interesting analogy to the Polish case. Condern used Bakhtin's idea of the carnival, in which the traditional order is reversed, to understand the position of women in the oppressed nation. The 'abnormal' situation of men regarding their national aspirations created an 'abnormal' situation for women. The former were

---

2 During the Polish uprising of 1863, the authorities introduced a new criminal code in the Russian partition. Henceforth women were punished as severely as men for political crimes. See Andrzej Chwalba (ed.), *Historia Polski: Kalendarium* (Kraków, Wydawn-Literackie, 1998), p. 554.

to fight and die for the nation (sacrificing only themselves) while the latter were to sacrifice themselves for the next generation of national fighters. Women would sacrifice both themselves and their husbands and sons. Women's participation in political life symbolically reversed the hierarchy of the oppressed and oppressing nations.[3]

Emancipated but subordinated: male politicians' attitude to women

Bakhtin's idea of the carnival is also useful for the description of women's role in the Polish nation at the time of the Partitions. In the first place, Polish men were excluded from the political life of Russia, Germany and Austria. Under these circumstances Polish women gained access to a broad range of civic (national) rights and duties, and took part in modern Polish political structures born at the end of the nineteenth century. They participated in both the nationalist movement (National Democrats, Endecja) and the Independence Camp (Independents, Obóz Niepodległościowy). These two political forces created two distinct concepts of the nation and two visions of the future of Poland, yet shared a similar view of women's role in Polish society.

Roman Dmowski, the leader of the National Democrats, rejected the idea of military uprisings, which he believed would lead the Polish nation to destruction. An independent Poland was, in his opinion, impossible. Instead of the dangerous daydreams of Independents, he proposed reunification of the Polish nation within the Russian Empire as a separate and autonomous Poland. This he hoped to achieve by diplomatic and political means, in collaboration with Tsarist authorities. By contrast, Józef Piłsudski, the leader of the Independence Camp, rejected the idea of autonomy, especially within Russia, which was, in his opinion, the eternal enemy of the Polish nation. He believed it possible to win independence for Poland through another insurrection. By analysing the history of the January 1863 uprising, Piłsudski articulated conditions for future success: the outbreak of a European war, during which Russia would be defeated by Germany and Austro-Hungary, with the help of Polish military forces with civilian support. After 1917 Piłsudski saw a new opportunity for Poland. Now that Russia had collapsed he could accept the demise of

---

3 Mary Condern, 'Work in progress: sacrifice and political legitimation. The production of a gendered social order', *Journal of Women's History*, 6:4 (1995), 160–189, 168.

Germany and Austro-Hungary too. The Anglo-French Entente was now acceptable because Russia no longer counted. In effect he switched sides. Piłsudski and Dmowski did not differ on issues of tactics and visions of the future alone. On a fundamental level, they embraced different concepts of the nation. As the British historian Norman Davies wrote in *God's Playground*:

> The Nationalists conceived of the nation as a distinct ethnic community which possessed an inalienable right to the exclusive enjoyment of its ancestral territory; the Independence Camp, in contrast, favoured the concept of a spiritual community, united by bonds of culture and history, and looking to some form of association with the other oppressed nations of the area.[4]

In the inter-war years both Piłsudski and Dmowski moved to the right. The former carried out a coup in 1926. His regime, the Sanacja, was not at first clearly situated on the right, having been supported by elements of the national minorities and the left, but with time it became increasingly intolerant, dictatorial and conservative. Dmowski's National Democrats, meanwhile, assumed the role of a national opposition. Polish historians generally avoid using the notions 'extreme right' or 'fascism' to characterise the movements of Sanacja or National Democrats. In spite of all the differences between them, the Sanacja and National Democrats moved, in my opinion, close to fascism. The former has been compared to the Franco regime, which also contained a strong fascist element. In the late 1930s a new generation of politicians built political structures, such as the Great Poland Camp (of the Sanacja) and the National-Radical Camp (of the Endecja). Both espoused anti-Semitism, militarism, nationalism, state chauvinism, and a belief in the superiority of a great Polish state. Both also embraced a masculine anti-feminist discourse.

In spite of all their political differences, both Piłsudski and Dmowski saw the importance of women's activity in similar way. According to Polish nationalists, the principal duty of every member of the nation was the defence of national interests in all spheres of social life. Therefore around the end of the nineteenth century they formed not only a political party, the National Democratic Party, but also educational, social and economic structures such as the Polish Motherland (an educational society), the Society of Courses for Adult Illiterates, the People's Libraries, the Polish People's Association (an

---

4 Norman Davies, *God's Playground: A History of Poland* (Oxford, Clarendon, 1982), vol. 2, p. 56.

economic institution) or the Libraries for Women, to name but a few. Through this large network of organisations national activity went beyond political action, and every effort devoted to the nation or the future state was treated as political.

Focusing on a future uprising, Piłsudski also found women's involvement necessary. In his opinion, they could be very useful as liaison officers and as workers of auxiliary services in the rear. These conclusions resulted in a programme of military training for women in the 'Falcon Squads'[5] or scouting troops. Women also participated in the political work of the Independence Camp, but they never belonged to the narrow circle of decision-makers. In spite of the restricted positions open to them, numerous women joined illegal organisations, but most of them took part in educational and social organisations. As in the case of women nationalists, non-political work turned out to be political.

The multi-dimensional character of Polish nationalist movements gave many women opportunities to take part in political work accepted and promoted by politicians. The latter consented to women's activity, but this had nothing to do with the idea of the equality of the sexes or suffrage. The attitude of leading National Democrats and Independents to women's work was ambiguous. Dmowski was not exceptional in rejecting the idea of women's suffrage. Piłsudski forbade women soldiers to join the military troops formed in the beginning of the Great War. Even the few politicians who were aware of women's issues saw emancipation and equal rights as a secondary problem compared to such great ideas as the nation and the sovereign state. Women themselves equated their lack of political rights with the lack of an independent Polish state. This led them to believe that the struggle for sovereignty was more important than the fight for suffrage, for in the future Polish state women would be emancipated.

This brief sketch of women's role in the national movements (both nationalist and independence) before the Great War should help us to understand the political activity of women in the Second Republic. The first generation of women involved in politics was born in the 1870s and 1880s, and grew up under the partition with its 'reversed order'. Younger generations, though they did not remember pre-war times, generally followed the old patterns, which remained strongly implanted in independent Poland.

5 At first the 'Falcons Squads' were dedicated to the improvement of the physical condition of young men, and later young women. Then they created paramilitary structures designed to prepare Polish youth for a future insurrection.

Voters at last: the first suffrage laws in independent Poland

The year 1918 was a double turning point in the history of the Polish women's movement:[6] Poland became an independent state, and women gained political rights. The Second Republic witnessed a 'change of national powers'. The Polish nation evolved from a subordinated one into a dominating one. Poles, Jews, Ukrainians and Germans, living in one state, formed a multicultural and multinational society, especially in eastern and western regions – the 'Borderlands' (Kresy).[7] The inhabitants of these areas did not create a homogenous community, in which national identity would have been less important than citizenship. Throughout the inter-war period the relations between national groups were marked by conflicts and violence, springing from both the aspirations of Ukrainians and Belorussians to gain their own independent national states and the national character of Polish authorities'policy.[8]

The political emancipation of women in Poland – the reasons for which they were granted suffrage – was typical of Central Europe. Although there had been rather weak feminist movements, hardly any suffragist actions or demonstrations, and no struggle or direct demands, women gained the right to vote as soon as the first Polish authorities were created. In the opinion of numerous women at the time, they had been right to prioritise national over women's interests. Equal rights (initially only political) were a sort of reward for their patriotic involvement, especially during the war. During these five years, women from different political factions had co-operated in common structures, supporting national and pro-independence movements. Only in 1918 did they start to demonstrate: not to fight for

---

6 'Women's movement' is here considered to be women's organisations working for the improvement of women's situation.

7 See Zbigniew Kurcz (ed.), *Mniejszośći narodowe w Polsce* (Wrocław, Wydawnicto, Uniwersytetu Wrocławskiego, 1997).

8 Although the Second Republic was a multinational state in which 30 per cent of the population belonged to national minorities, the problem of co-existence of national groups has still not been adequately considered. Historians dealing with women's history in the inter-war period have tended to research national groups separately. None of the works devoted to the women's movement, whether Polish, Jewish or Ukrainian, paid any attention to the question of the nature of contacts beyond or because of the national barriers (whether conflicts or co-operation). Upper Silesia is a good example of this historiographic strategy. Despite the Polish-German character of the Silesian society, historians have created a simplified picture of homogenous Polish Silesians (inhabitants of the region) against the figure of an impersonal or absent (except in the context of national conflicts) 'German enemy'.

suffrage but to prove that they deserved political rights as members of the nation rather than because they were equal to men.

In November 1918 the political authorities of the future Polish state, established in all three partitions, granted women suffrage. The Prime Minister of the Polish socialist government in Lublin, Ignacy Daszyński, asked Irena Kosmowska to be the Minister of Social Affairs.[9] Also in November 1918, in Warsaw, Józef Piłsudski signed a decree on the election to the first Polish nation-wide Parliament (to be elected in January 1919). It stated that 'every citizen of the state, over the age of twenty-one, whether male or female, has the right to vote. All above-mentioned citizens – men and women – have the right to be elected.'[10] In the German partition (Upper Silesia in the west and Greater Poland – *Wielkopolska* – in the north-west) women had already been voters and candidates to the Polish Provincial Assembly and its local structures, the People's Councils.

A national secret weapon: women and politics in the former German Partition

That introduction of female suffrage is very interesting from a gender perspective. The former German partition, which was the scene of national conflicts between Poles and Germans in the early 1920s, provides a rare opportunity to analyse women's activities during the national struggle against the German menace and to follow the relations between the traditional social structures and women's involvement in national politics. The society of this region was quite traditional and patriarchal. The German partition was a province without strong socialist or liberal structures, and conservatives and Catholics were influential. The newly formed Polish authorities decided, however, that everyone aged over twenty, both male and female, had the right to vote. The extension of suffrage was motivated by the political and national situation.[11] At a time when conflict between Poles and Germans was mounting, the aim of the Polish authorities was to prepare the people's resistance and to organise a national uprising. The German menace to the nation was used to mobilise all Polish inhabitants of the German partition. Since the prevailing concept of national solidarity and power was based on the quantity of the nation's population, it was assumed that extension of

9 She was the only woman minister in inter-war Poland.
10 *Dziennik praw państwa polskiego*, 18 (1918), 46.
11 *Dziennik Sejmu Dzielnicowego w Poznaniu w grudniu 1918* (Poznań, 1918).

the vote to women would create a strong anti-German political weapon. Under democratic rules, national identity mattered more than sex.

Women were elected to local national assemblies. They were numerous especially in those regions where they had participated in the formation of new Polish authorities. In the Poznań People's Council ten out of a total of seventy-five members were women. Although the proportion of women in Polish local councils was not higher than 15 per cent, women were more numerous than in parallel German ones.[12] Women were elected because voters were aware of their previous activity in social, educational and national organisations (Aniela Tułodziecka, Zofia Sokolnicka, Janina Omańkowska). When the Polish Provincial Assembly gathered at the beginning of December 1918, 140 out of 1,398 delegates were women (10.1 per cent). One woman sat in the twenty-strong Presidium. Women also entered the Main People's Council, but in the three-member executive of the National People's Council there were no women.[13]

The Provincial Parliament passed an important resolution stating that political equality for women was *sine qua non* for the healthy development of Polish society.[14] Undoubtedly, this resolution stemmed from awareness of the importance of women's political activity at a time of war between nations. Nationalists also wanted to involve a high number of women in their political campaign and to gain women's votes in view of the forthcoming election. In the German partition in 1918 female Polish nationalists organised marches and political meetings, and delivered speeches promoting the Polish cause. Public consent to women's participation in politics at a time of national danger was still apparent at this time.

The concept of carnivalesque order reversal can be used to describe and explain the case of women's participation in the nationalist movements of Upper Silesia. Silesian society was especially influenced by gendered division of public/male and private/female spheres. National interests and goals and Polish–German conflict altered the status of women with regard to suffrage and citizenship. Yet in spite of politi-

12 Zbigniew Dworecki, 'Udział kobiet ziem dzielnicy pruskiej w polskim ruchu narodowo-politycznym u progu II Rzeczypospolitej (listopad-grudzień 1918)', in Helena Kaczyńska (ed.), *Działalność społeczno-narodowa i polityczna kobiet na Górnym Śląsku w XX wieku* (Opole, Societas Scientiis Favendis Silesiae Superioris Instytut Górnośląski, 1997), p. 36.

13 Franciszek Serafin, *Stosunki polityczne, społeczne i ruch narodowy w Pszczyńskim w latach 1918-1922* (Katowice, Uniwersytet Śląski, 1993), pp. 46-7.

14 *Dziennik Sejmu Dzielnicowego*, p. 64.

cal emancipation, women accepted and still abided by unchanged patriarchal rules of gender. Since 1918 that region, or rather its division, had been a source of conflict between Poland and Germany. Industry and coal mines made Upper Silesia important for both states because of its economic and military potential. That is why the struggle between Germans and Poles there was especially hard-fought. Before the decision about Upper Silesia was settled during the Versailles Conference, Poles had started two uprisings against Germans. Finally, as diplomats in Versailles decided, the new border would be established according to the results of a plebiscite.

The plebiscite concerned only the national identity of Upper Silesians. Both sides counted on the women's votes. Silesian women, neither German nor Polish, were reduced to being voters.[15] Some of the Polish nationalist activists had been working in the province for years. In 1918, just before Poland became independent, women had formed a huge new nationalist organisation called the Polish Women's Association (PWA, Towarzystwo Polek). Between 1918 and 1922 it had about 35,000 members. The success of the PWA resulted from its ability to establish structures in every commune, and to exploit the tradition of women's engagement in local associations.

In 1921 nationalist women joined the plebiscite campaign, co-operating with the Polish Plebiscite Commissioner. They organised lectures, meetings and demonstrations, and prepared propaganda materials, among which was a very interesting leaflet drawn up during the meeting of the PWA. It contains a sort of national Ten Commandments:

1 Thou shalt not have any country over Poland.
2 Thou shalt not use thy vote against the Nation.
3 Thou shalt remember to do thy duty on the day of the Plebiscite.
4 Thou shalt not kill the future of the children.
5 Thou shall revere faith, Country and thine mother tongue.
6 Thou shalt not sell thine soul to the Germans.
7 Thou shalt not abuse thine Country's trust.
8 Thou shalt not vote against thy conscience.
9 Thou shalt not covet the wealth of thine enemy.
10 Thou shalt not believe betrayed promises.

15 In my research I did not find any publications devoted to the gender aspects of German propaganda in the plebiscite, which is why I present here only the Polish side of the story. Comparison between the Polish and German women's campaigns would nevertheless be interesting. The question of national and cultural differences (if there were any) arising from women's identity would also add to our understanding of the phenomenon known as 'Upper Silesia'.

For ever and ever, as long as the world continues,
Germans will not be brothers of Poles.[16]

This text, constructed on the basis of the Bible and ending with the
famous proverb from the Time of the Partitions, was distributed to
female voters during the so-called 'whispered campaign'. It consisted
of private (or what looked like private) visits to Silesian homes.
During informal conversations, women agitators tried to convince
housewives to vote 'for Poland'. This tactic seems to have been
specific to women's campaigns. Political activists replaced the hierarchical relation of speaker-listener with more personal contact. Women
paid special attention to this form of political work, for they believed
in the power of women's influence over their families. The belief in
women agitators' influence was common to all political parties at that
time: socialists, nationalists, as well as advocates of 'Sanacja'.
Propaganda addressed directly to women was accompanied by indirect
influence over husbands, sons, and even fathers. This whispered
campaign was very useful just before the plebiscite, for there was a
complete ban on public agitation.[17]

'Always faithful': women, morality and religion

The aforementioned ten commandments of the plebiscite in Upper
Silesia provide an excellent example of the symbiotic relationship
between religion and national identity. Traces of this symbiosis can
be found in the slogans of different organisations, of which the most
famous is the 'God, Country, Honour' of the nineteenth-century
national movement. Few today are aware of its female equivalent,
'God, Country, Family' – the motto of the Polish Women's
Association of Upper Silesia. The National Organisation of Women
(NOW, Naradowa Organizacja Kobiet), a political formation
connected to the National Democrats, had its motto 'God and
Country'. The attachment to religious moral values was common in
women's organisations. Even socialists and communists did not reject
religious symbols and language. Women nationalists, Catholics and
the admirers of Piłsudski, who started their career in the Polish
Socialist Party (Polska Partia Socjalistyczna, PSP), organised religious or semi-religious ceremonies. Among the more remarkable

16 Serafin, *Stosunki polityczne*, p. 144.
17 Jolanta Kamińska-Kwak, *Polski ruch kobiecy w województwie śląskim w latach
   1922–1939* (Katowice, Wydawn, Uniwersytetu Śląskiego, 1998), pp. 35–40.

examples of religious imagery in nationalist movements were the solemn oaths and symbolic gifts of women's organisations in Częstochowa, a special place on the religious map of Poland. The monastery of Jasna Góra is the most famous national sanctuary of the Virgin Mary. For centuries pilgrims from all over Poland have gone there to pray to the miraculous Icon of the Virgin Mary, usually called Our Lady of Częstochowa. Since the nineteenth century Jasna Góra has been the national sanctuary of Poles. In that holy place Polish women pledged to guard the faith and the purity of the national spirit (whatever that meant).[18]

After 1917 the emergence of atheistic revolutionary Russia dramatically changed the religious map of Eastern Europe. One purpose of women's national activity after the Russian Revolution was to fight against atheism and secularisation. This goal was articulated in the NOW programme, where it was stressed that the main priority was to defend religious education in schools. Together with other women's organisations (the Women Landowners Union, the Catholic Women's Association), NOW sent representatives to the Prime Minister in 1930, and asked the government to support a programme of children's education based on Christian (Catholic) values. One proposal was to protect youngsters from the dangerous influence of immoral literature and films.[19]

The defence of morality in women's activity was a legacy of the nineteenth century, when private virtues and duties acquired a public, patriotic meaning. The ideals connected with the Mother Pole were still current in the inter-war period because she epitomised values considered to be essentially female. Advocates of women's equality stressed that after Poland had become independent, female virtues remained important in (re)building a new, better Polish society. Women were able to imbue public life with positive values springing from their 'natural' altruism, caring and devotion. In the performance of their private duties they could influence public – and especially national – life. The most popular manifestation of this concept, in the inter-war discourse on women's issues, was the idea of 'the perfect housewife'.

In a new, post-war reality of the independent state, a perfect Polish housewife had to be aware of her national duties. A director of a

18 *Kobieta w Sejmie: Działalność posłanek Narodowej Organizacji Kobiet. Zarys sprawozdania za lata 1919–1927* (Warsaw, Narodowa Organizacja Kobiet, 1928), pp. 51–2.
19 *Gazetka dla Kobiet*, 2 (1930), 5.

household school for girls, Teresa Leszczyńska, thus described the role of a Polish housewife: 'Thanks to a wise, resourceful woman, cities and countryside will develop, prosperity will be a common experience, misery will disappear for ever'.[20] Proper housekeeping was seen as a necessary condition for the 'happiness and fate of the whole nation', contended a journalist. Referring to history, she reminded her readers that in the past women who neglected their duties had often caused nations to fall.[21]

What kind of activity derived from the concept of 'the perfect housewife'? Housewives were concerned primarily with economic life. Shopping became an economic weapon that women could use to support Polish national production and industry, and through their personal choices they created a national market. In the opinion of Polish nationalists, nationally motivated shopping was to be used particularly against the Jews, who largely monopolised commerce, and especially retail trade and crafts. Women in nationalist and Catholic organisations agreed that housewives had to support national, i.e. Christian, producers by boycotting Jewish and other foreign shops.[22] Łucja Charewiczowa, a Polish historian and a nationalist, encouraged women to follow the example of Ukrainian women who were boycotting Jewish products, claiming this to be an effective, though not 'spectacular' activity.[23] The concept articulated in the slogan 'do not buy from the Jews' was very popular in inter-war Polish society, but it was not a uniquely Polish phenomenon. Economic anti-Semitism was probably shared by all non-Jewish nationalities living in the Second Republic.

Women's organisations also claimed to raise the prestige of house-keeping as a socially and economically important professional occupation. They stressed the role of housewives in the defence of national interests. Thus, women who belonged to Sanacja argued that women's domestic activity was important to the development of the state. Among the numerous organisations connected with Sanacja were family organisations such as the Military Family and the Police Family, which united wives and daughters of soldiers, policemen or veterans. These family structures were important not only because of

20 Teresa Leszczyńska, 'Czy powinniśmy kształcić nasze córki?', *Gazetka dla Kobiet*, 2 (1924), 2.
21 Maria Zawadzka, 'Nowe stanowisko kobiet', *Kobieta Polska*, 1 (1919), 1.
22 *Gazetka dla Kobiet*, 4 (1926), 5.
23 Łucja Charewiczowa [as C. Mikułowska], *'Ukraiński' ruch kobiecy* (Lwów, Skupienie Lwowskie Zarzewie, 1937), p. 23.

their specific activity, but because of their propaganda significance – through them Sanacja activists demonstrated their attachment to traditional values and non-revolutionary order.

Voters and candidates: women nationalists and the first election campaign

During the first years of the independent state women were very active in political life. They participated in the foundation of the first Polish political structures. In connection with the election campaign to the first Polish parliament, the National Organisation of Women[24] (NOW) was formed in December 1918. Members of NOW participated in the campaign, registered those entitled to vote, and agitated for the People's National Association (Związek Ludowo-Narodowy) (the official name of the National Democrats' political party). In every town groups of women were formed under the banner 'God and Nation', the slogan of this nationalist formation. Female supporters of the National Democrats organised meetings, gave speeches and edited leaflets.[25]

The National Democrats attacked both Jews and the more or less anonymous 'enemies of Poland'. The same ideas can be found in NOW's programme. The following is an example of the connection between the nationalist ideology and women's issues in the NOW:

> The woman's task in the public sphere, according to the NOW, is to bring an element of social solidarity, ideological purity and disinterested devotion. In this way, woman's participation in public life is a mainstay of society's moral values and protection from influences causing its break-up, from the disintegration of virtues, and from the hegemony of egoism. NOW aims to raise national awareness in the country and purge the society of all alien cultural influences.[26]

Anti-Semitic ideas were articulated in the NOW's programme rather vaguely. However, campaign leaflets prepared by women nationalists left no doubt as to who the 'alien' was, or what 'purge' meant. The anonymous author of a 1919 leaflet told the female reader that 'every vote ... is like a bayonet directed against Jews and enemies of Poland'. A journalist writing for *The Polish Working*

24 The original name of the NOW, the National Organisation of Women for Election, was changed just after the elections of 1919.
25 Urszula Jakubowska, 'Kobiety w świecie polityki Narodowej Demokracji', in Anna Żarnowska and Andrzej Szwarc (eds), *Kobieta i świat polityki. W niepodległej Polsce 1918–1939* (Warszawa, Wydawnicto, Sejmowe, 1996), p. 149.
26 *Kobieta w Sejmie.*

Woman (a newspaper edited by the Society of Catholic Maidens) tried to convince her female voters that 'there will be no Jewish woman, sick old lady or the poorest beggar, who will not vote'.[27] According to nationalist editors, Polish women could play an important role as voters in counterbalancing the Jewish influences, and could prove their commitment to the nation. Thus participation was the act less of an emancipated woman, than of a 'real, Polish patriot'.

In the first elections in 1919 all political parties strove to appeal to women, for they constituted half of all voters, and were a serious but unpredictable political force. Almost all parties included female candidates on their lists. Most of these women were social and educational workers. Female candidates were quite visible on the lists of the socialists, nationalists and liberals. There were even women among the candidates of the peasants' parties, which had a very conservative attitude to women's issues and which underestimated the importance of voting women.

On the National Democrats' list the prestigious third place belonged to a woman, Gabriela Balicka. She was placed immediately behind two national 'heroes'– Ignacy Paderewski, a famous composer and 'spokesman' for Poland in Versailles, and Roman Dmowski, the unquestioned leader of the nationalist formation and the chief opponent of Józef Piłsudski.[28] Balicka probably appeared in this exhalted position not on the strength of her merits, but because her surname would remind the voters of her late husband, Zygmunt Balicki, the famous ideologist of Polish nationalism. Balicka was nothing more than a living monument to her famous husband and a purely symbolic element in the political campaign.

Women's presence on the lists of candidates did not follow from the support of their male colleagues for emancipation and women's equal participation in political life. The National Democrats put women on their lists yet proclaimed a deep attachment to tradition and the 'natural', hierarchical gender order. Dmowski himself was (in)famous for his anti-feminist and misogynistic opinions. In his two novels published in the 1930s, *In the Middle of the Way* and *Heritage*, Dmowski claimed that a woman could be happy only in her family and home. Outside the private sphere she would never find satisfaction or self-fulfillment. In their memoirs women nationalists often recalled discussions and quarrels with Dmowski, provoked by his

27 Ludwik Hass, 'Aktywność wyborcza kobiet w pierwszym dziesięcioleciu Drugiej Rzeczypospolitej', in Żarnowska and Szwarc (eds), *Kobieta i świat polityki*, p. 75.
28 Jakubowska, 'Kobiety w świecie polityki Narodowej Demokracji', p. 149.

refusal to see any reason to allow women to participate in politics.

His negative attitude towards women's activity – and in this respect Dmowski was exceptional – did not mean the exclusion of women from real political activity. On the contrary, men's ambivalence about emancipation helped nationalist women to make up their minds to form and preserve their own autonomous political structure. The socialist example proves how wise that choice was. Independent women's structures in the PSP were dissolved in 1922. Throughout the 1920s female socialists had to fight for the inclusion of women's issues in the party programme and had to struggle to convince their colleagues that women's interests were important and that a clear strategy was required for their defence. Although they ultimately achieved their goal, forming the Women's Department in 1924, they were unable to persuade many members of the PSP of the need for women's separate representation or autonomy.[29]

In spite of the formal independence of the NOW, nationalist women co-operated politically with the National Democrats, the People's National Association, especially in election campaigns. In 1927, a year after Piłsudski's *coup d'état*, the NOW congress passed a resolution concerning political alliances. It was proclaimed that co-operation was possible only with parties whose programme was based on the principle of national solidarity. Like the National Democrats, women nationalists refused to enter into agreement with the socialists, even though both were critical of the new Piłsudski regime.[30]

The state above all: women and the Sanacja

The *coup d'état* in May 1926 dramatically changed the Polish political scene. Since 1921 Józef Piłsudski, who had officially withdrawn from political life, had endlessly criticised the party system and the personal ambitions of party leaders who, he said, did nothing but quarrel. He proposed to replace sick and weak democracy with a programme of 'return to political health', which involved liberation from the rule of ideological division and political chaos. The under-pinning of this new political movement was the prestige and war-legend of its charismatic leader – Józef Piłsudski. He relied on the still loyal veterans of the Polish Legions (the troops who had

29 Adam Próchnik, *Kobiety w polskim ruchu socjalistycznym* (Warsaw, Wydawnictwo Wiedza, 1948).
30 *Gazetka dla Kobiet*, 1 (1928), 3.

fought against the Russians during the Great War) and his many other followers in various political parties. In 1928, during the parliamentary election campaign, Piłsudski's followers created a new 'anti-party' structure in the form of the Non-Party Bloc for Co-operation with the Government. The Sanacja was constructed as a hierarchical network of political and non-political organisations, in which the Bloc was the leading formation.

Like the nationalists in 1919, Piłsudski's women supporters organised their own association, the Union of Women's Civic Work (UWCW, Związek Pracy Obywatelskiej Kobiet). Among its members were Zofia Moraczewska (a leader of the organisation), Michalina Mościcka, Zofia Daszyńska-Golińska and Maria Jaworska. All of them had previously belonged to the PSP and were experienced parliamentarians. Like many male socialists they left the PSP and joined the Sanacja. Their choices were sometimes as much personal as ideological, for some of them (Mościcka, Moraczewska) were wives of politicians who supported the new regime. In the first months of its existence the new women's organisation concentrated on the election campaign. Their work did not differ from that of the NOW, but their programme used distinctive slogans. Among women demands for a new political order liberated from personal ambitions, quarrels and 'immoral' behaviours had been especially strong. From the early 1920s women's magazines and female journalists had argued for the need for new rules and values to govern political activity. It was said that it was women's duty to educate politicians and guard ethical values, for women were more moral and sensitive than men. In a way, women of the Sanacja did nothing but adopt postulates articulated in women's discourse prior to 1926, and they claimed to be the only true representation of a 'women's world'. The UWCW, which in 1930 had over 25,000 members, seemed to be attractive to women because its programme mixed tradition, feminist issues, patriotism and state ideology. The main aim of the UWCW was civic education for women and state service. Beside these progressive slogans, one finds the traditional conservative conception that women's activity should primarily be in the circle of social and family affairs. The political character of the organisation was revealed only during the election campaign and through demonstrations of loyalty to Piłsudski.

Protecting women, children, and 'adult' boys – women in the Polish parliament

As a reward for their contribution to the campaign of 1928, UWCW women won nine seats in the Parliament – they became the largest group of women Members of Parliament in inter-war Poland. Also after the final collapse of democracy in 1930, the UWCW effectively obtained permanent representation in the next parliaments because of the government's ability to manipulate elections. In fact, Sanacja women took over from the NOW as the most numerous group of female Members of Parliament. The two women's organisations therefore had few opportunities to confront each other as parliamentary groups. Nevertheless, aside from the distinctive ideologies, programmes and strategies of the political parties to which these women belonged, female MPs shared similar biographies, attitudes to women's issues and visions of their role in the Parliament.

Like their colleagues in the Provincial Assembly of the former German partition, most female MPs had a significant experience of working in national 'non-political' organisations.[31] Before they entered Parliament, these women had obtained university diplomas and proved their ability and readiness to work in a variety of professional settings. Most had begun their careers in nationalist or socialist organisations and societies. Typically women political activists (from both movements) had been involved in a love affair and marriage with colleagues whom they met in these organisations, and during the Great War these women participated in the fight for independence. In 1918 many joined feminist campaigns for women's suffrage in the future independent Poland, and were then politically active in their parties.

Women elected to Parliament were highly conscious of the special character of their role as MPs. In spite of political and ideological disagreements, they co-operated in parliamentary commissions and in drafting laws dealing with issues important for women. Nationalists like Irena Puźynianka, Wanda Ładzina and Maria Holder-Eggerowa implemented the 'feminist' ideas of the NOW, while women from the Sanacja like Zofia Moraczewska, Zofia Praussowa and Eugenia Waśniewska also devoted their efforts to legislation concerning women's interests. Women parliamentarians were involved in the fight against so-called social ills, such as alcoholism, prostitution and the illegal slave trade in women and children. Women wrote new laws

31 *Kobieta w Sejmie*, p. 54.

concerning the rights of illegitimate children, and prepared a new labour law concerning working women and children, while Wanda Ładzina prepared a bill protecting women's and children's work. Praussowa helped author the Social Protection law. For a while these concerns unified female MPs from different parties.[32] It soon turned out, however, that women were as deeply divided as male MPs on other issues. During debates on state affairs (the presidential election, the budget, foreign policy), women followed their parties' lines rather than attempting to build a women's group with a female perspective. During the twenty years between the wars, only a few cross-party initiatives were proposed – for example there was a joint campaign against the Upper Silesian region's discrimination against married public servants and teachers but these were short-lived and concerned specific issues.[33] In reality all attempts at building a female lobby collapsed, though the myth of a unitary women's world survived.

The political reality and everyday experience of the Parliament encouraged women to become conscious of their distinctive position in a men's world. One UWCW member recalled her first impressions of Parliament thus: 'It seemed to me, that I had quit my pedagogical work to play a crazy game with naughty boys. The Educational Commission barely permitted me to feel the reality and importance of the parliamentary work.'[34] This feeling of being lost among naughty boys and misunderstanding their crazy games caused women to conclude that they should educate childish men and teach them how to be grown-up and reliable.

Gender before ideology

The NOW and the UWCW, although connected with rival political camps, shared the same history. Because they had been organised primarily to mobilise women electorally, their independence was constrained by the political priorities of the National Democrats and the Sanacja. The separate organisations of women permitted them to focus on women's issues between elections, both at the local level and in Parliament, and they were more successful than socialist women in maintaining their autonomy. Nevertheless, the instrumental character

---

32 Dobrochna Kałwa, *Kobieta aktywna w Polsce międzywojennej. Dylematy środowisk kobiecych* (Kraków, Historia Iagellonica, 2001), pp. 125–34.

33 Ibid., pp. 152–3.

34 Helend Ceysingerówna, 'Wśród pracodawców. Wywiad z posłanką Marią Jaworską ze Lwowa', *Kobieta Współczesna*, 26 (1928), p. 3.

of women's political structures is unquestionable. Women's organisations existed because of their usefulness during political campaigns; women appeared on lists of candidates in order to gain women's votes; women worked in election committees in order to reinforce the efficacy of political propaganda.

Despite women's involvement and participation in political life, male opinions about emancipation and equality of the sexes hardly changed. Those who considered women's natural place to be the circle of the home and family still opposed their political activity, even if they kept silent publicly (unless women claimed 'too much equality' as in 1924, when the Parliament rejected the project of women's general military service). The notion of women's military service was promoted by feminists and later women's organisations connected with Sanacja. Ranged against the idea were anti-feminists and most MPs. Women too could be counted among those who espoused the traditional view of women's place. They included the first ladies of Sanacja establishment, Aleksandra Piłsudska and Michalina Moraczewska, the wife of the President, who sponsored activity devoted to housework, children and families. In a climate of post-war cultural and moral change across Europe, evident in women's fashions and behaviours, Polish women in independent Poland still reproduced values epitomised by the figure of the Mother Pole.

11

France

Cheryl Koos and Daniella Sarnoff

Following the Great War, 'gender trouble' loomed large in French political discourse. Both policy debates and ideological campaigns during the
1920s and 1930s often centred on concerns about a falling birth-rate and
weak families. In these discussions, publicists and polemicists across the
political spectrum shared a common understanding that France's future
depended on clarifying not only the centrality of the family in national
life, but also on defining appropriate roles and duties for men and
women. The parliamentary left and right and extreme and fascist right
anti-democratic leagues all agreed that more ordered gender and family
relations would guarantee the nation's well-being. Fascist leagues, in
particular, emphasised gender ideologies in their understanding and
articulation of state structures. Without exception, the extreme-right
organisations consistently positioned 'real' women as essential to
France's national vitality in a vision that deployed competing images of
female passivity and activity, public and private.

   Given the centrality of gendered and familial rhetoric in inter-war
political discourse, it is no surprise that political and military leaders
would single out 'gender trouble' and its by-product depopulation as
a major culprit in the nation's quick defeat at the hands of the German
army in June 1940. Leaders of the quasi-fascist, authoritarian Vichy
regime that followed the capitulation enshrined the French family and
'traditional' notions of gender at the very heart of the new government. Vichy's National Revolution, armed with its agenda of *travail,
famille, patrie* (work, family, country), would wage war against those
who violated its prescriptions for 'new men and new women', albeit
to varying degrees of success.

   This chapter addresses the relationship between gender and extreme-
right politics in both the inter-war fascist leagues and the Vichy regime.

It explores how Vichy and the fascist leagues such as the Légion, the Jeunesses Patriotes, the Solidarité Française and the Croix de Feu/Parti Social Français (PSF) utilised similar notions of femininity and masculinity, particularly constructions of motherhood and fatherhood, and examines the roles that women played or were to play in state and group organisational structures. Five individuals – four from the fascist leagues of the 1920s and 1930s and one from the Vichy regime of the early 1940s – and their political activities and organisations will serve as sites from which to explore issues such as domesticity, female suffrage and paid labour. To this end, Antoine Rédier of the Légion, Marie-Thérèse Moreau of the Jeunesses Patriotes, Lucienne Blondel of the Solidarité Française, Colonel François de la Rocque of the Croix de Feu/PSF and Marguerite Lebrun (Vérine) of the Vichy government allow us to map the deployment of gender both in ideology and in practice within inter-war fascist leagues and the Vichy regime. They provide an additional window on the complex and often contradictory connections between gender, sexuality and the construction of the modern nation-state, specifically the role gender plays in the philosophy and operations of fascist movements within both France and the larger constellation of European fascisms.

Until the mid 1990s, most historiographical discussions of French inter-war conservatism, the extreme right, and fascisms only glanced at the role of women and gender in these movements and ideologies.[1] With

1 See Robert Soucy, *French Fascism: The First Wave, 1924–1933* (New Haven, CT, Yale University Press, 1986); Robert Soucy *French Fascism: The Second Wave, 1933–1939* (New Haven, CT, Yale University Press, 1995); William Irvine, 'Fascism in France and the strange case of the Croix de Feu', *Journal of Modern History*, 63 (June 1991), 271–95; Samuel Huston Goodfellow, *Between the Swastika and the Cross of Lorraine* (DeKalb, IL, Northern Illinois University Press, 1999); Kevin Passmore, 'The French Third Republic: stalemate society or cradle of fascism', *French History*, 7:4 (1993), 417–49; Kevin Passmore, 'The Croix de Feu: Bonapartism, national populism or fascism?', *French History*, 9:1 (1995), 67–92; Kevin Passmore, '"Boy scouting for grown-ups?": paramilitarism in the Croix de feu and the Parti social français', *French Historical Studies*, 19:2 (1995), 541–4; Kevin Passmore *From Liberalism to Fascism* (Cambridge: Cambridge University Press, 1998); Roger Griffin, *The Nature of Fascism* (New York, St Martin's Press, 1991), pp. 133–6. For explorations of gender and the extreme right in France see Daniella Sarnoff, 'In the cervix of the nation: women in french fascism, 1919–1939', Ph.D. dissertation, Boston College, 2001; Kevin Passmore, '"Planting the tricolor in the citadels of Communism": women's social action in the Croix de feu', *Journal of Modern History*, 71:4 (1999), 814–52; Kevin Passmore 'Femininity and the right: from moral order to moral order', *Modern and Contemporary France*, 8:1 (2000), 55–69; Mary Jean Green, 'The Bouboule novels: constructing a French fascist woman', in Melanie Hawthorne and Richard J. Golsan (eds), *Gender and*

several notable exceptions, this lacuna plagued examinations of the Vichy regime as well.[2] By the late 1990s, however, histories of French fascism have begun to explore these issues and are going beyond discussions that focus on whether fascism existed in France and whether its origins were socialist or conservative.

Central to this newly emerging literature is an awareness that women occupied an important place in the formulation and production of extreme-right political ideology as well as its practice during the inter-war period and the Vichy regime. Unlike the parliamentary right, which did not attempt to mobilise women until 1935, the fascist leagues envisioned women as key political players as early as 1924. Gender as well figured prominently in these initial conceptions of ideal authoritarian state structures. Women – both literal and figurative – were central to the theory and practice of French fascism in the 1920s and 1930s. When representatives of the extreme right came to power in the Vichy regime under the German occupation, however, there was little room for women as political players, even though their symbolic presence permeated the regime.

Antoine Rédier and the Légion

Antoine Rédier founded the first extreme right and fascist league, the Légion, in June 1924, following the electoral triumph of the Cartel des Gauches, a centre-left coalition. Central to his league's political philosophy and his personal world-view were women – both 'real' and imagined. Rédier's ideas about the nation-state, politics and the family, which were never isolated within the rhetoric of the fascist leagues, revealed much concern about women, both figurative and literal. In Rédier's schema, multiple representations of 'women' existed and found their way into the structure of France's first, though

---

Fascism in Modern France (Hanover and London, University Press of New England, 1997), 49–68; Mary Jean Green, 'Gender, fascism and the Croix de Feu: the "women's pages" of *Le Flambeau*', *French Cultural Studies*, 8 (1997), 229–39.

2 Hanna Diamond, *Women and the Second World War in France 1939–1948* (London, Longman, 1999); Miranda Pollard Pollard, *Reign of Virtue: Mobilizing Gender in Vichy France* (Chicago and London, University of Chicago Press, 1998); Sarah Fishman, *We Will Wait: Wives of French Prisoners of War, 1940–1945* (New Haven, CT and London, Yale University Press, 1991); Francine Muel-Dreyfus, *Vichy et l'éternel féminin* (Paris, Seuil, 1996); Cheryl Koos, 'Engendering reaction: the politics of pronatalism and the family in France, 1919–1944', Ph.D. dissertation, University of Southern California, 1996.

short-lived, fascist movement.[3] First, there were the literal women: both 'real women' (those who behaved as he desired within largely a state of reproductive materiality and were the feminine complement of men who reigned over the foyer and within the league as social networkers and propagandists) and *filles-garçons* (those who did not and represented what Rédier and many conservatives considered to be the worst of French womanhood, personified in the figure of the dreaded *femme moderne* who behaved brazenly, cut her hair, had forsaken or postponed motherhood, and acted the part of the *garçonne*). Second, and perhaps most crucial for understanding Rédier's conception of the social and political order, were those 'women' who were biologically male, but aside from 'equipment' did not embody what it meant to be a 'true man' and the saviour of the French nation. Rédier began formulating these ideas early in his writing career as a journalist, memoirist and novelist, and then expressed them in the structure and tenets of the Légion.

Through a close examination of Rédier's pre-Légion writings, the gendering of males as either feminine or masculine, characterisations that without exception broke along political lines, is readily evident. Republican men appeared as effete and effeminate, while those that subscribed to conservative ultra-nationalist ideas embodied the notion of the virile 'true men' who would restore France to glory and prominence through heroism, bravery, and many children. Republican men – and thus the Third Republic – received much gendered opprobrium. At one point, he opined that United States President Theodore Roosevelt's epithet for the French bourgeoisie – *femmelettes* (little women) – was correct in describing why France had 'sterile households'.[4] Elsewhere in his war memoirs he described them as 'dreamers', 'babblers', 'old grandmothers', and 'queer figures of men'.[5]

In his 1919 novel *Le Capitaine*, Rédier contrasted hyper-intellectual republicans with what he considered 'true leaders': true men who were strong and powerful. As he did in his earlier writings, Rédier

3 See Denise Riley, 'Some peculiarities of social policy concerning women in wartime and postwar Britain', in M. R. Higonnet et al. (eds), *Behind the Lines* (New Haven, CT, Yale University Press, 1987); Joan Scott, *Gender and the Politics of History* (New York, Columbia University Press, 1988); Joan Scott, *Only Paradoxes to Offer* (Cambridge, MA and London, Harvard University Press, 1996).

4 Antoine Rédier, 'La Necessité pour les familles nombreuses', *Revue française*, 6:34 (21 May 1911), p. 197.

5 Antoine Rédier, *Comrades in Courage*, English Translation of *Les Méditations dans la tranchée* (Garden City, NJ, Doubleday Books, 1919), p. 258.

often referred to the need for virility to reinvigorate French society
and politics. Here, when the young lieutenant Olivier asks the captain
to clarify what he meant by extolling virility, the captain replied that
Olivier, and by implication all young French men, must 'become a
man ... [for] all men today are women. You will only be a leader
provided that you fortify your effeminate soul. You, a *maître*
[master]? Only when male blood colours your veins!'[6]

Rédier's ultimate remedy for society's ills was that each person
take his or her place in the 'natural' order. Females, too, according
to Rédier, needed to take their place in the natural, thus complemen-
tary social – and political – order as well. Those who did earned his
respect and praise. Just as he defined 'true men', Rédier also
described his vision of the ideal woman within his new authoritarian
order. Women were to stay at home and raise strong sons who would
be the true men of the future. When they needed to venture out of
their households, women were to function in their 'natural' roles as
mothers and carers. Women who did not conform to his standards of
appropriate womanhood received outright condemnation. Along these
lines, he enjoined his readers to remember that 'young women are not
boys', and those he blamed for aspiring to non-traditional roles were
not 'real women'; they were *filles-garçons* (girl-boys).

Rédier rejected the 'young modern woman who did more harm than
Von Kluck's army', as his soldiers in the 1916 novel *Pierrette* asserted,
and the wartime 'modern dolls', such immodestly dressed women, with
the 'necklines down to their stomachs' and 'absurd fingernails'.[7]
Following the war, Rédier launched an attack on the 'young modern
woman' through a series of journal articles outlining the threat she posed
to the survival of the nation. Though 'sometimes charming', she
smoked, dressed provocatively, used slang and vulgar language, was
inappropriately outgoing, and embraced a host of other vices.[8] Rédier
was alarmed; throughout the ages, according to Rédier, French women
had grown up with 'spirit' and 'aplomb', but always knew their responsibilities. This generation was different; these young women were not
learning their duties and traditional roles as future wives and mothers.
The majority of these young women were 'selfish' and 'arrogant'. They
participated in questionable leisure activities including 'risqué new
dances' and wore 'brazen dresses'. These 'unbridled' women were,

---

6 Antoine Rédier, *Le Capitaine* (Paris, Payot, 1919), pp. 53, 155.
7 Antoine Rédier, *Pierrette: Aux jeunes filles pour qu'elles reflechissent* (Paris, Payot,
    1916), pp. 110, 137; *Le Mariage de Lison* (Paris, Payot et Cie, 1918), pp. 59–67.
8 Antoine Rédier, *Revue française*, 17:15 (9 April 1922), 397.

according to Rédier, lost to the *foyers* (homes) of France, and were shifting this 'criminal disorder previously found among the elite' among the working class. Most devastatingly, these modern women were compromising the safety of the country.[9]

While condemning this corrupting influence, Rédier held out hope that the majority of young French women would come to their senses and forsake the dangerous route tempting them. The 'good' *femme moderne* knew that her duty was to serve France; she saw her freedom as a burden and recognised, according to Rédier, the need to found strong households.[10] He encouraged them to rediscover modesty and timidity, feminine virtues of another time. These honourable girls should avoid cosmetics, lower their eyes while in the street, and desire to populate their future *foyers* with many children.[11]

Central to Rédier's condemnation of the *femme moderne* was her unwillingness to have children. Rédier insisted on traditional gender roles not only to re-order a post-war world riddled with chaos and gender trouble, but also to repopulate a France decimated by a century-long decline in the birth-rate and a catastrophic war. To regain its past glory, France, according to Rédier, needed its men to be strong fathers and its women willing wombs for its future sons.

In forming the first fascist league, the Légion, in 1924, Rédier found the vehicle with which to bring his ideas into the tumultuous national political debate. While the Légion's platform echoed many of the basic beliefs held by ultra-conservatives and mid-1920s fascists, it also expressed Rédier's own convictions regarding ideal state structures, as well as gender relations that he had detailed in his earlier writings. The official programme of action of the organisation included a triad of principles that summed up Rédier's politics: authority, discipline and firmness. He articulated a state structure that provided a counterpoint to the 'flabbiness' of mind and body of the Third Republic and its devotees who instead promoted decadence and egoistic individualism.[12] The Légion's 'politics of national vigour' stood in stark contrast to the 'impotent' parliamentarianism of the Third Republic which was 'ruin[ing] and betray[ing] the nation'.[13]

9 Antoine Rédier, *Revue française*, 17:16 (16 April 1922), 425.
10 Antoine Rédier, *Revue française*, 17:17 (23 April 1922), 453–4.
11 Antoine Rédier, *Revue française*, 17:18 (7 May 1922), 510.
12 Archives Nationales, Paris (hereafter AN) F7 13208, 'La Légion: Sa programme, sa methode'.
13 AN F7 13208, 'Les Ligues nationales: Un appel de la Légion'; *L'éclair*, 30 April 1925.

According to Rédier, 'true men' would populate the Légion's ranks. War veterans and fathers were naturally predisposed to fulfilling this programme. Fathers would play a central role in Rédier's ideal state structures.[14]

While favouring the pre-eminence of the father in his new authoritarian political order, Rédier made clear early on that women were not to function in the same political arena. While a champion of the family vote, he opposed one version of the idea that included the vote for mothers of large families (defined as having five or more children).[15] Rédier also weighed in on the side of excluding women from participating in the electoral process. With the exception of widows who had the same responsibilities as fathers, he opposed the vote for married women. In addition, Rédier saw 'no necessity' for women to be eligible for election to the Chamber of Deputies. Though he recognised that some type of women's suffrage was inevitable, he steadfastly resisted, extending it to women at the hypothetical expense of fathers; to Rédier, it was a question of 'justice, duty, and necessity' – and patriarchal authority.[16]

Rédier's antagonism to women's suffrage was uncommon in the milieu of the political right.[17] For example, Louis Marin's Fédération Républicaine and Alexandre Millerand's Ligue Republicaine Nationale both favoured the vote for women since most rightists presumed that women, if enfranchised, would vote conservatively. As we shall shortly see, other fascist leagues such as the Jeunesses Patriotes, Solidarité Française and the Croix de Feu, among other fascist leagues of the 1920s and 1930s, also advocated women's suffrage.

Rédier's view, however, was consistent with his overall philosophy regarding the strict definition of gender roles within society, culture, and above all the family. He attempted to preserve and perhaps recreate a vision of womanhood that was as distinct in appearance and activity as possible from that of manhood. His goal was to keep men 'men' and women 'women'. To do this, he keenly differentiated women's roles in the family, society, and even the Légion itself from

14 Ibid. For more on the central role of fathers in the Légion, see Cheryl Koos, 'Fascism, fatherhood, and the family in inter-war France: the case of Antoine Rédier and the Légion' *Journal of Family History*, 24:3 (1999), 317–29.

15 AN F7 13208, Antoine Rédier, 'Chronique des Chefs de famille', *Le Rassemblement*, 1 March 1925, 38.

16 Ibid.

17 See Goodfellow, *Between the Swastika and the Cross of Lorraine*, p. 55.

that of men's roles. Rédier attempted to apply his strict delineation of gender roles to society, culture, the family, as well as politics. When he formed the Légion in the summer of 1924, he explicitly stated that women had no role in politics and thus could not join the new organisation. They could, however, influence their husbands, sons and brothers to join.[18] Within six months, though, he decided to allow women to join special women-only sections. It is not clear if the large female readership pressured Rédier to allow women to join the Légion. Rédier explained his change of heart by asserting that 'we do not have the right to distance women from this great movement which grows and develops irressitably beneath the surface'. He attempted nevertheless to preserve and perhaps recreate a vision of womanhood that was as distinct in appearance and activity as possible from that of men's. Women, though allowed to join, were not to engage in politics like the men; Rédier emphatically stated that 'we do not want amazons in the streets nor suffragettes in our gatherings'.[19] He desired women to be 'ardent agents of propaganda for the cause of national health' who would fortify and excite the souls of the men in the organisation 'with the flame that is in every feminine heart'.[20]

A tract distributed at Légion gatherings further detailed the role of women within the organisation. First, women of the Légion were to remind their husbands and brothers of their duties and raise their sons to know their duties as men. Secondly, these women needed to be moral examples to others. They should 'repudiate certain ways of behaving' such as 'painting themselves' with cosmetics, 'dancing, talking inconsiderately, reading' trashy stories and novels and 'applauding vile performances [*spectacles*]', and uphold the true virtues of womanhood which included an irreproachable purity of action and thought.[21] They must embrace their calling as mothers in order to combat France's declining birth-rate and morality along with the threat posed by her foreign and domestic enemies.[22] If they did

18 'La Légion', *Revue française*, 19:32 (10 August 1924).
19 'Les femmes et la politique', *Revue française*, 19:51 (24 December 1924), 673. Pierre Taittinger published an article entitled 'Ni Amazones, Ni Suffragettes', in the 16 January 1926 issue of *La Liberté*.
20 Ibid.
21 AN F7 13208, 'Schema de la Légion', Commissariat Spécial of Strasbourg No. 368 (5 March 1925).
22 Rédier advocated this view in a *Revue française* article in which he announced the creation of the women's sections of the Légion. See Antoine Rédier, 'Les Femmes et la politique', *Revue française*, 51 (24 December 1924), 673. See also Soucy, *French Fascism: The First Wave*, p. 35.

not, the women's sections of the organisation would 'not tolerate' those that refused.

By instituting the first women's section, Rédier and the Légion created a precedent for female political participation in right-wing political parties and organisations. Not only did fascist and extreme-right leagues follow the Légion's example in creating women's sections, but the most prominent parliamentary right parties, including Louis Marin's Fédération Républicaine and the Alliance Démocratique, pressured by the success of the fascist leagues in mobilising women, also set up organisations for women.[23] Prior to Rédier and the other league leaders establishing women's sections, right-leaning women's only political outlets were Catholic women's organisations.[24] By enlisting their aid within their 'natural' sphere of relationships, family and home, the Légion in theory kept women separate from men, thus avoiding potential disorder like that which plagued French society, and succeeded in involving them in modern mass politics on some level. In this manner, Rédier created an outlet for the 'good modern woman' whom he had lauded previously; she could stay truly a woman by remaining true to her natural roles of wife and mother and by operating in a sphere of influence different from that of men, but she could also be 'modern' by being involved in politics, fighting for the preservation of the French nation, her larger *foyer*. Reality, though, was much more complicated, as women would inhabit the public as well as the private space of meetings and group actions, both in the short-lived Légion and in the other fascist leagues.

Marie-Thérèse Moreau and the Jeunesses Patriotes

Marie-Thérèse Moreau was a member and leader of the Jeunesses Patriotes, a league founded by Pierre Taittinger in 1924. Like Rédier's Légion, the founding of the Jeunesses Patriotes should be seen in the context of the success of the Cartel des Gauches, a political victory that the extreme and fascist right viewed as a repudiation of the 'true France'. Moreau was the President of the Jeunesses

---

23 For a discussion of the women's sections of the Fédération Républicaine and the Alliance Démocratique, see Siân Reynolds, *France Between the Wars: Gender and Politics* (London, Routledge, 1996), pp. 168–9.

24 For an exhaustive study of these groups, see Anne Cova, *'Au service de l'Église, de la patrie et de la famille': Femmes catholiques et maternité sous la IIIe République* (Paris, L'Harmattan, 2000).

Patriotes' women's section, as well as a lawyer, a Legion of Honor chevalier, and an outspoken supporter of women's rights who also worked with the National Union for the Women's Vote, a Catholic women's suffrage league.[25] In her capacity as President, Moreau was present at numerous meetings of the Jeunesses Patriotes, even if just to say a few words on women's roles. She was generally 'on tour' for the Jeunesses Patriotes from 1925 to 1928. Moreau's presence, speeches and work within the Jeunesses Patriotes reinforced the notion that women could and should be part of the movement and were important to the group's propaganda work.

Central to the ideology and philosophy of the Jeunesses Patriotes, particularly Moreau, was the idea that the nation was a large family. This conception of the nation meant that the league brought together, under the rubric of public and political interests, all areas of private and family life. In this way the Jeunesses Patriotes broke down public and private distinctions. Articles by Moreau, featured on the front page of *Le National,* the Jeunesses Patriotes newspaper, exposed the false dichotomy of politics and family life. The league journal showed support for women's suffrage and described as 'radical' those who opposed giving women full citizenship. In reviewing the arguments over female suffrage Moreau noted that 'people who claim that politics is the reserved domain of men, and the home life is that of women, commit a grave error. The life of the *patrie* is that of a *grande famille* and there is not a firm divide between the two domains.'[26] Therein lay the crux of the political argument of the Jeunesses Patriotes: all areas of life were legitimate areas of political concern. There was no public and private, all was potentially public and political. This mode of argument also insured a safe entry for the league to comment upon women and politics. Instead of claiming that women needed to be involved in the same areas as men because they were equal in abilities, *Le National* claimed that it was natural for women to be concerned with the family and, by extension, all that affected the family, which could be politics.

The breakdown of public and private, even as the leagues might use separate spheres ideology in other areas, was an important philosophical approach for the leagues and one with significant implications for the understanding of gender within extreme-right politics. On the one hand, gender was an essential category for league

25 See publications of '*L'Union National Pour le vote des Femmes*', (Bibliotheque M. Durand, Paris).
26 *Le National de L'ouest* (June 1931), p. 1.

organisations and ideology (whether in the actual structure of many
leagues which created women's sections separate from the more
general organisation of the league, or in discussions of labour in
France which almost always brought up believed distinctions of
gender). On the other hand, leagues did not make distinctions between
the high politics of the French state (on such issues as the stabilisa-
tion of the *Franc* or foreign policy) and the private politics of
domesticity. In this way the role of men and women and traditional
assumptions of gender were often effaced along with the effacement
of public and private.

The complexity of gender use in the extreme right means that it is
often difficult to separate league attitudes and propaganda which
addressed female suffrage and imparted a message of female autonomy, from those that discussed women almost exclusively in terms of
the family. Even articles that began by discussing female enfranchisement almost inevitably ended by reasserting the primacy of the
family in women's lives. Moreau's many speeches illustrate that
paradox.

At a February 1927 meeting Moreau, 'loudly cheered by the
members', spoke about the role of women in France and discussed
what brought the 'Jeunesses Patriotes to seek her help'.[27] Moreau
argued that the Jeunesses Patriotes needed to bring women into their
organisation and attract them to non-leftist politics because as it stood
the communists were in a position to profit from women's suffrage.[28]
The Jeunesses Patriotes needed and wanted to support female suffrage
because the communists did – that was the reality of the political
context in the 1920s.

Moreau went on to discuss the position of women in France:

> Next, it is undeniable that women play a primordial role in the house-
> hold, just as important as that of the man; if one acknowledges that the
> *patrie* is the extension of the *foyer*, one must conclude that the inter-
> vention of woman in the affairs of the state is logical ... woman must
> voice her opinion on the running of public affairs.[29]

This speech intertwined all the reasons to extend the vote to women
(as well as a new conception of the relationship between domesticity
and politics): the *foyer* is the *patrie* (and vice versa); women define

---

27 AN F7 13234, Commissaire Central to Minister of the Interior, Nantes, 20
    February 1927.
28 Ibid.
29 Ibid.

the former so they must be part of the later; women were part of the economic world so they must be part of the political world.

Within the same newspaper the Jeunesses Patriotes showed the kind of conflict and social and gender tension that was part of the inter-war years, on the questions of female labour, women's suffrage, and the role of women in the extreme right's visions of the new France. The same tensions would be present in the debates and discussions of the Solidarité Française.

Lucienne Blondel and the Solidarité Française

Millionaire newspaper and perfume magnate François Coty founded the Solidarité Française in 1933, shortly after the electoral victory of another left-wing coalition government. The global depression by this point had rocked France. The perilous economic instability promoted political instability as well; over the course of four years, France would have six governments, each illustrating to the far right the ineptness of the Third Republic's parliamentary system. As a result, fascist leagues like the Solidarité Française and the Croix de Feu that criticised the Third Republic found receptive audiences.

Lucienne Blondel was the Solidarité Française's most conspicuous woman. Blondel, a leader in the league whose name appeared within the pages of the group's journal consistently from 1934 to 1938, began her work with the organisation's press as a writer for the column 'La Maison et le monde'. The title itself, 'The Home and the World', illustrates the blurring of the boundaries of public and private, domesticity and politics within the leagues. As with the Jeunesses Patriotes, the home was a microcosm of the nation and the world for the Solidarité Française as well. Further, Blondel and the Solidarité Française acknowledged that the world had an impact on the home; to this end, women should be aware of and involved in 'la monde' as much as 'la maison'. The column's title also shows the way the group reaffirmed the separation of public and private even as it minimised the distinction between them. Through her missives and speeches, Blondel urged Solidarité Française men and women to contemplate the connection of the domestic and political world and to be engaged in both.

An October 1935 article appearing on the first anniversary of the *Journal de la Solidarité Française*, also the first anniversary of François Coty's death, repeated claims that the Solidarité Française was continuing in its work and, despite some difficult times, was on the right path. The article featured two photos, leaders of the Solidarité Française who would inspire the reader with confidence in the strength and tenacity of the movement: Jean Renaud and Lucienne Blondel.[30] Blondel eventually became Secretary General of the *Journal de la Solidarité Française*. Her influence within the group and across the spectrum of the extreme right was well known; according to political rivals, other fascist league members knew her well and feared her.[31]

Lucienne Blondel, as spokeswomen for the Solidarité Française, supported women's political right – namely, the vote – as well as their rights within the corporatist state that the organisation envisioned. In contrast to François Coty's earlier support for the family vote, Blondel, in a number of *Journal* articles, particularly a December 1935 article on 'Le Vote des Femmes', advocated women's suffrage in addition to a corporate vote, when the state reform would mean organisation by *métiers*. While supporting women's vote in both those areas, she strongly argued that the vote was neither a remedy nor a solution for the nation's ills, and she was much more inclined to see depopulation as France's greatest problem.[32]

In contrast to the parliamentary right and left which did not specify when women should receive suffrage, the Solidarité Française believed that women should have some immediate access to the nation's official political and economic life. As the group most intimately involved in everyday life, women, Blondel argued, may have comprehended the problems of the late Third Republic better than men. Because of this, she believed, women should be included in the economic considerations of the country.[33]

The Solidarité Française, like other leagues, both recognised the contribution of women's labour inside and outside the home and considered women's attention to the household to be the best course for France. Articles in the Solidarité Française press, notably 'La Solidarité Française et les femmes', were illustrated with pictures of women at work: a secretary, nurses, women working at an atelier or an office, as well as women in Solidarité Française uniforms at

30 'La Solidarité française', *Problèmes Actuels*, October 1935, p. 13
31 *Le droit de vivre: Journal des juifs et non-juifs unis pour le rapprochement des peuples*, 29 February 1936.
32 Lucienne Blondel, 'Le Vote des Femmes', *Grand reportage sur la Solidarité française*, 1 December 1935. Much of this article is a repetition of earlier articles cited.
33 Ibid.

demonstrations. Further, there were often pictures of Lucienne Blondel, behind her desk at the league's headquarters, presumably penning another article for the paper.[34] The presence of these images is some indication that the Solidarité Française supported women's work – and to some extent it did. The article that accompanied these pictures played the role of tempering some of that support. Again, while the group acknowledged the necessity of women's paid labour, it also saw it as an indication of the difficult economic times.

Blondel, on behalf of the Solidarité Française, also demanded that 'the civil code be revised to give women not exceptional or particular rights, but simple equality before the law' and supported the 'partial elimination of salaried work for women'.[35] She acknowledged that women 'have always worked' and claimed that 'we will always be the defenders of the interests and rights of woman, whether in the legal order or in the economic struggle' and then declared female labour was one of the main causes of French depopulation.[36]

Labour, both male and female, was thus integrally connected to the family and pro-natalist concerns of the group. The organisation roundly condemned the Third Republic because it had been 'a regime which has encouraged the exploitation of a poorly defended workforce and the disintegration of the home'.[37] The Solidarité Française linked these issues through women. The group believed that most women worked because it was necessary, 'because they are single or supporters of their families'. If France was to experience a regeneration, morally, socially, and in the population, women would have to be at the vanguard of that regeneration. They could not possibly do that if they were forced to 'suffer, without joy, the necessity of work'.[38] For the Solidarité Française, French depopulation, the symbol of much that was wrong in France, was directly attributable to female labour. Only a 'strong and energetic regime' could create the proper moral and economic climate in France to allow for the end of financially necessary female labour. The league had no doubt that most women would be happy to give up their jobs if men earned a 'fair salary'.[39] For the Solidarité Française and the other fascist leagues, the fact that

---

34 'La Solidarité Française', *Problèmes Actuels*, October 1935.
35 Ibid.
36 Ibid.
37 Ibid.
38 Ibid.
39 Ibid.

women had to work was fodder for their battle against the parliamentary system. The war, inflation, economic depression, and depopulation were somehow connected to female labour. The leagues presented themselves as the groups that could best deal with these problems, and they highlighted the extent to which the government of the Third Republic not only could not address these problems, but also, in fact, had caused them.

Colonel de La Rocque, the Croix de Feu/Parti Social Français, and women's social work

The Croix de Feu/Parti Social Français, through the words and actions of its best-known leader Lieutenant-Colonel François de La Rocque, shared many of the ideas and sentiments of the Jeunesses Patriotes and Solidarité Française. Financed by the Solidarité Française's founder François Coty, the Croix de Feu began in 1928 as a loose association of veterans. After becoming its President in 1931, La Rocque transformed the group into an extreme-rightist league, aided by the creation of the Sons and Daughters of the Croix de Feu, the National Volunteers, as well as its paramilitary branch, 'the dispos'. When the leftist Popular Front government banned the fascist leagues in 1936, La Rocque created the Parti Social Français, which had close to 800,000 members in 1939.[40]

While women had been members in the organisation, generally under the category of the 'Régroupement National', in March 1934 the Croix de Feu formed a women's section specifically dedicated to social work.[41] The women's group, a sub-group of the 'Mouvement Social Français des Croix de Feu', claimed that its goal was to be 'the defense of the moral forces of the nation menaced by revolutionary elements'.[42] Specifically the group consisted of visiting nurses and social work programmes, distributed clothing to the unemployed, provided children's programmes, served free meals and ran vacation

---

40 The debate about the fascist nature of the Croix de Feu is ongoing and filled with more intensity than discussion about other groups, at least in part because it garnered the greatest amount of support. Some historians, such as René Rémond, view the Croix de Feu as an example of the more traditional right. Others, including Robert Soucy and Kevin Passmore, see the Croix de Feu as connected to fascism. Soucy, *French Fascism: The First Wave,* and *French Fascism: The Second Wave*; Irvine, 'Fascism in France'; Passmore, *From Liberalism to Fascism.*
41 AN 451 AP 87 (Papiers de La Rocque), 'Oeuvres sociales Croix de feu'.
42 AN 451 AP 87 (Papiers de La Rocque), 'Oeuvres sociales Croix de Feu: Section féminine du Mouvement social des Croix de feu.

camps, one specifically honouring Nadine de la Rocque, La Rocque's deceased daughter.[43]

The league's social work was an area of near total female control within the Croix de Feu. Madame de Gérus, Madame de Préval and Mademoiselle Féraud, among others, were in charge of the many different programmes within the social work of the group. While these areas may strike one as traditional areas of female work and thus marginalised, women's engagement speaks not only to women's interest in the league, but also represents one of the many ways in which domestic ideals were an intrinsic part of Croix de Feu ideology.

The league's social action, the major undertaking of Croix de Feu/Parti Social Français women, had an important political role: turning communist workers and families into league partisans.[44] Robert Soucy further acknowledges the political purposes of female work that was purported to have purely charitable motivations.[45]

Women's apparent subordination within the league to seemingly marginal areas that served as extensions of the domestic sphere does not address the complexities of the organisation's gender ideology. The position of women cannot be reduced to an extension of the familial role, not least because of the uncertainties in the discourse and practices of the leadership.[46] La Rocque himself called upon the language and idea of the social world throughout the various formulations of league ideology, hence, areas that may be considered purely social (and by extension more feminine than masculine) are, indeed, deeply political.[47] Because of this there were often contradictions within La Rocque's statements on women and women's work within the league. Even as women's social work might be rationlised as apolitical and maternal work, certainly, as Passmore argues, 'the unintended consequence of the contradictions in the movement's discourses was that female activists were able, within the limits represented by their own relative lack of power resources, to invest the women's sections with their own purposes'.[48]

The contradictions of La Rocque's and league discourse are also

43 AN 451 AP 87, 8 July 1935; 451 AP 82, Illustrated Supplement *of Le Flambeau*, May 1936.
44 Passmore, 'Planting the Tricolour'; Green, 'Gender, fascism and the Croix de Feu', pp. 229–39.
45 Soucy, *French Fascism: The Second Wave*, pp. 110–11.
46 Passmore, 'Planting the Tricolour', p. 825.
47 Lieutenant-Colonel François de La Rocque, *Service Publique* (Paris, Bernard Grasset, 1934), pp. 75–77, 112–19.
48 Passmore, 'Planting the Tricolour', p. 828.

apparent in discussions of female suffrage. Like the Solidarité Française, Croix de Feu/PSF at least by 1936 simultaneously supported women's suffrage, the family vote, and making the vote obligatory.[49] Throughout its pamphlets and press, the Croix de Feu claimed that is was interested in 'making the vote obligatory for all voters. Instituting the family vote ... the vote for women in municipal and departmental elections first, in preparation for the introduction of the family and women into full universal suffrage.'[50]

The Croix de Feu/PSF made women's morality an essential part of its platform, as well as part of its recruiting tactics for women. This sentiment is clear in the address of Charles Vallin, PSF Executive Committee member, to the female delegates of the women's social action group: 'It is a certainty that history gives us: We will not save France without women, because we will not save France if we do not first create the moral climate without which one cannot do anything serious nor durable'.[51] All the leagues utilised and shared this belief and dependence on women's moral strength. They cast the perceived French political crisis as a moral crisis; women's moral strength would be the vehicle that saved the nation.

Like other leagues, the Croix de Feu/PSF appreciated the impact a woman's voice might lend to the organisation. *Le Flambeau,* the league's journal, published a front page article by Marcelle Tinayre on 16 March 1935. Tinayre, a novelist, nominee for the Legion of Honor, and winner of the French Academy's Prix Barthou, contemplated in 'Action des Femmes' what women could do to help France.[52] She concluded that there needed to be a total reform of state institutions, particularly suffrage, 'which will allow the values of all kind, masculine and feminine, to serve the country efficiently'.[53] The Croix de Feu must have believed Marcelle Tinayre was an asset to its organisation, that it was more powerful to have these sentiments come from a woman, that it would be more persuasive to its members, men and women. A caption under her picture in *Le Flambeau* called

49 *Le Parti Social Français, Devant les problèmes de l'heure* (Paris, SEDA, 1936), p. 409 and the pamphlet *Pourquoi j'ai adhère au Parti social français.*
50 Marcel Acouteurier, *Au Service des Croix de feu, October 1934–19 June 1936 et du Parti social français* (Paris, SEDA, 1937), p. 231.
51 Charles Vallin, *'Aux femmes du Parti Social Français' Conférence faite aux déléguées des Groupes d'Action Sociale du P.S.F. (Région Parisienne)* (Paris, SEDA, July 1937).
52 Jennifer Waelti-Walters, *Feminist Novelists of the Belle-Epoque* (Bloomington, Indiana University Press, 1990), p. 186.
53 *Le Flambeau*, 16 March 1935.

Tinayre 'one of our premiere propagandists of the women's section'.[54] Mary Jean Green acknowledges the presence of articles for and by women *in Le Flambeau* and notes that this illustrates both an interest in attracting female members to the league and the assumption of female readership.[55]

The Croix de Feu, like all the leagues considered here, was deeply involved in the national debate about women's political roles and the particular question of female suffrage. Further, the groups examined here and the work of the individual women considered here illustrate the extent to which women were important in inter-war extreme-right movements, not only as subjects of discussion, but also as agents within the leagues. In their discussions of female work, suffrage, domesticity and politics, the leagues propagated clear ideas of masculinity and femininity. Playing numerous and varied roles in practice and rhetoric, women were central to the politics of the far right of the 1920s and 1930s. This presence would set the stage for what was to come in the early 1940s.

Vérine and the Vichy regime

With many on the right crying 'Better Hitler than Blum', referring to Léon Blum, the leader of the leftist Popular Front, many fascist league members hailed the fall of the Third Republic in June 1940 following France's defeat to the Germans. The Third Republic's successor, the authoritarian Vichy regime, placed the family – and thus gender – at the centre of its political programme as embodied by the triptych *travail, famille, patrie* (work, family, fatherland). With the creation of Vichy's 'new men' and 'new women', women faced much more limited opportunities for political involvement than they had in the Third Republic. Even those politically minded *Pétainistes* who desired to become involved in far-right politics, like their predecessors on the extreme right Lucienne Blondel and Marie-Thérèse Moreau, found even more circumscribed opportunities. Some women did join Jacque Doriot's Parti Populaire Français (PPF) and Marcel Déat's Rassemblement National Populaire.[56] In 1942 a women's group broke off from the PPF to form the Jeunesse Française

---

54 Ibid.
55 Green, 'Gender, fascism and the Croix de Feu'. Some of these ideas are also expanded upon in her 'The Bouboule Novels'.
56 Diamond, *Women and the Second World War*, p. 91; Philippe Burrin, *France à l'heure allemande, 1940–1944* (Paris, Seuil, 1995), p. 433.

Feminine, which consisted of 'uniformed girls, often cavorting with German officers, often bored adolescents'.[57] Similarly, Pétain's Légion des Combattants formed a 'ladies social-medical service' which conducted its activities *en uniforme* on the department level.[58] Additionally, La Rocque's PSF, with its legions of female social workers, initially supported the National Revolution. Renamed Progrès Social Français, the organisation increasingly distanced itself from the regime as collaboration with the Germans became more apparent, and it operated resistance activities under the aegis of its social services branch primarily populated by women.[59]

One prominent woman, however, found her way into the ranks of the Vichy government. Marguerite Lebrun became one of two women to serve on Vichy's National Council.[60] Better known by her pseudonym 'Vérine', Lebrun, like Moreau, Blondel, and the women of the Croix de Feu/PSF, also illustrates the conflicted and ambiguous place of women in the far right. A writer, journalist and conservative pro-family activist, Vérine cut her political teeth within the social and political networks of the far right during the late 1920s and 1930s, largely through her involvement in the Ecole des Parents (Parents' School) which she founded in 1930. She became a consistent fixture – all the more prominent because she was one of few women – in the forefront of the pro-natalist and pro-family movement. Her Ecole des Parents sponsors and benefactors were luminaries across the political and para-political networks of the right and far right; pro-natalist and pro-family parliamentary representatives, including Antoine Rédier, were among the patrons and participants of the Ecole des Parents' many conferences. Vérine, the mother of five children herself, was one of few women who received praise across the spectrum of the largely all-male cadre of the political right and its ideologically affiliated movements and causes.[61]

To this end, Vérine even approached the office of Antoinette de Préval, perhaps the most prominent woman in La Rocque's PSF,

57 Paul Jankowski, *Communism and Collabouration: Simon Sabiani and Politics in Marseille, 1919–1944* (New Haven and London, Yale University Press, 1989), p. 133, quoted in Diamond, *Women and the Second World War*, p. 91.

58 Rita Thalmann, 'Vichy and l'antifeminisme', in Christine Bard (ed.), *Un siècle d'antiféminisme* (Paris, Fayard, 1999), p. 237.

59 Passmore, 'Planting the Tricolour', pp. 850–1.

60 On the Conseil National de Vichy, see Michèle Cointet, *Le Conseil national de Vichy, 1940–1944* (Paris, Aux amateurs de livres, 1989).

61 Little has been published about Vérine. See, for example, Muel-Dreyfus, *Vichy et l'éternel feminin*; Thalmann, 'Vichy and l'antifeminisme', p. 236.

about the possibility of writing columns for the PSF's newspaper, the *Petit Journal*. Her association with PSF social service section chief Robert Garric gave her inquiry a cachet among the women staffing the social services office, as did, no doubt, her support of the PSF's central tenets of *travail, famille, patrie*.[62]

Following the defeat to the Germans, Vérine became a vocal supporter and defender of Maréchal Philippe Pétain's National Revolution. With its slogan, *travail, famille, patrie,* the Vichy regime embodied the values that Vérine – and many of those on the extreme right – had lauded during the inter-war period and on which she had modelled her own organisation. As the co-director of the pro-Vichy journal *Éducation*, Vérine echoed the tenets of the 'new order' in her columns – which, by the way, did not differ much from her earlier treatises, insisting that parents had the duty and responsibility to inculcate the values of work, family, fatherland, discipline, respect for authority, moral and social hierarchies, and order, into their children.[63] She was also selected as the only female contributor to the official thematic manifesto of the National Revolution published by Pétain's associates and assorted government officials.[64] To this end, Vérine asserted the primacy of the family in the regime's *révolution nationale*; she condemned the change occurring within the structure of the family over the last centuries (read: since the Revolution of 1789) which had 'violated eternal principles' and had 'revolted against the laws of fertility, authority, purity, and love'. As a result, man 'created his own hell' and made himself an animal (bestialised himself).[65] She refused, though, to blame only 'anti-familialist' policies that emphasised pleasure and leisure; 'infertile and sterile men and women whose souls had been ossified by *egoisme*, withered by materialism, not able to "think French", do not know anymore how to "think family". As a result, disorder is the order of the day in France. According to Vérine, only France's rich moral and intellectual patrimony would be saved through 'familial virtues which would revive [its] sluggish forces'.[66]

While Vérine was involved in promoting the regime in ways that

62 See AN 451 AP 187, Dossier 'Travail et Loisirs 1936–40', PSF (Dossier Vérine).
63 See, for example, Vérine, 'Climat familial 1942', in *Les Devoirs présents des éducateurs* (Angoulême, Coquemard, 1942).
64 Vérine, 'La Famille', in *France '41: La Revolution Nationale constructive, un bilan et un programme* (Paris, Editions Alsatia, 1941), pp. 191–214. See also Muel-Dreyfus, *Vichy et l'éternel féminin*, p. 181.
65 Vérine, 'La Famille', p. 193.
66 Ibid., p. 194.

few other women would, she occupied liminal space in its structures. She spoke publicly about women playing political roles as child-bearers, child-raisers and wives, thus defying the intended gender ideology of the regime, one that attempted to relegate women to the home. In doing so, she highlighted, as did the fascist leagues earlier, the contradictions and complexities involved in the ways in which women acted as agents of an ideology that both utilised them for their traditional position as carers and mothers and simultaneously marginalised them within a pronounced masculinist ideology and later regime.

The individuals considered here – Rédier, Blondel, Moreau, La Rocque and Vérine – help illustrate the extent to which issues relating to 'women', both real and imagined, were central to the theory and practice of the extreme right, fascist or quasi-fascist. As agents within the leagues (as seen by Blondel, Moreau, and the women of the Croix de Feu/PSF), as subjects of discussion and debate within the leagues (as also seen by Rédier and La Rocque), and as participants and propagandists within the Vichy regime (as seen by Vérine), they occupied a central place in the formulation and production of political ideology and the practice of it in the streets, in offices, at the podium, or in print. By placing 'women' and gender within the debate about the extreme and fascist right in France, like the other scholars in this anthology have done within the context of their respective parts of Europe, we can begin to bring to light the ways in which women and 'women' were far from 'being antithetical to the real business of politics'.[67]

---

67 Scott, *Gender and the Politics of History*, p. 46.

12

Spain

Mary Vincent

According to the Ministry of Tourism in the 1960s, Spain was different. Several generations of scholars have since argued that Spain was nothing of the sort, but if the country has a claim to historical distinctiveness, it rests on the experience of neutrality in the First World War. Spain was the largest European power not to take part in a conflict which mobilised virtually the entire continent. The nation was thereby spared the trauma of military defeat or large-scale mortality; its townscapes were not reshaped by war memorials nor its politics reconfigured by the need to accommodate returning soldiers. Spanish manhood was not conditioned by the experience of the trenches. Among women, the grieving mother had no immediate symbolic status, the black-clad widow no abnormal claim to welfare. The experience of the war could have little rhetorical resonance in a non-combatant country. Yet the post-war experience of the two sexes in Spain would have been recognisable to men and women in belligerent countries.

In Spain, as throughout Europe, the end of the First World War brought with it the collapse of the old liberal order. The closed political systems run by urban elites in collusion with the *fuerzas vivas* of rural society imploded in Spain, just as they did in Portugal and Italy. From 1917 to 1923, Spain experienced deep political and social crisis: riot and rebellion seemed endemic, while revolution was threatened both from Barcelona, which spent much of this period under military rule, and from the southern countryside.[1]

1 The classic statement is Juan Díaz del Moral, *Historia de las agitaciones campesinas andaluces* (Madrid, Alianza, 1967). For Barcelona see Temma Kaplan, *Red City: Blue Period: Social Movements in Picasso's Barcelona* (Berkeley and Los Angeles, University of California Press, 1992), pp. 147-57 and Enric Ucelay Da Cal, *La Catalunya populista: imatge, cultura i política en l'etapa republicana (1931–1939)* (Barcelona, La Magrana, 1982), pp. 67–92.

Wartime neutrality and the ensuing political crisis had a determinant effect on both left and right. The experience of 1917, in both Spain and Russia, suggested that revolutionary solutions to social problems were possible – a notion taken up vigorously by sections of the Spanish left. To the right, especially to what would become the extreme right, this meant that not only socialism but also liberalism were tarred with the revolutionary brush. To them, democracy was a system of warring factions and atomised individuals; it provided no guarantee against disorder, as the crisis years of 1917 to 1919 demonstrated. This preference for strong government and an ostentatiously stable social order seemed confirmed in 1923, when an army coup not only removed the civilian government but also led to direct military rule.

The Primo de Rivera dictatorship

Under the leadership of General Miguel Primo de Rivera, the army undertook to 'regenerate' the nation. The language of regeneration had formed part of the common currency of politics since Spain's humiliating military defeat by the United States in 1898. It could thus easily feed into the palingenetic ideologies espoused by fascist movements in the 1920s and 1930s. For some on the Spanish right, however, regeneration was replaced by essentialism, and a mythic idea of true imperial Spain.[2] Although regeneration was synonymous with modernisation, patriotic essentialism did not necessarily mean stasis: modernisation held different meanings for liberals and conservatives, democrats and corporatists, just as it did for communists and fascists. For liberal republicans, it was inextricably linked to the internal regeneration which would be brought about by the secular processes of democratisation. For others, however, particularly on the right, the nation would be regenerated by mobilising its people.

For the Primo de Rivera dictatorship, political modernity was to be achieved largely on the basis of mobilisation. Yet any such project posed immediate problems in terms of who exactly should be mobilised, not least because it highlighted the right's ambivalence towards mobilising women. The language of class harmony and corporatism was not generally couched in gender-inclusive terms. Rather, it was used to enhance a sense of national unity, suggesting that the military coup had put an end to the bitter class struggles of

2 Sebastian Balfour, *The End of the Spanish Empire 1898–1923* (Oxford, Oxford University Press, 1997), pp. 230–4.

1917 to 1921. The Bolshevik revolution had confirmed populism as the language of the left: 'respectable people' were looking to mobilise the nation but only against the mob. Similarly, the failure of a revolutionary solution to Spain's social crisis before 1923 had ensured that the 'regeneration' of the nation effectively became the regeneration of a more-or-less existing system rather than the creation of a new one.

In this way, the Primo regime conflated the language of the nation with the language of the right. The adoption of the national idiom reinforced the conservative right's claim to patriotism, as against the internationalism of much of the left. While this was to change, at least on the far right, with the rise of fascism, the elision between 'right-wing' and 'patriotic' marked the contrast with the 'debased' liberal language of party politics. It also disguised the class nature of Primo's support which persisted despite the socialist party's temporary collaboration with the regime.

This preference for lofty, 'eternal' values was reflected in the reassertion of traditional gender roles which provided a reassurance of social order throughout post-First World War Europe. After the upheavals of war, domesticity exerted a powerful attraction, with its sense of inviolate space and 'natural' patriarchal order. The organic language of living communities was common currency on the political right – a trope which emphasised gender as a central, if not always articulated, way of understanding the distribution of social and political power. Unlike adherence to a traditional class structure – over which right and left divided sharply – ideas of gender cut across political divides. The newly united nation had, of course, to comprise both men and women. But, in contrast to most combatant countries, in Spain women were not granted the vote, although universal manhood suffrage had been granted in 1891.

From 1923 voting was suspended. This had less impact than might have been expected: in Spain, as in much of southern Europe, influence-peddling and electioneering had effectively disenfranchised much of the electorate in any case. Regeneration required corrupt 'old politics' to be swept away. Henceforth, new forms of social and governmental organisation were to consolidate the nation, even though the panoply of monarchism continued to symbolise the social order. In 1926, for example, a spate of telegrams requested commemorative 'medals of homage to their majesties'.[3] Such rituals provided

---

3 Archivo Histórico Nacional (henceforth AHN), Presidencia del Gobierno (henceforth PG), legajo 228, expedientes 368, 524–5, 528; half a million such medals were issued to the public. Shlomo Ben-Ami, *Fascism from Above: The Dictatorship of Primo de Rivera in Spain 1923–30* (Oxford, Oxford University Press, 1983), p. 160.

some connection, however slight, between the monarchy and its citizens. By the 1920s, it was clearly impossible for monarchs to continue as remote figureheads, divorced from all but an aristocratic elite. Nor could they simply symbolise an abstract and reified 'nation', particularly not in countries with a burgeoning republican movement. Rather they represented a certain, hierarchical conception of the social order, one which was given a recognisable content by gender and class.

This particular social order was, of course, that envisaged by the right. Primo de Rivera's mobilisation of the nation was to be achieved through two institutions, the Unión Patriótica (UP), or single party, and the Somatén, or national militia. This was to be a mobilisation of the *citizenry*, understood in the oligarchic terms of the liberal franchises inherited from the American and French revolutions and similar in form to those 'civic unions' of anti-Bolshevik defence which sprang up all over Europe after 1917.[4] The decree reconstituting the Somatén as a national militia spoke of it as bringing together 'men of good will, lovers of order, eager in their duties as citizens'. The institution was quite explicitly conceived of as an auxiliary to the constituted authorities, giving 'strength and vigour to the civic spirit'. While women were not specifically excluded from the ranks of the Somatén – the decree speaks only of 'individuals' over twenty-three years of age – it was clearly a masculine institution.[5]

Both the Somatén and the UP functioned according to an explicitly masculine understanding of politics, bringing together 'good Spaniards, honourable and fitting'.[6] The entire project rested on a notion of civil defence which implicitly contrasted citizens and populace, social peace and social strife, hierarchical order and populist disorder. But it also crystallised a different opposition, that between the protectors and the protected. For one propagandist, the Somatén required 'the citizen's active collaboration, neither passive nor indifferent'.[7] For Primo, his movement was a 'virile' endeavour.[8] Citizens

---

4 See Eduardo González Calleja, 'La defensa armada del "orden social" durante la dictadura de Primo de Rivera', in José Luis García Delgado (ed.), *España entre dos siglos (1875–1931): continuidad y cambio* (Madrid, Siglo XXI, 1991), pp. 61–108 and Ben-Ami, *Fascism from Above*, pp. 33–52.

5 *Gaceta de Madrid*, 18 September 1923, in AHN, Gobernación Serie A, leg. 59ª, exp. 9.

6 Cited in José Luis Gómez Navarro, *El régimen de Primo de Rivera* (Madrid, Cátedra, 1991), p. 220.

7 José Andrés y Morera, 'La defensa contra la revolución: El Somatén y sus similares en el extranjero' (1927), typescript, AHN, PG, leg. 177, exp. 9494.

8 Quoted Ben-Ami, *Fascism from Above*, p. 131.

were men, not simply by function of their anatomy but also by the cultural understanding which reserved to them the right of bearing arms. These active citizens then protected other categories of Spaniard, including women, children, and 'the people', whom paternalist social thought had long since infantilised.

Spain's neutrality in the First World War had not prevented the elaboration of a militarised understanding of both social and political organisation. The UP brought a new generation into politics and, to some extent at least, a new class, mobilising younger Catholic men from metropolitan and provincial cities throughout Spain.[9] The UP in Illescas (Toledo), for example, called on all citizens 'whatever their social condition', claiming that the UPs 'are the nurseries from which the men needed for the regeneration of our Fatherland must come'.[10] *Fiestas de fraternidad* were celebrated, emphasising the comradeship of brothers-in-arms, although a lack of weapons and complaints of undignified behaviour undermined their noble image.[11] Even so, under Primo citizenship and military service were interconnected and both excluded women.

In looking to supersede class divisions, the military regime asserted a highly gendered sense of the social order. Education for boys, for example, was to be reconstituted on a basis of national defence. Recommendations for gymnastics as 'pre-military physical education' were drawn up and approved by the King, and a National Committee for Physical Culture was established, with members drawn from the teaching staff in military academies.[12] Some governmental effort was put into exploring this question, though limited financial resources and the state's woeful shortfall in educational provision make it unlikely that such schemes had much impact among the general school population.

In a parallel and equally symbolic move, the national Domestic and Professional School for Women (Escuela del Hogar y Profesional de la Mujer) had its staff replaced on grounds of nepotism and in June

9 Mary Vincent, *Catholicism and the Second Republic in Spain: Religion and Politics in Salamanca, 1930–6* (Oxford, Oxford Historical Monographs, 1996), pp. 135–40; José Luis Gómez Navarro, 'Unión Patriótica: análisis de un partido del poder', *Estudios de Historia Social*, 32–3 (1985), 93–161.

10 'Al vecindario de Illescas', April 1927, AHN, PG, leg. 177, exp. 9516.

11 Letter from Andrés Grau, Cabo de Distrito, 18 October 1926, AHN, Gobernación Serie A, leg. 59ᵃ, exp. 12; correspondence, exp. 14. See further, Ben-Ami, *Fascism from Above*, pp. 168–73.

12 Minute, 23 September 1924, AHN, PG, leg. 213, exp. 4; letters from General José Villalba, 30 March, 10 April 1929, AHN, PG, leg. 201, exp. 15014.

1924 its teaching 'reduced to that of a purely domestic character'.[13] No longer would girls be able to follow the general syllabus which, along with domestic and professional subjects (such as typing), had formed part of the original curriculum. Yet, in 1924–25, these classes were the most popular, with maths attracting 117 students and French 151 as against dressmaking's 89, housekeeping's 39 and corsetry's 16.[14]

This slightly curious example suggests how the rhetoric of conventional femininity served within the political right as part of the lexicon of modernisation. Open access to official posts and professional qualifications were important components of meritocratic state institutions and the sweeping away of placemen was generally applauded. The notion of a specialisation of function, naturalised through contemporary understandings of biology, underpinned much of the rhetoric of separate spheres in this period. Although there were practical gains – the teaching staff at the Escuela del Hogar was now entirely female – they were won at the expense of a constricting delineation of women's sphere of action.

The educational policies of the Primo dictatorship seemed to be the trenchant restatement of separate spheres perhaps unsurprising in a military regime. Yet, despite the dominant rhetoric of domesticity, women were increasingly incorporated into the public body of the nation, not least through their ceremonial presence in the dinners, displays and demonstrations of loyalty that punctuated civic life in the 1920s. Their presence was particularly welcome when the regime's ideology was on show.[15] Once the militia became a national institution, for example, no self-respecting branch was complete without both a flag and a ceremony to bless it. These inevitably served as microcosms of the desired corporative social order: in one village near Bilbao the 'entire *pueblo*' heard addresses from the military, civil, ecclesiastical and naval authorities as well as from the flags' godmothers.[16]

---

13 Mª Rosa Capel Martínez, *El trabajo y la educación de la mujer en España, 1900–1930* (Madrid, Ministerio de Cultura, 1982), pp. 450–6.

14 'Escuela del Hogar y Profesional de la Mujer (sobre su reorganización)', AHN, PG leg. 213, exp. 12.

15 Jesús María Palomares Ibáñez, *Nuevos políticos para un nuevo caciquismo: la dictadura de Primo de Rivera en Valladolid* (Valladolid, Universidad de Valladolid, 1993), pp. 82–3.

16 Telegram from Besauri, 12 July 1925, AHN, Gobernación Serie A, leg. 59ª, exp. 11.

In a confessional state, these ceremonies were liturgical as well as civic events. The office of godmother (*madrina*) to the flag reinforced this conflation of the sacred and the secular, not least because it was the only institutional feminine presence in military life. The role was widely mimicked. Under the Second Republic, political parties across the right of the spectrum had not only flags but also *madrinas*. As the leader of the Somatén in Olivenza (Badajoz) put it, the sight of the flag 'in the hands of such a beautiful and distinguished godmother . . . representing our Race and our blood, stimulated our patriotism still more, for the participation of the Spanish woman in these ceremonies, with her beauty, love and virtue, induces heroism'. The local Somatén was 'profoundly grateful for her patriotic participation'. [17]

The role of the *madrina* was thus both highly symbolic and essentially abstract. They would customarily address the assembly, but their speeches were formulaic and usually short.[18] As the role was essentially decorative, it was often played by unmarried girls who were, in this militaristic age, rewarded with medals.[19] The ceremonial presence of Spanish womanhood symbolised the entirety of the nation and patriotic sacrifice. War widows, for example, could be awarded the 'Medal of Suffering for the Fatherland', while ranking officers attended ceremonies for the award of Red Cross arm-bands.[20] National sentiment was thus writ large in a self-conscious attempt at modernising political life. Endless military and civic display also pointed to a new form of politics, one modelled on Mussolini's virile Fascist spectacle.[21] But, while women were being incorporated into national and public life, they were not necessarily there as political actors.

In many respects, full, active citizenship remained the preserve of men. As in other European countries, women's rights were primarily a cause for the bourgeois left. Rhetorically, anti-feminism provided the mainstay of the political right, although, as the regime looked to reconstitute itself on a civilian basis, corporatism provided a suitable

---

17 Handbill (undated), AHN, PG, leg. 440.

18 Clive Beadman, 'Official nationalism of the Primo de Rivera regime: some findings from the pages of *Unión Patriótica* and *Somatén*', *International Journal of Iberian Studies*, 11:2 (1998), pp. 69–75 sees the *madrinas* as representing purity and tradition.

19 Correspondence over award of *medalla madrina Somatén,* AHN, Gobernación Serie A, leg. 59ᵃ, exp. 13.

20 Letter to Serafina Alvarez, 10 October 1927, AHN, PG, leg. 177, exp. 9392; telegram from Lérida, 17 April 1927, AHN, Gobernación, Serie A, leg. 59ᵃ, exp. 12.

21 Ben-Ami, *Fascism from Above*, esp. pp. 155–60.

idiom for those women looking to develop a more active presence without challenging men's position. Some in Valladolid, for example, referred to themselves as 'co-citizens' (*conciudadanas*).[22] This was indeed a fair proximity to their legal position, as a Royal Decree of 12 April 1924 enfranchised women who were over twenty-three years of age and not subject to 'paternal authority [*patria potestas*], marital authority or guardianship'. Such a formulation ensured that enfranchisement did not undermine the paternal hierarchies of the family, now enshrined as an 'organic' foundation of the state. Single and widowed women could, though, take full part in public life, serving in municipal government and, from 1927, in the dictator's consultative National Assembly.[23]

As the first corporative political body established in Spain, the National Assembly had to embody the nation, with designated representatives of the state, the provinces, the municipalities, Unión Patriótica and 'activities, classes and values'.[24] The thirteen women who took up seats there not only represented their sex within the body of the nation, but also exercised various professional functions, generally beneficence or education. María de Echarri and María de Maeztu were public figures, the first a Catholic trade-union organiser and prison reformer, the second a prominent educationalist and university teacher. Both were feminists, albeit within a conservative context, and their public roles depended directly upon their professional identities.[25] Such a relationship between professional and public life was peculiarly appropriate to corporatism, and neither woman was politically active under the Republic, perhaps also because of the rapid radicalisation of the right after 1931.

Another of the female deputies in the National Assembly was Josefina Olóriz Arcelus, who taught at the Escuela Normal de Maestras de Guipúzcoa and was a municipal councillor for San Sebastián. She believed that pioneering activists would open public

22 Open letter published *El Diario Regional* (Valladolid), reproduced Palomares Ibáñez, *Nuevos políticos para un nuevo caciquismo*, p. 137.

23 Mercedes Ugalde Solano, *Mujeres y Nacionalismo Vasco: Génesis y desarrollo de Emakume Abertzale Batza, 1906–1936* (Bilbao, Universidad del País Vasco, 1993), pp. 180–1, 184; Elisa Garrido, Margarita Ortega, Pilar Folguera and Cristina Segura, *Historia de las mujeres en España* (Madrid, Síntesis, 1997), pp. 484–5, 488. Elections were either local or plebiscitary.

24 Ben-Ami, *Fascism from Above*, p. 221.

25 Susana Tavera (ed.), *Mujeres en la historia de España: enciclopedia biográfica* (Barcelona, Planeta, 2000), pp. 493–6, 575–80; Capel Martínez, *El trabajo y la educación de la mujer*, pp. 510–12, 515–18.

service to other women, whose traditional role would be adapted to their new function. Careful always to avoid charges of 'masculinisation', Olóriz emphasised that women were 'always men's loyal collaborators' whose public role stemmed directly from their domestic expertise and natural competence. As councillors, they should be concerned with education, welfare, hygiene, and the appearance of buildings, squares and gardens.[26]

This kind of specific, practical political involvement could be seen as a simple reassertion of women's nurturing role.[27] As changing ideas of citizenship and national representation led to women's greater political involvement, so a process which was potentially both dangerous and dissolvent – for the family as well as for the nation – could be kept in check by an insistence on natural gender roles. Modernising the political process was accomplished while the limits to women's (expanded) sphere of action remained clear. In public life, women were the mothers of the nation, not least in the symbolic way reaffirmed by the endless involvement of right-wing and Catholic women in charitable activity. But not all of these women were mothers; if not widows, National Assembly delegates were, by legal requirement, unmarried. In the heavily clericalised culture of right-wing, bourgeois Spain, motherhood was only an option for married women.[28] As the careers of Maeztu, Olóriz and Echarri – a member of a religious community – show, unmarried women were both familiar and valued in Spanish society. The language of philanthropy, for example, played a large part in the life of married women, but the bulk of Spain's social and welfare services was provided by unmarried and semi-professional nuns.

By the end of the Primo dictatorship, women had accessed the public sphere. Political activists were still a small and legally circumscribed minority, but even the supposedly silent public platform

26 'La actuación de la mujer católica concejala en los distintos secores de la Administración Pública' précised in Ugalde Solano, *Mujeres y Nacionalismo Vasco*, pp. 185–6.

27 See Geraldine Scanlon, *La polémica feminista en la España contemporánea, 1868–1974*, 2nd edn (Madrid, Akal, 1986), pp. 154–7.

28 Here, I am arguing against Mary Nash, 'Un/contested identities: motherhood, sex reform and the modernisation of gender identity in early twentieth-century Spain', in Victoria Lorée Enders and Pamela Beth Radcliff (eds), *Constructing Spanish Womanhood: Female Identity in Modern Spain* (Albany, NY, SUNY Press, 1999). See also Frances Lannon, 'Los cuerpos de las mujeres y el cuerpo político católico: autoridades e indentidades en conflicto en España durante las décadas de 1920 y 1930', *Historia Social*, 35 (1999), 65–80.

occupied by the more-numerous *madrinas* and benefactresses gave women a presence in civic life. Despite the tiny number of female delegates, the National Assembly gave women a political voice and status that they had hitherto been denied. Women participated in the 1926 plebiscite which ratified the Assembly both as voters and as campaigners.[29] When, under the Second Republic, women's political mobilisation became a crucial component of anti-Republican political strategy, it was neither simply an opportunistic response to liberal legislation giving women full electoral rights – though this is the conventional interpretation[30] – nor a function of the common assumption that women favoured the religious right. Rather, such considerations added impetus to a developing process of women's politicisation which, under the emergency conditions of Republic, was less circumspect than either before or after.[31]

The Second Republic

The rise of fascism and anti-fascism, the Great Depression and the retreat from democracy ensured that forms of political activity changed markedly in Europe during the 1920s and the 1930s. The times were not propitious for democracy: when Spain declared a Republic in April 1931, it bucked an international trend; when the Republic collapsed into civil war, many on the corporatist right believed democracy's day was done. These international circumstances reinforced the inability or unwillingness of substantial sections of the right to come to any genuine acceptance of liberal democracy. However, in 1931, they did little to insulate the right from the shock of the collapse of the monarchy. As Primo's regime had demonstrated, a hierarchical understanding of social order – underpinned by Catholicism and always conceived of in paternalist terms – ran through all the groups on the Spanish right. This was far more important than was loyalty to the person of the King. Before 1932 the Carlists, despite their ostensible adherence to the utterly anachronistic concept of the divine right of kings, experienced various schisms

29 Ben-Ami, *Fascism from Above*, pp. 213–15.
30 For example, Giuliana Di Febo, 'Memorialistica dell'esilio e protagonismo femminile degli anni Trenta', in Giuliana Di Febo and Claudio Natoli (eds), *Spagna anni Trenta: società, cultura, istituzioni* (Milan, FrancoAngeli, 1993), pp. 370–3.
31 On enfranchisement, see the chapters by Judith Keene and Gerald Alexander in Enders and Radcliff (eds), *Constructing Spanish Womanhood*, pp. 235–374; Mª Rosa Capel Martínez, *El sufragio femenino en la Segunda República española* (Granada, Universidad de Granada, 1986).

over both the identity of the true pretender and the movement's accommodation with liberalism.[32]

As the frantic manoeuvrings of the first weeks of the Republic indicate, the right looked to make common cause against the new regime. While the right divided into those 'catastrophists' who remained convinced that the Republic should be overthrown by direct assault, and the much larger number of 'accidentalists' who looked to rewrite the constitution via an absolute parliamentary majority, the Republican period demonstrates the fluidity of the boundaries between 'moderate' and 'extreme' right-wing positions.[33] With the monarch gone, the right was forced to confront its own ideological underpinnings and this process was reinforced by the rapid legislative secularisation of the Republican state. In the legally constituted order, at least, neither King nor God now reigned supreme. In these circumstances, the language of 'natural' hierarchies like gender was used to suggest a divinely ordained social ordering which was easily contrasted with the disorderly chaos of a reformist Republic. Disturbing the natural order provoked some disquiet. One public lecture claimed that the current Parliament 'had created a kind of inter-sexual', having 'made from a woman a man to govern the Nation' – an attack on the Prime Minister, Manuel Azaña.[34]

Though this particular slander resulted in six months' internal exile for the speaker, he was rehearsing an established theme, albeit one not usually discussed in mixed company.[35] The Spanish right was not simply or uniformly reactionary, though its commitment to the Republic was contingent at best. When a parliamentary party (Confederación Española de Derechas Autónomas, CEDA) did emerge, some of its members and some of its ideological positions certainly shaded into the far right. Corporatism, in particular, exerted

---

32 Martin Blinkhorn, *Carlism and Crisis in Spain, 1931–1936* (Cambridge, Cambridge University Press, 1975), ch. 1.

33 The classic statement of accidentalism as a tactic to win legislative control of the Republic is Paul Preston, *The Coming of the Spanish Civil War: Reform, Reaction and Revolution in the Second Republic 1931–1936* (London, Macmillan, 1978; 2nd edn Routledge, 1994). Cf. Stanley Payne, *Spain's First Democracy: The Second Republic 1931–1936* (Madison, University of Wisconsin Press, 1993).

34 Telegram from Zaragoza, 23 November 1931 and reply 24 November, AHN, Gobernación A, leg. 18, exp. 8.

35 Scurrilous posters in Pamplona, for example, referred to Azaña as 'Manolita' (AHN Gobernación A, leg. 49[a], exp. 40) while Francoist depictions of him incorporated both miscegenation and homosexuality. Ángeles Egido León, *Manuel Azaña: Entre el mito y la leyenda* (Valladolid, Junta de Castilla y León, 1998) esp. pp. 33–45.

a powerful attraction.[36] But, despite its rhetorical denials, CEDA still espoused much of the apparatus of liberal constitutionalism. The right had adopted the language of the nation but the need for popular legitimation was still clear. As the experience of the UP had shown, this was to be achieved by mobilising support, the strength of which could then be demonstrated by mass rallies, elaborate liturgical events and, increasingly in the 1930s, paramilitary displays.

As mobilisation was translated from a national, state idiom into a party political one, its most enthusiastic adherents were to be found among both the most parliamentarian forces on the Spanish right and the most reactionary. The 'new men' of the UP began to mobilise support through Catholic agrarian networks, establishing the nucleus of Acción Popular (AP: later the CEDA), the largest parliamentary Catholic party ever seen in Spain.[37] At the same time, the Carlists, as the Comunión Tradicionalista, began to win new recruits for the first time since the 1870s. The attraction of the Traditionalist cause was presumably its overtly ambiguous relationship with liberalism, yet this also limited potential recruitment. Until 1936, the hegemony on the right lay with the parliamentary groupings uneasily joined together in the CEDA.

CEDA was Spain's first modern party of the right, although for both pragmatic and ideological reasons it was established as a confederation of local right-wing groupings. Such an organisational structure ensured that the CEDA remained a broad, even disparate alliance of anti-Republican elements. It stood in a wide variety of electoral coalitions, determined according to local conditions and pacts with Carlist and Alfonsist monarchists were common.[38] Various shades of right-wing opinion thus benefited from the CEDA's up-to-date methods of electioneering, including radio broadcasts and aeroplane journeys. This modernising lexicon reinforced CEDA's mission to nationalise the masses. The experience of the Primo regime, together with the historic weakness of liberalism in Spain, meant that elite models of politics were

---

36 Mary Vincent, 'Spain', in Tom Buchanan and Martin Conway (eds), *Political Catholicism in Europe 1918–1945* (Oxford, Oxford University Press, 1996), pp. 97–128.

37 The literature on the CEDA is usefully reviewed in Leandro Álvarez Rey, *La derecha en la II República: Sevilla, 1931–1936* (Sevilla, Universidad de Sevilla, 1993), pp. 448–53.

38 See José Ramón Montero, *La CEDA: el catolicismo social y político en la II República*, 2 vols (Madrid, Revista de Trabajo, 1977), Vol. 2, pp. 293–6, 311–12. There were convinced Republicans within the CEDA, some of whom tried to exclude 'catastrophist' monarchists from party slates in the 1936 elections.

espoused by few in the 1930s: the right spoke the language of nation, the left that of the people; both had a notion of citizenship but neither now spoke of the citizenry. And, in contrast to the 1920s, the process of politicisation now necessarily involved women.

Full female enfranchisement created a new political constituency in Spain and one which was characterised in a curiously unsophisticated way. Although no one seriously suggested all women would vote the same way, their higher rates of religious practice led to both right and left assuming that women would vote predominantly for the right. The Carlists and the incipient CEDA organisations were thus among the first to establish active women's sections. These had expressly electoral aims, and their members worked tirelessly, particularly in the 1933 elections, to register voters and win them over to the right.[39] The numerous female orators and propagandists provided by the CEDA, the Comunión Tradicionalista and, to a lesser extent, the Alfonsist monarchist group Renovación Española, made much of the moral imperative which would take women into the polling booths. At the same time, feminine practicality and resourcefulness would guarantee the mundane but essential work of checking censuses and updating electoral rolls.

The mobilisation of women as a 'natural' constituency for the right was imperative, rather than simply expedient, but it was also problematic. Domestic ideology, anti-feminist rhetoric and an acute sense of patriarchal authority meant that women's sudden full entry into the civic arena could not be straightforward. As even a cursory look at the electoral propaganda of the time will show, the public justification was quite simple: women came out of the home in defence of the home.[40] But this could not happen unless they were given genuine responsibilities, some degree of organisational independence and, crucially, a public presence. Active engagement in the public arena by women who participated both as rational beings and as full citizens could not but undermine the gendered ideology which these same women were purporting to defend.

Awareness of this conundrum has led to an emphasis on the

---

39 See Mary Vincent, 'The politicisation of Catholic women in Salamanca, 1931–1936', in Frances Lannon and Paul Preston (eds), *Elites in Twentieth-Century Spain: Essays in Honour of Sir Raymond Carr* (Oxford, Oxford University Press, 1990), pp. 105–26 esp. pp. 115ff.; Isabel Morant Deusa and Rafael Valls, 'Acció Cívica de la Dona, secció femenina de la DRV' in *Homenatge al Doctor Sebastià García Martínez* (Valencia, Generalitat Valenciana, 1988), Vol. 3, pp. 431–45.

40 Valls, 'Acció Cívica de la Dona'; Vincent, 'Politicisation of Catholic women'; Álvarez Rey, *La derecha en la II República*, pp. 330–40.

women's lack of autonomy, on the fact that the CEDA women's committees, for example, were nominated by the male party leadership, and on the close family ties between male and female elites.[41] These links were plain to see, though the absence of archival evidence means that we have very little sense of the informal negotiations which lay behind formal nominations.[42] Nevertheless, keeping it in the family supposedly ensured women's subordination by reinforcing the patriarchal relationship which already existed between them and their husbands, fathers and brothers. The prominence achieved by women like Pilar Velasco, leader of the Madrid women's section and a considerable figure in the national party, Abilia Arroyo, a tireless orator and propagandist from Salamanca, or Francisca Bohigas Gavilanes, elected deputy for León between 1933 and 1936, is simply seen as exceptional.[43] Yet, this underplays the substantial amounts of female labour mobilised by the right. None of the women mentioned above had husbands who were prominent in the party. Bohigas was unmarried and worked for a living as a primary school inspector. Arroyo was a mother of twelve, yet her offer to send her well-practised orators wherever they were needed is unlikely to have been made on the instructions of the male leadership, any more than was Velasco's request for full autonomy for the women's sections.[44]

It is not surprising that certain families should be prominent in right-wing circles, particularly in close-knit provincial towns. The CEDA women's committees were made up of names from 'good' families, predominantly the professional and landed bourgeoisie, and so reflected a class identity more clearly than they did a direct kinship between male and female leaders.[45] However, the relationship between family and politics was fundamentally important to all parties

41 Montero, *La CEDA*, Vol. 1, pp. 664–88 and, after him, Helen Graham, 'Women and social change', in Helen Graham and Jo Labanyi (eds), *Spanish Cultural Studies: An Introduction. The Struggle for Modernity* (Oxford, Oxford University Press, 1995), pp. 104–5. For examples, see Rafael Valls, *La Derecha Regional Valenciana, 1930–1936* (Valencia, Edicions Alfons el Many̆anim, 1992), pp. 115–16, 133–4; and Miguel Angel Mateos Rodríguez, 'Formación y desarrollo de la derecha católica en la provincia de Zamora durante la Segunda República', in Javier Tusell, Julio Gil Pecharromán and Feliciano Montero (eds), *Estudios sobre la derecha española contemporánea* (Madrid, UNED, 1993), pp. 445–66.
42 Abilia Arroyo, for example, was involved in a series of private meetings before being acclaimed leader of the Salamanca women's section at its first rally, *La Gaceta Regional* (Salamanca) 21, 26 October 1931; 16 March 1932.
43 Montero, *La CEDA*, Vol. 1, pp. 682–3.
44 Both quoted Montero, *La CEDA*, Vol. 1, 685–6.
45 Álvarez Rey, *La derecha en la II República*, pp. 117–18.

on the Spanish right. Monarchists, both Alfonsist and Carlist, had the clearest understanding of politics as a family matter. Indeed, Carlist adherents were literally born into the cause. Aspirants to the women's section, known as the Margaritas, were defined as 'all the daughters of those belonging to the Communion, from birth to sixteen'; the association would take cradle gifts to families with new-born babies: a daisy (*margarita*) for a girl, the militia's red beret for a boy.[46]

Such examples suggest a distinct sense of public and private within monarchist circles, one directly inherited from the closed world of titled elites. The Alfonsist monarchist group Renovación Española had an orator and parliamentary candidate, Pilar Careaga, who was both daughter to the count of Cadagua and the first Spanish woman to qualify as an industrial engineer. She was chaperoned to all university classes, at which she wore a hat and sat apart from the other students. Her aristocratic culture may help to explain why, when she stood for election in 1933, ostensibly so that women could win the right not to take part in politics in the future, she returned to public life under Franco, serving as mayoress of Bilbao. Her objection was presumably to liberal, democratic politics. A more congenial authoritarian, corporatist regime merely confirmed the birthright of her class to govern others.[47]

Renovación Española was a tiny, elitist group. Less clear-cut was the case of the Carlists, who attracted cross-class support.[48] Admittedly, until 1934 the Carlist leader was the count of Rodezno, whose countess was nominally the national leader of the Margaritas. Yet, Rodezno was the only man of his class prominent in either Carlism or parliamentary politics and, while the landed classes figured prominently in the Comunión Tradicionalista, they also did so in the CEDA. Peasant loyalties were fundamental to Carlism's appeal, particularly in its heartlands of Navarre.[49] Here, Carlism was a

46 Florencia Carrionero Salimero, Antonio Fuentes Labrador, Mª Angeles Sampedro Talabán and Mª Jesús Velasco Marcos, 'La mujer tradicionalista: las Margaritas', in Instituto de la Mujer, *Las mujeres y la Guerra Civil Española: III jornadas de estudios monográficos. Salamanca, octubre 1989* (Madrid, Ministerio de Cultura, 1989), p. 190.

47 Capel Martínez, *El trabajo y la educación de la mujer*, pp. 477–8; Ugalde Solano, *Mujeres y nacionalismo vasco*, p. 238.

48 Jeremy MacClancy, *The Decline of Carlism* (Reno and Las Vegas, University of Nevada Press, 2000), pp. 51–6.

49 Martin Blinkhorn, 'Politics and society in Navarre, 1931–6', in Paul Preston (ed.), *Revolution and War in Spain, 1931–1939* (London, Methuen & Co, 1984), pp. 59–84 and 'Land and power in Arcadia: Navarre in the early twentieth century', in Martin Blinkhorn and Ralph Gibson (eds), *Landownership and Power in Modern Europe* (London, Harper Collins, 1991), pp. 216–34.

'cause' not a political programme, adherence to which ran through generations, as communities venerated the memory of those lost in the Carlist civil wars and families passed down the testimonies and artefacts – particularly the iconic red berets – of those who had gone before.[50]

In this particular political tradition, parents played a crucial role in the transmission of Carlist identities to future generations.[51] This again places the family at the heart of politics, helping to explain the prominence achieved by some women in what was ostensibly the most reactionary element on the Spanish right. María Rosa Urraca Pastor, for example, was among the Traditionalists' best-known propagandists. As she had been fined, arrested and detained by the Republican authorities, her claim to be 'a soldier' of the Communion who 'occupied a place in the vanguard' had some force.[52] Hyperbolic rhetoric was quite usual on the extreme right – as it was among many sections of the CEDA – and Urraca Pastor's appropriation of masculine imagery and rhetoric was not uncommon, despite its obvious paradoxes.

These paradoxes were apparent in Urraca Pastor's own career. Avowedly anti-parliament, and committed to democratic politics only as 'a legal weapon' against the Republic, she nevertheless stood for election in 1933. Originally selected for Logroño, her name was vetoed, apparently by the most prominent CEDA deputy, Tomás Ortiz de Solórzano. It is not clear why this happened: hers was not the only Traditionalist name to be discarded and her sex may not have been the only factor. However, as Ortiz de Solórzano's involvement suggests, the parameters of political action were set by men, who monopolised the national offices of all these parties and who may well have been unprepared to accept a female candidate. Even so, women's political involvement reflected female action and agency, their candidatures being the result of an unequal process of negotiation, and even conflict, with their (male) party superiors. As the Logroño case shows, there were limits to both female activity and female autonomy. But the arguments which took place over women's candidacy for public office illustrate the existence of a contested space.

50 Francisco Javier Caspistegui Gorasurreta, 'Navarra y lo carlista: símblos y mitos', in A. Martín Duque and y J. Martínez de Aguirre (eds), *Signos de identidad histórica para Navarra*, Vol. 2 (Pamplona, Caja de Ahorros de Navarra, 1996), pp. 355–70.

51 MacClancy, *Decline of Carlism*, pp. 56–72.

52 Urraca Pastor, 'A mis amigos y correligionaries' and 'Dios lo ha querido', *El Pensamiento Navarro*, 4 November, 7 December 1933.

Urraca Pastor ran instead in Guipúzcoa where she narrowly failed to win a seat. She had stood in Logroño in 'an attitude of discipline', 'at the service of the rightist cause', knowing that, as a woman, her candidature was exceptional. When she then lost in Guipúzcoa, she accepted her defeat as God's unwillingness to see 'a Traditionalist woman go to what may be Spain's last parliament. Human beings are too vain – women even more so – and the liberal air [*polvillo*] they breathe there is dangerous. Perhaps I would have been infected with the virus of great debates, quorums, guillotines etc.'[53]

This contrast between the masculine virtues demonstrated by right-wing women and the inherent fragility of their sex runs through all the right's political discourse, whether written by men or women. The Carlist leader Manuel Fal Conde eulogised right-wing women after the 1933 elections for demonstrating 'the virtues considered appropriate to the male', particularly 'that masculine compendium of all other masculinities: valour'. Future generations would be told to 'vote like women if you want to behave like men'.[54] Yet, the emphasis on voting easily instrumentalised women; the CEDA 'had to create men, had to educate youth, had to capture the female vote'.[55] The familiar tropes of active male and passive female were thus conserved at the same time as women's supposedly superior capacity for proselytism undermined them. Politically, women were clearly visible only at election times, being otherwise occupied in charity work (with which all the women's groups were concerned) and collecting census data. It was with some justice that an unusual, explicitly feminist, CEDA publication complained that the male leaders 'forget us, as if we didn't exist (after accepting our work)'.[56] But this work had made a difference. The sheer groundswell of female activism on the right in the 1930s marked a clear change from the 1920s, despite the constraints under which women operated.

Seeing women as ballot papers is less emancipatory than imagining them as frontline soldiers, largely because it denies female agency. The difference in rhetoric between the CEDA and the Carlists reflected the latter's greater disdain for the atomised politics of liberal democracy, which divorced government from the society over which

53 Ibid.
54 Fal Conde, 'Honor a las mujeres españolas', *Pensamiento Navarro*, 26 November 1933.
55 José Monge y Bernal, *Acción Popular: Estudios de Biología Política* (Madrid, Sáez Hermanos, 1936), p. 145.
56 *Aspiraciones*, 29 December 1933.

it ruled. But, while they wanted the vote to be reserved for heads of families, the Carlists retained a unique tradition of female heroism which militated against domestic subservience. Women such as Indalecia Bravo had donned the red beret to fight disguised as men during the Carlist wars, showing courage and honour in their exploits of action, imprisonment and escape.[57] Carlism's fighting tradition was very much alive. Carmen Villanueva, a popular orator from Pamplona, appealed for votes by calling on youth 'capable of soaking itself in patriotic blood'.[58]

As Villanueva's rhetoric suggests, Carlism had a vexed relationship with democratic legality. The party's militia, the Requeté, effectively substituted for any formal male youth movement, and paramilitary training continued throughout the Republic's existence.[59] The CEDA, however, did have a youth wing, the Juventudes de Acción Popular (JAP), which became increasingly prominent after 1933. The ambivalence of the CEDA's attitude to fascism crystallised in the JAP, which came to exemplify the rapidly blurring line between parliamentary and extreme right. A centralised, uniformed movement, the JAP, like the Requeté, was clearly affected by 'the vertigo of fascism', affecting a half-Roman salute and a khaki shirt.[60] Mass rallies, military march pasts, roll-calls of 'martyrs' and a pronounced leadership cult around Gil Robles combined with a large membership and an ideology of youth, vigour and direct action to make the JAP a more overtly masculinist movement than any yet seen on the parliamentary right.

Traditional notions of the social order rested on age as well as gender hierarchies, and while the idea of paternal authority was never overtly challenged, the role of youth changed fundamentally between 1931 and 1936. Though the JAP was occasionally disciplined by Gil Robles, it accepted this as an act of leadership rather than paternalism. As with the women's groups, political praxis altered, and even subverted, political ideology. While they were ridiculed by their rivals

---

57 'La veterana "Margarita"', *Pensamiento Navarro*, 30 November 1933.

58 *Pensamiento Navarro*, 31 October 1931; for Villanueva see also AHN, Gobernación A, leg. 51, exp. 17 and Gloria Solé Romeo, 'Mujeres carlistas en la república y en la guerra (1931–9): Algunas notas para la historia de las "Margaritas" de Navarra', *Principe de Viana*, 15 (Segundo Congreso General de Historia de Navarra 3) (1993), pp. 581–4.

59 Josep Carles Clemente, *El carlismo: historia de una disidencia social, 1833–1976* (Barcelona, Ariel, 1990), pp. 111–14.

60 The phrase is from Stanley Payne, *Fascism in Spain, 1923–1977* (Wisconsin, University of Wisconsin Press, 1999), p. 48.

in the overtly fascist Falange as 'a sad caricature' and 'cold-cut fascism',[61] the JAP was much less trammelled by bourgeois respectability than were the CEDA women. As girls were already incorporated into the women's groups, their role in the JAP effectively reverted to the ceremonial one of the *madrinas* favoured under the Primo dictatorship. Their rhetoric had changed with the times, with talk of 'enthusiast youth ... before the martyrs of our ideals'.[62] But it was quite clear that only the boys were to display the fighting spirit that informed the JAP's rhetoric. In the Castilian city of Salamanca, for example, a separate girls' section was only established in autumn 1936; at no point before the war did younger women escape the chaperonage of their mothers.[63]

Middle-class convention was undoubtedly more constricting for women than it was for men, as it affected dress, deportment, social relationships and professional opportunities. There were tasks which right-wing women simply could not undertake. This meant that, as street-fighting became increasingly characteristic of Spain's political life, so the public advocacy of adult bourgeois women was eclipsed, even though their practical work continued. The mobilisation of youth was emblematic of the transition from elite to mass politics which was taking place under the Second Republic. The women's sections of the CEDA, like the party itself, were established by political elites, which designated leaders and trained activists who in turn went forth to capture the support of the masses. The CEDA was only populist in that it looked to capture the popular vote, but its youth movement introduced a new dynamic which shifted power to the streets. The same process could be seen in Carlism, but those monarchist groups without any sort of a mass base, like the Alfonsists, were effectively sidelined.

While the right-wing parties did not simply lose control of their members, even the young male ones, or see their leaders sidelined overnight, mobilising youth along quasi-fascist lines created a clear tension within right-wing politics. As the elite groups which ran the parties became divorced from those who were joining them, the crisis of the Spanish right deepened. This was itself a manifestation of the wider crisis of European conservatism. When the Popular Front won

---

61 David Jato, *La rebelión de los estudiantes: apuntes para una historia del alegre SEU* (Madrid, CIES, 1953), p. 99; *F.E.* (Organo de Falange Española), 26 April 1934.
62 Rosarito Román Arroyo (daughter of Abilia), *Gaceta Regional*, 20 February 1934.
63 Ibid, 4 October 1936.

government back for the Republican left in February 1936, the right's response was paralysis. As its youth movement haemorrhaged away and the Comunión Tradicionalista abandoned legalism altogether, the CEDA effectively imploded.

As the parliamentary option collapsed, so the Requeté and the miniscule fascist party, Falange Española, expanded. The Falange – which perhaps best represented the dynamic politics of the radical right – was now recruiting seriously. Formed in 1933 under the leadership of José Antonio Primo de Rivera, son of the dictator, the Falange was made up of groups of young men, many of them friends. Dedicated to the virile politics of fascism, the party emphasised sacrifice, combat and militarism. The commitment to violence meant that José Antonio originally opposed women's entry into the Falange, and the first women to join did so illicitly, as students.[64] The promptings of these few girls, however, led to the establishment of a separate women's section (Sección Femenina), led by José Antonio's sister, Pilar, in a re-run of the familiar pattern of women negotiating active participation within the confines of ideologically determined sex roles.

Mobilising women was, if anything, an even more ambiguous process for the Falange than for other right-wing parties. The SF was explicitly auxiliary to the main (male) party, yet it only existed because of some girls' insistence that they join. The emphasis on discipline and hierarchy meant that the women's leaders were ultimately subordinate to their male superiors. Much of their time was spent sewing. But as well as making the eponymous blue shirts, they also wore them, so becoming the first uniformed female activists on the Spanish right.[65] Falangist women thus achieved a visibility denied to their Carlist or CEDA counterparts. This was enhanced when the party designated the care of those detained by the Republican authorities to be women's work.[66] Yet, this compassionate feminine duty also required masculine virtues such as courage and steadfastness.

---

64 Justina Rodríguez de Viguri substituted an 'o' for the 'a' in her name in order to join: Jato, *Rebelión de los estudiantes*, pp. 52–3.

65 See further Mary Vincent, '*Camisas nuevas*: style and uniformity in the Falange Española, 1933–43', in Wendy Parkins (ed.), *Fashioning the Body Politic: Dress, Gender, Citizenship* (Oxford, Berg, 2002).

66 *FET y de las JONS: la Sección Femenina, Historia y organización* (Madrid, n.p., 1951), pp. 13–14; copy held Archivo Documental de 'Nueva Andadura', Real Academia de la Historia (henceforth ANA) carpeta 1–B.

The Civil War and Franco's 'New State'

After the elections of February 1936, as the Falange's centres were shut down and its leaders arrested, activism outweighed compassion. The Sección Femenina now acted as a conduit between the gaoled leaders and those outside.[67] As the party became clandestine, so women became essential to it, not despite their sex but precisely because of it. Women were less likely to be searched or detained, attracted less suspicion as prison visitors, and generally enjoyed more freedom of movement than their male comrades.[68] They were excluded from street-fighting – as Pilar Primo de Rivera put it, 'the men of the Falange were too much men to involve us in those duties' – but girls had always aided and abetted male violence.[69] They provided cover for street-fights and hid firearms and documents, ferrying guns under their clothing, worried lest an unwitting movement should reveal or trigger them.[70]

Involvement in the Falange could thus be exciting, perhaps especially for those who found social convention constricting. The Falangist medical student who launched a cry of 'Arriba España' in her hospital ward inhabited a different university world from the one in which Pilar Careaga had worn a hat to lectures as if on a society visit.[71] For at least some of the predominately upper-class girls who first joined the Falange, the danger of underground political activity together with the self-conscious virility of fascist 'style' may have had a sexual charge. Some risked social notoriety for the 'cause'. Valladolid's Rosario Pereda, the party's only regular female orator, and Segovia's Angelita Ridruejo, for example, were imprisoned during the 'days of persecution'. Most were not, but their actions were rewritten as examples of courage, action and heroism. During the Civil War many had to escape the revolutionary violence which broke out immediately in Republican-held territory. In Málaga, for example, Carmen Werner escaped on a false Mexican passport, her

67 'Historia de la Sección Femenina escrita por Pilar Primo de Rivera', pp. 10–11, 13; typescript held ANA, carpeta 1-B and published in *Y* (Revista de la mujer nacional-sindicalista), January 1938 – May 1939.

68 Luis Suárez Fernández, *Crónica de la Sección Femenina y su tiempo* (Madrid: Asociación Nueva Andadura, 1993), pp. 28–9.

69 Pilar Primo de Rivera, *Recuerdos de una vida* (Madrid, Dyrsa, 1983), p. 70.

70 'Informe de la camarada Carmen Aramayona', ANA, carpeta 16, doc. 16; 'Historia de la Sección Femenina', p. 28; María Teresa Gallego Méndez, *Mujer, Falange y Franquismo* (Madrid, Taurus, 1983), pp. 20, 25–6.

71 Interview with Carolina Zamora de Pellicer, *Medina* (Semanario de la Sección Femenina) 39 (1941).

hair dyed blond, after her father and brothers were shot by a revolutionary patrol in August.[72] A more formal escape network from the 'red zone', which became known as Auxilio Azul, was gradually established to provide safe passage to foreign embassies. Those credited with its foundation, María Paz Unciti in Madrid and Carmen Tronchoni in Barcelona, were both surprised, detained and shot, one aged eighteen, the other twenty-two.[73]

Like the other fifty-six Falangist women executed or killed at the front, Unciti and Tronchoni were endlessly commemorated after the war. All were awarded posthumous honours, including the 'Y' medal which was commissioned specifically for members of the Sección Femenina. Their hagiographies were conventional, dwelling on their heroic deeds, their resolve and steadfastness, and the exemplary manner of their deaths. It was a point of pride that 'our women have never worn trousers'.[74] Rather, they acted as women, displaying masculine virtues when appropriate but otherwise relying on the dextrousness, abnegation and *simpatía* natural to the female sex.

War work was also defined by this view of women's nature. Unlike their Republican counterparts, Francoist women never took men's jobs. Rather, Sección Femenina members helped supply Falangist militia units – which were not assimilated into the army until after April 1937 – with clothing and blankets. After unification with the Carlists, the Sección Femenina was charged with both the production and the storage of uniforms, employing 20,000 women in its workshops and warehouses. Laundries – which employed a further 1,140 – were established to wash, disinfect and mend soldiers' clothes, carrying out humble, women's duties in the military environment of the battlefront.[75] This female mobilisation, which provided essential services and drew civilians into the war effort, was the Sección Femenina's most substantial contribution to the war.

Female Falangists also staffed hospitals, dining-rooms and soup-kitchens. Such services had previously been the preserve of nuns, and while religious sisters continued to be crucial to welfare provision,

72 'Del 18 de julio a la liberación de Málaga (relato de Carmen Werner entregado en sept. 1987)', ANA, carpeta 57, doc. 5.
73 Hagiographies abound: for example, 'La primera mujer caída en Cataluña por el ideal', *Y*, 14 (March 1939), 34–5; Tomás Borras, *Seis mil mujeres* (Madrid, Editorial Nacional, 1965).
74 '18 de julio', *Medina*, 19 July 1942.
75 'Lavaderos de frente' and '"Mutilada de Guerra"', Sección Femenina de Falange Española Tradicionalista y de las JONS', *Anuario de 1940* (n.p., n.d.), p. 232. Party statistics for war-work quoted Scanlon, *La polémica feminista*, p. 317.

they were now joined by middle-class lay-women. In the administrative uncertainty that characterised the early Francoist war effort, the Falange, aided by its burgeoning membership and distinct identity, was effectively able to claim certain areas of competence as its own. For example, in response to the acute shortage of hospital nurses, official recognition was given to the party's qualifications for nurses. These were clearly deficient – training lasted only a few months – but the party's 8,000 nurses took women into the military for the first time.[76] The provision of nurse training was also a means of out-manoeuvring the Margaritas, who were given nominal charge of 'Hospitals and Fronts' after unification in April 1937.

In other respects, too, the Carlist women were soon eclipsed. Though Urraca Pastor was named national delegate for hospitals, she was substituted in August 1938, and the delegation was disbanded by decree in May 1939.[77] In contrast, the Falangist Auxilio Social went on to become Spain's first systematic welfare service, eventually mobilising 300,000 women. Originally called Auxilio del Invierno (Winter Aid), this was set up in Valladolid early in the war by Mercedes Sanz Bachiller, widow of the Juntas Ofensivas Nacional-Sindicalistas (JONS) leader Onésimo Redondo, who had previously had no official role in the party.[78] Essentially, Sanz Bachiller took an opportunity that presented itself, and the organisation's success cannot have been foreseen. Yet, in Franco's New State, social service for women became the equivalent of military service for men. Auxilio Social thus brought women into the apparatus of the state for the first time.

As well as providing the regime's rudimentary welfare services, Auxilio Social expanded professional opportunities for women, creating new posts for health visitors (*divulgadoras*) and 'social nurses'.[79] Health campaigns for vaccination or infant nutrition then took these new uniformed officials all over the country. When interviewed many years later, it was these new horizons which Sección Femenina

---

76 Letters dated 8 February and 11 April 1937 and 'Orden', ANA, carpeta 16–1, docs. 1, 2, 4. See also Priscilla Scott-Ellis, *The Chances of Death: A Diary of the Spanish Civil War*, ed. Raymond Carr (Norwich, Michael Russell, 1995).

77 Ricardo Chueca, *El fascismo en los comienzos del régimen de Franco: un estudio sobre FET-JONS* (Madrid, Centro de Investigaciones Sociológicos, 1983), p. 246.

78 'Mercedes Sanz-Bachiller', in Paul Preston, *Palomas de guerra: cinco mujeres marcadas por el enfrentamineto bélico'* (Madrid, Plaza y Janés, 2001), pp. 21–96 and Mónica Orduña Prada, *El Auxilio Social, 1936–1940: la etapa fundacional y los primeros años* (Madrid, Escual Libre, 1996).

79 ANA, carpeta 26–1, doc. 3 and *Reglamento: Cuerpo de Enfermeras* (Burgos, n.p., 1938).

activists remembered and saw as validation.[80] They presented their political protagonism as a modernising project, one which improved the lot of Spanish women – a very different perspective from that taken by many historians. Under the Franco regime, the Sección Femenina is usually categorised as Catholic and conservative, preaching the traditional values of submissiveness and decorum, while taking over the Escuela del Hogar's custom of offering practical training in housekeeping.[81]

This domestic discourse seems entirely appropriate to a regime which demobilised hospital nurses the moment the war was won. In the New State, gender became a more powerful signifier of social order and hierarchy than ever before in twentieth-century Spain. Women were again minors before the law, their rights as citizens or Spanish nationals coming from their husbands or fathers. Yet, despite these legal disabilities and what Stanley Payne has termed the relentless conservatism of their discourse, the Sección Femenina became the Falange's most successful component, being the only one to surpass its Italian counterpart in size or role.[82]

It is, of course, paradoxical that a movement which preached the virtues and rewards of marriage and female subservience deployed activists who were single and economically self-sufficient. The rhetoric of domesticity was employed even as the massed cadres of Spain's fascist womanhood marched through the streets on behalf of the *Caudillo*. The style and the aesthetics of the incipient Franco regime were taken directly from the Falange. The visual appearance of the Sección Femenina conveyed conflicting messages yet its uniformed displays put women at the heart of the regime.[83] Both Pilar Primo de Rivera and her organisation played a part in the imagery of the Franco regime which quite escaped the SF's Italian and German counterparts.

---

80 Victoria Lorée Enders, 'Problematic portraits: the ambiguous historical role of the Sección Femenina of the Falange', in Enders and Radcliff (eds), *Constructing Spanish Womanhood*, pp. 375–98.

81 For example, Gallego Méndez, *Mujer, Falange y Franquismo*; Paul Preston, *Comrades: Portraits from the Spanish Civil War* (London, HarperCollins, 1999), pp. 111–39; Rosario Sánchez López, *Mujer española, una sombra de destino de lo universal* (Murcia, Universidad de Murcia, 1990).

82 Payne, *Fascism in Spain*, p. 477; the SF claimed 580,000 members by 1939, ibid, p. 301.

83 Enric Ucelay Da Cal, 'Problemas en la comparación de las dictaduras espñola e italiana en los años trenta y cuarenta', in Elio d'Auria and Jordi Casassas (eds), *El estado moderno en Italia y España* (Barcelona, Universitat de Barcelona, 1992), p. 163.

This cannot be explained simply by the Franco regime's reliance on the politics of display. These were fundamental to the New State, particularly in the period of the 'first Francoism' (1939–1943/5), but they were hardly unique to it, as numerous visual references to Fascist and Nazi spectacle make clear.

Unlike the Axis regimes, Francoist Spain survived the war to reinvent itself as a repository of traditional Catholic values, the 'spiritual reserve of the West'. This downplaying of fascism was appropriate to the post-war European order, but it could not excise the fascist period.[84] Despite Franco's personal conservatism and the religious character of the regime, military victory in the Civil War had depended on modern technology and the mobilisation of a people for battle. Nor was the regime's Catholicism simply reactionary. In the mid twentieth century, divine providence alone could not provide a sufficient or convincing legitimation for a dictatorial regime, particularly not one which used its resources against its own people. Franco's legitimacy depended on mobilising supporters in the streets, filling public spaces with blue-shirted citizens. The regime had, once again, to nationalise the masses.

In demonstrating its own right to rule, particularly against the memory of the Republic, the Franco regime stressed the involvement of women, not against their 'natural' aptitudes and social role but because of them. Women's supposedly apolitical nature allowed them to demonstrate the Franco's regime's natural order, its moral superiority to the Republic, and its compatibility with the essence of traditional Spain. As heir to the right's experience of both mobilising women and insisting on their ideological subservience, the Franco regime continued to develop women's activism. Far from marginalising or suppressing women's political role, the Francoist state made it central to its own legitimacy.

---

84 Explored in Paul Preston, *The Politics of Revenge: Fascism and the Military in Twentieth-Century Spain* (London, Unwin Hyman, 1990).

13

Britain

Martin Durham

When Britain entered the First World War, a number of anti-socialist and ultra-patriotic groups had already come into existence. More emerged during the war itself, and at times the claim circulated that the country's war effort was being sabotaged by enemies within. Ultimately, Germany's defeat and the sheer size of the British Empire precluded the nationalist resentment so crucial to the rise of fascism elsewhere. In other ways, however, the possibilities for the extreme right appeared more promising. The rise of insurgent nationalism within the Empire led to fears that the nation's pre-eminent role in the world was in danger, while at home the industrial unrest which was ultimately to culminate in the 1926 General Strike polarised political opinion and led to the creation of a swathe of organisations committed to the defeat of the unions. The Labour Party, though markedly different from socialist parties on the Continent, still appeared to represent a danger to property, while to its left, the impact of the Russian Revolution, most evident in the emergence of the Communist Party of Great Britain in 1920, was to add an even more frenzied tone to the dark warnings of anti-socialist organisations.

For both socialists and anti-socialists alike, the granting in 1918 of the vote to women over the age of thirty marked a crucial moment in the development of mass politics. Women were organised into separate branches (in the case of the Conservatives) or sections (in the case of Labour) and both parties sought to find a way in which to benefit from women's key role as fund-raisers and canvassers while trying to minimise the tension between the sexes that arose within their ranks. For Labour, this involved, for instance, disputes over whether married women were taking men's jobs, while Conservative women, concerned that they be seen as labouring for a common cause rather than promoting feminist demands, supported a party that lamented that women were leaving the home but 'perhaps even at the eleventh hour' might be won back.[1] It was against this background, then, of industrial conflict, insurgent nationalism and the rise of women's involvement in politics that fascism first emerged in Britain.

The British Fascisti

Established in 1923, the British Fascisti, subsequently the British Fascists (BF), for the remainder of the decade would prove to be the most significant form of British fascism.[2] While determination to stop 'any nonsense from Communists or Socialists' played the central role in its concerns, from early on its propaganda linked the Bolshevik threat to a German Jewish conspiracy [3]

Although men played a crucial role in its leadership, the BF was highly unusual in being founded by a woman who, until her death shortly before its dissolution in 1935, remained of central importance to the organisation. In early 1923 Rotha Lintorn-Orman had placed an advertisement in the leading far-right publication of the time, the *Patriot*, and in the months that followed, men's and women's units of the organisation spread across the country, with the women being particularly involved in the provision of first aid, the organisation of canteens and the driving of vehicles.[4] A number of prominent women in the organisation had only a few years earlier engaged in just such activities as part of the war effort. Lintorn-Orman had served with the

1 G. E. Maguire, *Conservative Women: A History of Women and the Conservative Party, 1874–1997* (Basingstoke, Macmillan, 1998), pp. 75, 77, 79, 81; P. Graves, *Labour Women: Women in British Working-Class Politics 1918–1939* (Cambridge, Cambridge University Press, 1994), pp. 23, 115, 128, 157–8; D. Jarvis, 'The Conservative Party and the politics of gender, 1900–1939', in M. Francis and I. Zweiniger-Bargielowska (eds), *The Conservatives and British Society, 1880-1990* (Cardiff, University of Wales Press, 1996), p. 176; B. Campbell, *The Iron Ladies: Why Do Women Vote Tory?* (London, Virago, 1987), p. 53.

2 Estimates of British Fascists membership in the mid 1920s greatly differ, from as low as a 'few thousand' to as high as 150,000. For the problems of a reliable estimate, see T. Linehan, *British Fascism 1918–39* (Manchester, Manchester University Press, 2000), pp. 152–4; K. Lunn, 'The ideology and impact of the British Fascists in the 1920s', in T. Kushner and K. Lunn (eds), *Traditions of Intolerance: Historical Perspectives on Fascism and Race Discourse in Britain* (Manchester, Manchester University Press, 1989), pp. 145–6.

3 *People*, 25 October 1923; *Fascist Bulletin*, 20 June 1925, 12 September 1925.

4 *Bulletin* (April 1925); R. B. D. Blakeney, 'British Fascism', *Nineteenth Century and After* (January 1925), p. 139.

Women's Reserve Ambulance, then with the Scottish Women's Hospital Corps. The Vice-President of the Scottish Women's Units, Mrs Hamilton More Nesbitt, had been an inspector in the Women's Police Service, while the County Commander of Women's Units in Yorkshire, Lady Downe, had been in charge of the Royal Flying Corps Auxiliary Hospital. While women's wartime activities had on occasion been argued in terms of their equal claims to citizenship, they had often been explicitly seen as auxiliary to those undertaken by men, and in the BF, too, women's units were seen as performing an auxiliary function. Indeed, in 1924 Lintorn-Orman laid down that with certain exceptions, when the need for mobilisation arose women officers were to place themselves and their units under the command of men of the same rank.[5] As we will discuss later, women were crucial to the organisation's intervention in the General Strike. But its preparations for industrial confrontation were only part of women's activity within the BF. Two other areas were particularly important - the Fascist Children's Clubs and Special Patrols.

The Children's Clubs were created in 1925, and by March 1926 the Assistant Director of Women's Units was reporting that around forty had been set up with a total membership of almost 3,000.[6] 'We started teaching them to salute the Flag, and then got busy on games', one article reported, noting 'the look of happiness on every child's face, as they went away fortified with a stick of Fascist rock or an orange'. In this combination of patriotism and play, the clubs were intended as a barrier to a development that the BF saw as particularly pernicious, 'the Socialist corruption of the minds of the British children'.[7] The BF's pamphlet on the subject drew little distinction between Labour activists' involvement in Socialist Sunday Schools, the Proletarian and Communist Sunday Schools organised by groups to Labour's left, and efforts by followers of the Theosophist and former Fabian Annie Besant to attract the young to a heady mixture of occultism and internationalism. All of these, the pamphlet declared,

5 B. S. Farr, *The Development and Impact of Right-Wing Politics in Britain 1903-1932* (New York, Garland, 1987), p. 55; R. M. Douglas, *Feminist Freikorps: The British Voluntary Women Police, 1914-1940* (Westport, CT Praeger, 1999), pp. 20, 106; *Fascist Bulletin* (1 May 1926); *Blackshirt* (12 June 1937); R. Robert, 'Gender, class, and patriotism: women's paramilitary units in First World War Britain', *International History Review*, 19:1 (1997), 52-65; *British Fascist Bulletin* (October 1924).

6 *Fascist Bulletin*, 13 June 1925, 27 March 1926.

7 Ibid., 13 February 1926; *British Lion*, 9 October 1926.

were opposed to Christianity and patriotism, and the Fascist Children's Clubs needed to be established in every area where 'anti-British feeling' existed.[8] In this women played the leading role, but men too could play a part. Thus in the case of West Kensington it was reported that three male activists had helped the Women's Units, while another article noted that 'Our helpers are drawn from all classes, hard-working East End mothers, city men, business girls and school teachers who are cheerfully giving up some of their scant hours of leisure, or society girls who have put off a dance or theatre engagement'.[9]

If the Children's Clubs existed in a number of localities, so did the Special Patrols. In Birmingham the 1925 programme of events included infantry drill, a lecture on ju jitsu, a talk on how to tend injuries in a street accident or riot, and a lecture on 'The perfect woman fascist', while the London Patrol sold papers, organised meetings and distributed leaflets to theatre queues and outside factories.[10] They also, one writer noted, were involved in what was described as 'Special Duty', but what it entailed, she went on, could not be revealed. What this might have been remains uncertain. We know that London Special Patrol members were trained to steward meetings and remove female opponents. 'The work of the Women's Special Patrol was admirable!', one report declared. 'The way they seized the female hooligans! The way they "outed" them!' But where this use of force was publicly acknowledged by the BF, a government report on the organisation described it as disrupting left-wing meetings, and it may be that such patriotic sorties were the kind of duty that members of its patrols sought to keep secret.[11]

These were not the only activities in which BF women engaged. In 1924, at a London Women's Units meeting, its Director of Social Propaganda emphasised the importance of insisting on only buying Empire products, and in 1928 the paper noted its support for the work of a League of Empire Housewives.[12] In 1925 the Assistant Director

8 British Fascists, *The 'Red Menace' to British Children* (London, British Fascists, n.d., 1927), pp. 2–11.
9 *Fascist Bulletin*, 13 February 1926.
10 Ibid., 12 September 1925, 27 February 1926; *British Lion* (June 1927) and 32 (1929).
11 *British Lion* 32 (1929), (20 November 1926); J. V. Gottlieb, *Feminine Fascism: Women in Britain's Fascist Movement, 1923–1945* (London, I. B. Tauris, 2000), p. 26.
12 *British Fascist Bulletin* (August 1924); *British Lion* 25 (1928).

of Women's Units called on women members to take part in another area of activity. 'We want to get a great scheme of social work going all over the country', she declared, 'we want to make our Fascist badge known everywhere, as something that stands for practical good and practical help then you'll find there won't be much Communism in the country.'[13] In order to raise funds and encourage camaraderie, women organised social events, while in 1925 a camp was initiated 'on service lines in order to accustom Women Fascists to discipline, camp routine, and the organisation of a community under canvas or in huts'. The camp reportedly came under attack from Communists but it was held again in 1926, 1927 and 1928, in the second case culminating with a performance entitled 'The spirit of fascism through the ages'.[14]

If Communist insurrection or general strike were the two crises for which the BF prepared, the coming of the latter in 1926 was to deal a grievious blow to the organisation. When, during the previous year, it became increasingly clear that the newly created Conservative government was preparing to defeat a general strike, the BF both sought to work with other right-wing groups and approached the government and chief constables to offer its services. The government, however, refused to accept the BF's assistance unless the organisation dropped any claim to function as independent units with their own officers. For some leading members this was acceptable, but for Lintorn-Orman and others it was not, and in April 1926 a number of activists broke away to form the Loyalists, a group which accepted the government's conditions. The following month, the Women's Units in Scotland broke away to form the Scottish Women Loyalists. The BF Women's Units, despite the government's stance, did play a part in the General Strike, with members driving vehicles, acting as special police officers, staffing canteens and distributing a daily news sheet.[15] But the departure of the Loyalists and, it should be emphasised, the fact that the general strike had been defeated were profoundly damaging to the BF, which would never again enjoy the following it had had when fear of industrial confrontation was at its height.

---

13 *Bulletin* (May 1925); *Edinburgh Evening News*, 2 April 1925.
14 *Bulletin* (April 1925); *Fascist Bulletin*, 15 August 1925, 31 October 1925, 20 February 1926, 12 June 1926; *British Lion* (October–November 1927), 25 (1928).
15 Farr, *Development of Right-Wing Politics*, pp. 57–60; R. Benewick, *The Fascist Movement in Britain* (London, Allen Lane: The Penguin Press, 1972), pp. 35–6; *Fascist Bulletin*, 29 May 1926.

In its diminished state, the BF, which had also experienced a split earlier in the decade, attempted to forge links with others on the extreme right. In what seems a distinctly unpropitious alliance for a group in which women's involvement was so emphasised, it established close links with one group, the Unity Band, which despite trying to set up its own women's section took a fiercely patriarchal stance in which men had a 'sacred trust' to preserve 'the true womanly ideal'. The alliance failed and ultimately financial ruin was to lead to the BF's demise.[16] But, as our reference to the Unity Band should remind us, we have focused on what women did in the BF while so far saying very little about the organisation's views on gender.

In 1927 one of its leading members, Nesta Webster, attacked the proposal to lower the voting age for women to twenty-one. 'The Socialists', she declared, 'have only to promise the mill and factory girls silk stockings and an easy life to get their votes.' General Blakeney, the movement's second President (and subsequent leader of the Loyalists), declared the previous year that socialism relied on the lowering of national morals and a stimulation of 'excitement, effeminacy, and all the nasty sex nonsense' to undermine society. 'Let us', he had gone on, 'wage implacable war on nastiness of every description, whether it be lack of true patriotism ... or effeminacy in men, or lack of feminacy in women.'[17] Yet what is most interesting with the BF is how little it addressed the subject. It did not speak with one voice on the extension of the vote to young women, and as the 1929 General Election approached, one of its writers argued that new woman voters would vote patriotically. Like others on the right of the time, it propagated the remarkable canard that the Bolsheviks had declared women to be collective property, and towards the end of its life, when the organisation was increasingly influenced by National Socialism, it called for the banning of cohabitation between white women and 'coloured men'.[18] But when we turn to the 1930s, we will be struck by how much was said about gender by British fascists. For the group that first took the name, women were undeniably important as both rank-and-file members and leaders. As a subject for propaganda, however, gender was almost wholly eclipsed by the issues of property and empire that underpinned its emergence and its development.

16 Farr, *Development of Right-Wing Politics*, pp. 56, 78; *Patriot*, 20 March 1930.
17 *British Lion* (May 1927); *Fascist Bulletin*, 20 March 1926.
18 *British Lion* 29 (1929); *Fascist Bulletin*, 20 June 1925; *British Fascism* Special Summer Propaganda Number (1933).

The Brititish Union of Fascists

By the early 1930s, it was not industrial unrest but mass unemployment and the Depression that was to give a very different fascist movement the chance to emerge. Where the BF had been entwined with the Conservative Party, the British Union of Fascists (BUF), the dominant group of the 1930s, developed out of a breakaway from the Labour Party. Resigning from the Labour government in 1930, Sir Oswald Mosley created the New Party to carry forward his proposals for economic restructuring. Politically ill-defined, while showing some fascist characteristics, the party was electorally humiliated the following year and Mosley decided to create an explicitly fascist organisation. After a brief alliance with the Conservative press-baron Lord Rothermere, which in part broke down due to the BUF's growing anti-Semitism, the movement sought to project itself as a revolutionary force opposed to the party system as a whole. Changing its name later in the decade to the British Union of Fascists and National Socialists, usually shortened to British Union, the BUF's opposition to the Second World War and intelligence reports on secret meetings between different groupings on the extreme right were to lead in 1940 to the internment of many of its key figures and the banning of the organisation.[19] Like the BF before it, it attracted some support from within the aristocracy and it was also successful in recruiting some former Conservatives. But it was more radical than the group of the 1920s on a number of counts, ranging from its elaborate scheme for a corporate state to its deliberate use of anti-capitalist and patriotic socialist rhetoric. This radicalism, although not without ambiguities, also applied to its stance on gender.

The creation of the BUF in October 1932 was followed six months later by the establishment of its Women's Section. Its organiser, Lady Makgill, was subsequently to write of 'the wonderful response of women all over the country' to the launch of the Section. 'We had then a few dozen women scattered about the country who were anxious to help the splendid young men supporters of Fascism.' One year on, she noted, there were 'Women's Branches in seventy-five per cent. of the districts where the Men's Branches are established; in some places they have separate Branches of their own'.[20]

19 While BF membership figures remain obscure, the evidence is clearer for the BUF, which reached between 40,000 and 50,000 in mid-1934 and then fell away dramatically before reviving to nearly 20,000 by the outbreak of war. R. Thurlow, *Fascism in Britain: A History, 1918-1985* (Oxford, Basil Blackwell, 1985), pp. 122–5.
20 *Fascist Week*, 23–9 March 1934.

Soon after, however, she was replaced amidst allegations of corruption, only for her successor, Mary Richardson, to be replaced first by Mosley's mother, Maud Lady Mosley, and then by two women, Anne Brock Griggs and Olga Shore, responsible for the organisation of women in the south and the north of the country respectively. In 1937 Griggs took on responsibility for the country as a whole and in 1940 she was replaced by the last Chief Women's Organiser before the dissolution of the organisation, Olive Hawks.[21] In addition to the turnover in the leadership of women's work, one of the most important developments concerning the Women's Section was the short career of its duplicated fortnightly newsletter, *The Woman Fascist*. Established in March 1934, it was initially described as dealing with 'news and problems peculiar to women members. The first issue contains an article on fascism and religion, branch news and some practical hints for women Fascists'. In September 1934, however, Lady Mosley announced that in future news of Women's Section activity and articles by and for women would appear in the BUF's weekly publication, the *Blackshirt*. *The Woman Fascist*, she suggested, did not reflect the importance of women's work, and given the vital need for men and women to work together, there should be no 'publication that might even suggest a separate existence'.[22]

Judging from extracts which appeared in the *Blackshirt* (only one issue of the newsletter is known to have survived), it had been at pains to emphasise the importance of co-operation between the genders. Plainly, however, this had not been enough to ensure its survival, and a closer examination of the BUF gives a number of clues as to why the issue should have been so difficult.[23]

The launch of the BUF had been marked by the appearance of Mosley's book on fascism, *The Greater Britain*. In a brief discussion of women, he noted that it had been claimed that in concentrating on the organisation of men, the movement had failed to give attention to the organisation of women. But if the movement was newly formed, how could any such criticism have been made? Although not stated in *The Greater Britain*, it would appear that the reference is not to the BUF at all but to its immediate predecessor, the New Party. As a book on the party had noted the previous year, arguments had broken

---

21 Public Record Office (PRO), HO144/20140/112; *Blackshirt*, 7 September 1934; *Action*, 21 November 1936, 13 February 1937, 20 March 1937; PRO HO283/13/65; A. W. B. Simpson, *In the Highest Degree Odious: Detention Without Trial in Wartime Britain* (Oxford, Clarendon Press, 1992), pp. 176–7.

22 *Blackshirt*, 23–29 March 1934, 7 September 1934.

23 Ibid., 6 and 20 July 1934.

out in its youth organisation as to whether or not women should be recruited, and members who objected to the decision to restrict it to males had compared the result to Nazism. In his later discussion, Mosley argued that while the focus had to be on men in the movement, this was not due to a failure to recognise women's importance. Instead, he claimed, it was because opposition took a violent form, something to which women should not be exposed.[24] This, however, was not a view that long survived. In February 1934 the *Blackshirt* reported that special Propaganda Patrol squads had been formed under the control of Miss Phyllis Davies and Miss Marjorie Aitken to sell literature and 'undertake other propaganda work as necessity arises'. In May, another of the BUF's papers, the *Fascist Week*, announced that the ban on women holding outdoor meetings had been lifted and that in South London a Women's Defence Force led by Miss M. Aitken was providing women stewards for meetings addressed by women speakers.[25] The following year, the first anniversary dinner of what was now described as the Special Propaganda Section (SPS) appeared in the pages of the *Blackshirt*:

> Miss Marjorie Aitken gave an interesting if somewhat unconventional account of what later became the SPS. It was interesting for those present to look back on the early days of the British Union of Fascists, and to remember how six women set forth to build up a Women's Defence Force, with little, save their own convictions and determination to serve the movement, to encourage them. From this nucleus has grown the most active branch of the Women's Section.

What might have been meant in describing Aitken's account as 'unconventional' remains unclear, although the fact that the officer in charge of the overall BUF Defence Force, Eric Hamilton Piercy, had been a vehement opponent of women being allowed to join the New Party youth organisation is highly suggestive in light of Aitken's allusion to the lack of encouragement the Women's Defence Force's founders had initially received. The use at one stage of a different name, Special Patrol, suggests another interesting possibility, that there was a continuity between at least some of the women in the BF and the BUF. We know that the BF formally removed honours previously awarded to a number of male and female members as a result of disagreement over whether or not to amalgamate with the new organisation. But while some men are

24 Oswald Mosley, *The Greater Britain* (London, BUF, 1932), pp. 40–1; C. F. Melville, *The Truth About the New Party* (London, Wishart and Co., 1931), p. 41.
25 *Blackshirt*, 23 February–1 March 1934; *Fascist Week*, 25 May 1934.

known to have crossed over to the BUF, no evidence has been unearthed that any women in the BF Special Patrol did so.[26]

This was not the only way in which the organisation of women in the BUF resembled the BF. The BUF set up children's clubs, emphasised women's role in fund-raising and organised women's camps.[27] But in other ways the two organisations were different. One crucial distinction was the emphasis on women as canvassers. The BF, which supported the Conservative Party, had played little role in electoral politics. The BUF, however, was committed to the election of a Fascist government and in January 1935 announced proposals for a reorganisation of the movement, whereby members would either be in uniformed Blackshirt Units or part of a separate political organisation. The latter was to be responsible for 'all existing women's organisations', which were expected to engage in constituency activity immediately. As comments in later issues of the *Blackshirt* made clear, the proposals caused some concern among women members and Mosley found it necessary to assure them that women would both retain their right to belong to Blackshirt Units and be eligible to be parliamentary candidates. But while plans to launch a separate political organisation were ultimately discarded, the belief that women were crucial for electoral work was retained.[28]

While the BUF saw a vital role for women in seeking to cultivate support on the doorstep, it envisaged other roles too. In an early account of the creation of the Women's Section, it was reported that either a class for prospective speakers or a study circle to discuss policy was the most important class in women activists' week and that a 'sound knowledge of Fascism' was essential if women were to be able to canvass effectively. The Propaganda Patrol was also crucial, and it was hoped that 'similarly trained groups of girls' would be set up 'in every branch in the country'. But there was much else to do, from selling literature and painting placards to helping in canteens and providing entertainment. 'Whatever your talent, there is a place for you in the Fascist Movement!'[29]

Later articles outlined other roles. One suggested that while some

26 *Blackshirt*, 3 May 1935; Benewick, *Fascist Movement*, p. 115; *T.N.T.* (July 1932); *British Fascism* Special Summer Propaganda Number (1933).
27 *Blackshirt*, 1 June 1934, 29 November 1935, 4 September 1937; *Action*, 27 August 1938.
28 *Blackshirt*, 18 January 1935, 1 February 1935, 22 March 1935, 24 May 1935, 27 March 1937.
29 Ibid., 1 June 1934.

women could sell papers on the streets, others could loan a room for
meetings, make goods for sale or keep the district headquarters 'clean
and in order'. Another proposed that as members of local organisations, from parents' groups in schools and co-operative societies to
women's institutes and women's citizens' associations, women
members could 'inspire a solid resistance' to Bolshevism.[30] Where the
BF had believed that the Soviet Union would attack Britain, the BUF
feared that conflict would break out with Nazi Germany. This was
crucial for the most distinctive of all the roles the BUF gave to women
- that of peace campaigner. As 'the givers of life', one leading BUF
woman declared in early 1938, women hated war. British mothers
were demonstrating for peace, another leading woman declared later
in the year. All over the country, she claimed, women were carrying
placards announcing that once they had been Labour, or Tory, or
Liberal, but now they followed Mosley for peace and security.[31]

The coming of war, rather than ending BUF women's anti-war
activity, intensified it. With the calling up of men up to thirty, the
organisation declared at the beginning of 1940 that women members
needed to 'work harder than ever' to bring the message of peace to
the women of Britain. A Women's Peace Campaign was launched,
and money was urgently solicited to cover the costs of meetings,
leaflets and posters. 'MR. CHURCHILL wants a million women to
prepare destruction and death for the world; he wants them to take the
places in civilian life of men who are then to be herded to the slaugh-
ter. Against this archaic remnant of a barbarous world, British Union
calls to the women of Britain to work for Peace – "new worlds are
born of life, not of death".' That the BUF should deploy a vocabu-
lary that not only identified women with peace but identified fascism
with it as well takes us some distance from assuming that such movements must always be bellicose and prioritise the role of the male
warrior. Nor is the only way in which the BUF is somewhat surprising. Its policies on women and work too are not what we might
expect.[32]

In 1932, Mosley argued in *The Greater Britain* that women's role
in the corporate state would be of considerable importance. Women
in the professions and in industry would be represented through the
relevant corporations, while the great majority of women who had
chosen 'the important career of motherhood' would be represented as

30 *Action*, 25 June 1938, 28 January 1939.
31 Ibid., 26 March 1938, 8 October 1938.
32 Ibid., 18 January 1940, 25 January 1940, 1 February 1940.

mothers. At present, he declared, their only representatives were professional women politicians whose sole idea was 'to escape from the normal sphere of women and to translate themselves into men'. Under Fascism, however, 'the normal woman and mother' would be 'one of the main pillars of the State'.[33]

These views were further expressed in a pamphlet, *Blackshirt Policy*, which appeared in 1934. While not treating 'women purely as mothers of the race', Mosley declared, they did perform this role and as such Fascism was vitally interested in their welfare. Women who chose to pursue an industrial or professional career would be free to do so, and the present conflict between the sexes would be ended by ensuring that there were 'enough jobs to go round'. Barriers to women's employment would be lifted and equal pay introduced. But those who 'desire to follow the great career of Home and children' would no longer be forced to leave their interests in the hands of a small number of women MPs, most of whom were 'elderly spinsters' whose knowledge of family life was less than that of the average married man. Instead, 'normal women' would be directly represented in Parliament and a Corporation of Motherhood. Socialists had long declared that housewives could teach the Chancellor of the Exchequer 'a thing or two'. Now Fascism, the pamphlet claimed, would make this a reality.[34]

Where equal pay had been absent from the views set out in *The Greater Britain*, other themes were to be found in both. Motherhood, seen as incompatible with a career outside the home, was privileged over female employment, but the BUF insisted that it did not oppose women's presence in industry or the professions. Women MPs were denounced as unfit to represent the 'normal' woman, but a specific representation, both for those women in paid employment and those in the home, was characterised as a key feature of Fascism. Pulled in different directions and articulated in different ways, the Fascist argument was remarkably ambiguous. At times it could appear surprisingly sympathetic to women's rights. At other points, however, it displayed exactly the characteristics its opponents alleged.

One local BUF publication, the *West London Regional Bulletin*, exemplified just such a 'traditionalist' approach. Many women members, it declared in April 1934, were uncertain as to women's role. They rightly felt that they could not help in most of the movement's activities, but they could produce and rear children, and this

33 Mosley, *Greater Britain*, pp. 41–2.
34 O. Mosley, *Blackshirt Policy* (London, BUF Publications, 1934), pp. 49–52.

is what Fascism expected of them. If they did not want to 'fulfill their natural functions', Fascism would not force them. But Fascists' duty was to serve the state, and for most women this meant bearing children.[35]

The previous month another article had appeared in the pages of the *Fascist Week*. Writing under the pseudonym 'Senex', the author noted that women were beginning to ask how they could help the movement. Mosley had 'denied the lie, invented by hostile propaganda, that Fascism is a purely masculine cult in which women have no part except to serve men'. But while some women were suited to be speakers, 'the average woman' was not; 'her duty and her inclinations alike keep her at home, looking after the children, cooking the family dinner'. Many were 'good cooks and providers', but there were, however, 'many shirkers among us in these days of canned food, ready-made cakes and cheap restaurants'. Nor was this the only area in which women were failing in their responsibilities. Some were 'frittering away' the family's earnings on 'sheer rubbish ... chiefly of foreign manufacture' and 'Far too many women consider it their privilege to be ill ... just ill enough to pamper themselves and evade their proper share of the family work'. Fascism was 'a tough creed', and if applied in the home, would make life better for this generation and the next.[36]

A subsequent letter by a woman Fascist attacked the article for seeking to deprive women of their recent gains. The article, the editor replied, had been written not by a man, as the complainant had assumed, but by a woman, and the existence of such sentiments among other women in the movement was illustrated by an article that appeared in the *Blackshirt* later in the year. Written by Jenny Linton, the BUF women's organiser for Aberdeen, and entitled 'Fascist women do not want equal rights with men. They desire only the true woman's place in the community', it declared that for women to claim equal rights was to put their happiness at risk. There was 'no place in Fascism for the militant woman, and in daily contact with the true Fascists she would readily find that she had made her life very uncomfortable'. Fascists wanted 'a happy and agreeable relationship between men and women', and sought to restore men's 'chivalrous care over "the weaker sex"'.[37]

---

35 *West London Regional Bulletin*, 5 April 1934.
36 *Fascist Week*, 16 March 1934.
37 Ibid., 23 March 1934; *Blackshirt*, 2 November 1934, 18–24 May 1934.

As we will discuss later, the period in which Linton's article appeared was marked by a dispute over Fascism's stance towards women in which those she described as 'militant' women and 'true Fascists' fell into bitter conflict and a number of the militants left the movement. It may well be that her article was a direct reference to these internal frictions, but this should not be taken to indicate that her position was victorious. Instead, the nominally egalitarian but deeply ambiguous view expressed by Mosley continued to define the movement's stance, but how its ambiguities played out in different articles and pamphlets demonstrated the existence – and persistence – of a range of views within the BUF.

This was particularly evident in discussions of equal pay. We noted earlier the closure of *The Woman Fascist* despite its insistence on the importance of co-operation between men and women. Writing at the end of 1933, its future editor, Elizabeth Winch, argued that 'many unthinking women' appeared to believe that to describe Fascism as wanting women's return to the home was a matter for condemnation. But when prosperity returned, as it would under Fascism, then women would indeed be able to 'look after their children, and administer to their husbands'. Women were currently employed because they were cheaper than men, but with equal pay, the men who had been denied jobs could now afford to marry while the women who had been forced to earn their living would have the security of marriage. Earlier in the year, the *Blackshirt* had published an imaginary conversation on the subject, in which equal pay was described as probably leading to 'a lot of women displaced from situations of work', but 'in the long run', it cheerfully continued, this would 'cancel itself out' since men would now be able to afford to marry and the necessity for the women they wed to go out to work would disappear.[38]

If some BUF writers envisaged equal pay facilitating married women's departure from the workforce, there were also suggestions that once women ceased to be cheap labour, only those jobs for which they were particularly suited would be effectively available to them. This latter argument could be found, for instance, espoused by one of the BUF's leading figures, Alexander Raven Thomson. Equal pay, he declared in the BUF's pamphlet on the corporate state, would both 'prevent the undercutting of men by women in industry, and lead to a more truly functional discrimination between the sexes, women

---

38 *Fascist Week*, 29 December 1933 – 4 January 1934; *Blackshirt*, 23–9 March 1934, 19-25 August 1933.

doing the work for which they are best suited and men likewise'. In an account of a training class for women speakers in 1933, the *Fascist Week* described a speech on 'women's rights under Fascism' which linked the two issues together. The higher wages that a corporate state would bring about, the speaker argued, would make it possible for families to live on the male wage while equal pay would ensure that women worked in the jobs 'ideally suited' to them and vacated those 'that are more suitable for men'.[39]

But if in some interpretations women's sphere within the labour force would be diminished by both departure and occupational differentiation, other BUF pronouncements had very different emphases. Indeed, despite explicitly describing itself as National Socialist in the latter part of the decade, some of the most seemingly favourable views towards women's employment were to appear in the late 1930s. A later edition of Thomson's pamphlet, in addition to dropping the comment on why equal pay was desired, also pledged that under Fascism the practice that presently existed of sacking women from certain jobs upon marriage would be ended, and where Olive Hawks was arguing in 1934 that a woman would not have to return home if she did not wish to and could remain employed and unmarried, five years later she was arguing that 'the purely personal factor of marriage' should not be seen as disqualifying women from working outside the home. Indeed, for another BUF woman, Agnes Booth, it was evident that 'every woman is not a born home-maker', and Fascism should not make her choose between staying at home and remaining unmarried. Instead, through their combined earnings, she and her husband could employ a woman who did enjoy home-making, and not just two but three people could find happiness.[40]

In the early version of his pamphlet, Thomson had argued that feminists were mistaken in believing Fascism saw women only as 'breeders of "cannon fodder"', and, contrary to our expectations, the organisation put considerable effort into trying to persuade feminists that it represented no danger to women's rights. Writing in 1938, one writer, Phylise Aldridge, claimed that National Socialism would realise feminist ideals, while a male author, E. D. Hart, declared his sympathy for the 'gallant struggle' of the suffragettes, and one note-

39 A. R. Thomson, *The Corporate State* (London, BUF Publications, n.d., c.1934), p. 43; *Fascist Week*, 17–23 November 1933.
40 A. R. Thomson, *The Coming Corporate State* (London, Action Press, n.d., c.1937), p. 26; *Blackshirt*, 24 August 1934; *Action*, 11 February 1939, 26 March 1938.

worthy characteristic of the BUF was the prominent role played in its activities by former suffragettes.[41] The BF too had success in this area, not only recruiting in Scotland Mrs More Nesbitt, who had been a suffragette before joining the Women's Police Service, but organising a London meeting in 1926 in which an eyewitness account of the horrors of Soviet Russia was presented by another former suffragette, Nina Boyle. Later that year, during the General Strike, BF women were enrolled in More Nesbitt's former organisation, which was now known as the Women's Auxiliary Service, and was led by another former suffragette, Mary Allen. In 1933 Allen was in touch with the BF and the following year spoke at meetings organised by the BUF. Indeed, there is a considerable coincidence of aims between the declaration made by Lintorn-Orman in 1934 that in the event of either foreign attack or civil war, BF Women's Units stood ready to drive vehicles, work in canteens and deal with gas attacks and Allen's creation of a Women's Reserve the previous year to provide transport, canteens and anti-gas instruction. But neither Allen nor Boyle joined the BF. It was the BUF that was to win Allen's support. More importantly, the BUF broke new ground in depicting itself as the culmination of the pre-war suffrage struggle.[42]

Allen, who only officially joined the BUF after the outbreak of war, although it has been suggested she was secretly involved far earlier, did not draw attention to her suffragette past in the material she wrote for the BUF press. Her friend and a member from shortly after its inception, Norah Elam, had no such reluctance. In a 1935 article, 'Fascism, women and democracy', she argued that those who fought for the vote had not done so for self-interest but because they recognised that the nation had to draw on the talents of both men and women. Only by 'co-operation in the corporate body of the state' could economic insecurity or foreign policy be properly dealt with, and in acknowledging this, 'the women's struggle resembles closely the new philosophy of Fascism'. Nor, she claimed, was this the only commonality between the two movements. Militant women had come from all classes and parties, they followed their Leader devotedly and had faced 'the brutality of the streets' and 'the loneliness of the prison cell'. In all this, they resembled the new movement. Fascism, she

---

41 Thomson, *Corporate State*, p. 43; *Action*, 11 June 1938; *Blackshirt*, 8 January 1938.

42 Douglas, *Feminist Freikorps*, p. 90; *Fascist Bulletin*, 30 January 1926; *British Fascism* (June 1934); M. S. Allen, *Lady in Blue* (London, Stanley Paul & Co., 1936), pp. 272–5.

held, would ensure that women enjoyed an equal status with men,
enabling them to 'direct and control the conditions under which they
shall live', and in this it would 'complete the work begun on their
behalf by the militant women from 1906 to 1914'.[43]

In 1940, when the government moved against the BUF, women
members were among those taken into custody. Allen was interro-
gated but not held. Elam was interned. The third suffragette member
of the BUF was not the subject of such attentions, and for good
reason. A member before either Allen or Elam, Mary Richardson
had already broken with the organisation. A socialist in the 1920s
and subsequently a member of the New Party, she joined the BUF
in late 1933 and, as we have noted, was subsequently appointed as
the organiser of the Women's Section. In June 1934 she appeared
in the pages of the *Blackshirt* defending the organisation's policies
against the former suffragette and anti-fascist Sylvia Pankhurst. 'I
was first attracted to the Blackshirts', she declared, 'because I saw
in them the courage, the action, the loyalty, the gift of service,
and the ability to serve which I had known in the Suffragette movement.' In November 1935, however, she wrote to a trade union
official embroiled in a slander action brought by the BUF's leader
that she had been expelled from the organisation 'for daring, with
other women, to put forward demands to the great Mosley, whereby
women would receive *some* measure of fair play. All the best women
left when I was expelled.' The following month a local newspaper,
the *Welwyn Times*, reported that the Honorary Secretary of a local
anti-war group, Miss Mary Richardson, had described at its meeting
how she had joined the BUF believing that it supported women's
equality and rejected anti-Semitism, only to find 'hypocrisy ... from
top to bottom' of the organisation. Mosley, she declared, had only
accepted women into his movement because Mussolini had told him
he would never succeed without them, and after her expulsion for
'attempting to organise a protest', she had told him: 'You will never
succeed in England because you have insulted the women'. Shortly
after this, Anne Brock Griggs replied, arguing that women would
have equality of pay and opportunity under Fascism and chastising
Richardson for engaging in 'personal criticism' of Mosley. It was
'Jewish sources', she proclaimed, who were particularly to blame
for claims that women's status would suffer under Fascism. Replying
in turn, Richardson argued that women in the BUF received less

43 PRO, HO144/21933/467; *Action*, 21 November 1936; *Fascist Quarterly* (July
   1935).

remuneration than men and that the Women's Section had been reduced from employing over thirty women in its own headquarters to occupying one room in the men's headquarters where the only woman official was assisted by 'a motley of casual voluntary helpers'. Forty women had gathered in her home the previous spring to protest 'against the unjust treatment of women in the B.U.F.', and one of the most vociferous in demanding a deputation be sent to Mosley, she declared, was Griggs herself.[44]

If Richardson's departure appears to have passed almost unnoticed, another departure was noted by the *Blackshirt*. In February 1935 a London daily paper, the *Star*, reported that the BUF Women's Organiser for North West London, Mrs H. Carrington Wood, had resigned her post because she had realised she had been wrong to believe in Mosley. 'It is my firm conviction', she declared, 'that under Fascism women will be infinitely worse off.' She had 'fought unavailingly for the equality of women within the Blackshirt movement', and had sent Mosley a memorandum stating that 'The promises made on Fascist platforms and in Fascist literature are inadequate to appease the anxiety of the women folk, who naturally do not want to risk going back to where they were before the days of the Suffragettes'. The *Blackshirt* in reply insisted that Carrington Wood had not resigned but been expelled and subsequently published a long article in which the author, identified only as 'an Old Suffragette', denounced the former organiser's 'exploitation' of the suffragettes' sacrifices. But the dispute did not die out. Writing in the *Hampstead and Highgate Express* the following month, Carrington Wood declared that she had become 'sadly disillusioned' with the BUF and that while women wanted equality of pay and opportunity, the only equality she had seen in the movement was 'the equal right to work and serve'. In response to the appearance in January of a scheme to reorganise the BUF, 'several women met at the house of one of the members to discuss proposals which would ensure the advancement under Fascism of the position of women in this country. It was then decided that four of the participants would go to Sir Oswald Mosley ... with a petition. The holding of this meeting became known at the

---

44 H. Kean, 'A suffrage autobiography: a study of Mary Richardson – suffragette socialist, fascist', in C. Eustace, J. Ryan and C. Ugolini (eds), *A Suffrage Reader* (London, Leicester University Press, 2000), p. 179; *Blackshirt*, 29 June 1934; *Fascist Week*, 22–28 December 1933; M. Richardson, letter to Mr Marchbank, 1 November 1935 Modern Records Centre, University of Warwick, MSS 127/NUI/GS/3/5D; *Welwyn Times* (19 December 1935, 2 January 1936, 16 January 1936).

Fascist Headquarters, and was ruled as being out of order.' [45]

In seeking to deny the claims of its opponents (including, on occasion, its ex-members), the BUF found it necessary to come to grips with a number of arguments. One of the most difficult was the contention that fascism must necessarily oppress women in Britain just as it did in Germany and Italy. In 1936, for instance, the former suffragette Sylvia Pankhurst argued that fascism opposed 'any participation in government by the mother half of the race'. In Italy, she declared, Fascist women's groups took their orders from men and adulterous women were punished when men were not, while in Germany, the Nazi Party forbade its women members to run for office, thousands of women were being sacked and women teachers were only allowed to occupy subordinate positions. Nor were such arguments only made outside the BUF. The same year, one woman member wrote to the organisation's journal criticising the treatment of women teachers and discrimination against women in sports in Nazi Germany. New members, she declared, needed assurance that the BUF did not stand for women's subordination.[46]

In both cases, a reply came from Anne Brock Griggs. Pankhurst, she argued, was misguided in her claims. Adulterous men were punished under Italian law and in Germany there were many woman professionals and female employment in general had risen. Furthermore, she insisted, in her criticism of the law in Italy, Pankhurst had failed to make any 'allowance for the difference in outlook between the Latin and Anglo-Saxon'. Griggs's reply to her fellow-fascist took a similar stance. Britain and Germany, she declared, had a different 'racial tradition' as regards attitudes to women, and the situation in both the professions and sports were more favourable than had been suggested. But her riposte here contained a different element. When the Nazis first came to power, she argued, there had been a reaction to the previous order in which 'the pendulum' had swung 'too far to the right'. Now, however, 'the German woman' was 'coming into her own'.[47]

While an explicit critique of fascist policy elsewhere was untypical, the suggestion that women's situation in both Italy and Germany was better than anti-fascists argued and that British fascist policy would necessarily differ from that followed abroad were crucial in

---

45 *Star*, 11 February 1935; *Blackshirt*, 15 February 1935, 22 February 1935;
   Hampstead and Highgate Express, 2 March 1935.
46 *Hibbert Journal* (January 1936); *Fascist Quarterly* (January 1936).
47 *Hibbert Journal* (April 1936); *Fascist Quarterly* (January 1936).

how the BUF replied to its critics. Thus E. D. Hart, who was cited earlier, accompanied his expression of admiration for the suffragettes with the observation that while fascism might 'appear anti-Feminist' elsewhere, 'an anti-Feminist policy' in Britain would be 'impossible'. The only copy of *The Woman Fascist* to have so far been recovered took the argument further, expressing admiration for maternity and child-care in fascist countries while arguing that Britain 'had advanced further along the road of justice and equality for the sexes'. Without access to other copies, we cannot be certain if such a remarkable distinction was typical of the ill-fated publication's approach to the question. Nor, in turn, can we tell how closely it was related to Mosley's claim that, as with previous movements, fascism would come to Britain with 'characteristics which are peculiarly British and in a manner which will strive to avoid the excesses and the horrors of Continental struggle'. It is clear, however, that the BUF's undoubted enthusiasm for the Mussolini and Hitler regimes did not mean that it felt obligated to argue that their policies towards women would necessarily be replicated when it came to power.[48]

For the BUF, like the BF before it, men and women were to work together in the struggle for fascism. Yet how this co-operation would work, and where the differences between the sexes would lie, could never be agreed. For Oscar Boulton, the leader of the Unity Band, writing in the year that he began his brief alliance with the British Fascists, women were invading men's jobs, were being urged to undertake men's sports and outnumbered men in the electorate. 'A masculine woman', he declared, 'is every whit as hateful and contemptible as an effeminate man, and both types are equally symptomatic of racial depravity.' For A. K. Chesterton, writing later in the decade, fascism stood for 'the great creative urge of the masculine spirit', determined to bring about a splendid future 'freed from all spiritual confounding of the sexes'.[49] But, as we have seen, these were not the only voices within British fascism. The BF, despite the prominent role played by women, did not find issues of gender of pressing importance. The BUF, however, had a great deal to say about it, and many of its pronouncements appear far more sympathetic than we would expect. Why this should be the case raises some crucial questions. Gottlieb has suggested that, despite the formal prohibition on women occupying such positions as District Leader, at local level

48 *Blackshirt*, 8 January 1938; *Woman Fascist*, 7 June 1934; Mosley, *Greater Britain*, p. 154.
49 *Patriot*, 20 February 1930; *Action*, 9 July 1936.

BUF women could be more significant than the man nominally in charge of them.[50] But both women and men could hold drastically different views on such issues as equal pay, and while the movement was undoubtedly sensitive to the balance of views within its ranks, it is most likely that the crucial variable was not how important women were in the BUF's membership, but how important they were in the BUF's strategy. Where the BF had not emphasised elections and had had doubts about the extension of the vote, its successor faced a preponderantly female electorate. Rather than representing an anti-feminist backlash, the BUF tried to appropriate feminist themes while simultaneously appealing to those, women and men, who believed women's place was in the home. Furthermore, as its comments on fascism elsewhere suggest, it was shaped by the very political culture it sought to transform. It was a British nationalism, rather than a nationalism *per se*, and as such it could not escape taking on at least some of the characteristics of the polity in which it operated. With women freshly enfranchised and important shifts taking place within both the labour market and the culture, the Britain of the time was uncertain about the roles of women and men. But so too was fascism internationally. In different permutations, disputes about women's role took place across much of the extreme right in inter-war Europe. The British case represents a particularly striking case of this – but not a unique one.

---

50 Gottlieb, *Feminine Fascism*, p. 61.

14

Europe

Kevin Passmore

Changes in the economic and social position of women during the Great War were greatly exaggerated by contemporaries and largely misconceived. All the same many soldiers were exercised by the suspicion that while they were suffering for their countries at the front, women were taking their jobs, and, perhaps worse, enjoying themselves. There was much fretting that the independence of the 'modern woman' – the British bachelor girl, the Italian *maschietta,* the French *garçonne* – would divert women from their 'natural' roles. Veterans, like many men who had not fought, viewed the modern woman with a mixture of barely suppressed desire and deep resentment at her unavailability and self-confidence.[1]

These fears were particularly sharp because they coincided with general social crisis, and negative images of femininity have been used throughout history to make sense of such upheavals. Misogynist stereotypes were all the more appealing because changes in women's position had followed the birth and development of organised feminism in the two decades preceding the war. Moreover, the war brought about a thorough militarisation of society, even in non-combatant Spain. Soldiering privileged allegedly virile values such as tenacity, selflessness, discipline and bravery. Once the war was over, many felt that order could be restored only by applying the male camaraderie of the front to a civilian society believed to have been rendered decadent by feminine materialism and selfishness. It was not just women themselves who were affected by these ills: striking

1 A literary example is Victor Margueritte's simultaneously titillating and moralising novel of 1922, *La Garçonne*, discussed in Mary Louis Roberts, *Civilisation Without Sexes: Reconstructing Gender in Postwar France, 1917–1927* (Chicago and London, University of Chicago Press, 1994).

workers and turbulent ethnic minorities too were considered to have been invaded by female passions. Anti-feminism and a more generalised fear of social decay converged, and many became convinced that 'normal' gender roles must be reasserted as the condition of a general restoration of proper social relations.

The perception that there was a crisis in gender relations must also be seen in the context of the crisis of liberal democracy between the wars, the major ramifications of which are well known. In politics the crisis was evident in, for example, the decline of liberal-democratic parties like the French Radical Party, the German Democrats (DDP) and the British Liberals in Western Europe, and in the supplanting of liberal-democratic nationalism by an altogether more exclusive variety in Eastern Europe. The women's movement was not spared this crisis, as the isolation of the liberal leadership of the Association of German Women (BDF) from an increasingly conservative rank and file, the growing indifference of European socialists to women's equality and the rise of New Feminism in Britain all demonstrated.[2] Liberalism was undermined from two directions. On the one hand many conservatives felt that the advance of democracy after the Great War had accorded too much to national minorities, workers and women. On the other hand, notwithstanding conservative fears, many of the national minorities, workers and women who had hitherto seen their causes as inseparable from democracy were disappointed by the product of voting in practice. Some women, including some feminists, now felt that communism represented an alternative way to realise the hopes once placed in democracy, while others saw the far right as a more appealing alternative. The far right therefore resulted from a convergence of disparate forces – democratic and anti-democratic, pro- and anti-feminist impulses.

Liberalism gave way to a rural, autarkic, ethnic conception of the nation. Those who subscribed to it believed that a nation's ability to survive in the face of hostile domestic and foreign enemies depended upon its ability to live off its own material and human resources. Nations with lower birth-rates would inevitably be displaced by those with higher fertility – hence the conviction that women should return to their child-bearing role. Demographers, doctors and racial hygienists also worried about the physical quality of the nation. Of particular concern were the spread of venereal disease amongst soldiers, the danger to women's reproductive faculties represented by factory

2 Karen Offen, *European Feminisms, 1750–1950* (Stanford, CA, Stanford University Press, 2000).

work, and alcoholism. Again the message was that women should be chaste and primarily domestic. Meanwhile, the drive for self-sufficiency placed a premium upon women's ability to manage the home frugally and consume only national products. While the British Fascisti urged housewives to buy imperial products, Yugoslav women's organisations' preoccupation with national costumes was linked to the drive for self-sufficiency. The autarkic project also placed a heavy emphasis on the population's relationship to the land. Again women were implicated, for they were conventionally seen as having a special affinity to the soil – the sphere of women was nature, while that of men was culture. All over Europe, movements and regimes of the extreme right idealised the chaste mother in peasant costume. This image might be predictable in Latvia, Croatia or Romania, but even the British Union of Fascists (BUF) promised to resurrect a rural 'Merrie England'. Neo-mercantilist autarky did not emerge primarily as a response to women's emancipation, but it did provide convenient weapons with which to beat feminists and women in general.

Neither was anti-feminism inevitably, or uniquely, a part of extreme-right discourses in this period. Rarely did the extreme right pay as much attention to feminism as it did to the socialist, communist or ethnic enemies. The extreme right's preoccupation with *women* was intermittent – Croatian fascists, for instance, virtually ignored women in the 1930s, but paid great attention to them during the war. Nevertheless, assumptions about *gender* subtly pervaded the discourses of all the right-wing extremist movements considered in this volume, and natural gender relations were seen as essential to the health of society as a whole.

Beyond this there was uncertainty. Resolution of the 'woman question' had to be weighed against other, possibly conflicting goals. The extreme right distinguished between women according to marital status, age and race. There was some disagreement about how to return women to the home, and some women were expected, as mothers, welfare workers and teachers, to help construct the homogeneous nation-states dreamed of by the partisans of autarky. Women themselves sought to redefine the extreme right's political goals according to their own ideas – drawn sometimes from the women's movement. Women's position in the fascist and non-fascist extreme right also differed, so we must begin with some definitional questions, focusing in the following section upon the *intentions* of the most powerful strands within each.

Authoritarian conservatism and fascism

In practice there were many similarities between these two types of extreme-right movement and regime, for they shared enemies, both believed in social inequality and both were nationalist.[3] In Poland, Piłsudski and Dmowski espoused basically similar views of women, even though they were political opponents. Yet there were important differences. Authoritarian conservatives defended the primacy of a constellation of conservative 'interests': property, Church, family, the military, the administration. They believed the nation to be actualised in the aforementioned interests, and in power authoritarian conservatives ruled through established institutions. While authoritarian conservatism was highly repressive, its intervention in social life was restricted by the need to defend the autonomy of these interests. So unlike fascists, they left some space for private initiative – they did not completely abolish 'civil society'. Similarly, preoccupation with established interests made them suspicious of mass parties. Where mass organisations were established, they were controlled by the social elites.[4]

As part of their 'disciplining' of society from above, authoritarian conservatives attempted to re-establish conventional gender roles. They saw the patriarchal family as one of the building blocks of society and nation, not least because succession through the male line was essential to the transmission of property in bourgeois and aristocratic families. State intervention in the family was, however, restricted by the conviction that the family was a bastion of the private sphere, and often by religious scruples about interference in the reproductive function of the family. Rather than regulate and politicise the family, as fascists attempted to, authoritarian conservatives were usually content to repress opinion considered harmful to the family and reinforce the pro-family, usually religious, component of education. They were more likely to introduce reforms designed to encourage the birth-rate than implement eugenic measures against the 'unfit'. They favoured assimilation rather than exclusion of national

3 Claudia Koonz, 'The fascist solution to the woman question in Italy and Germany', in Renate Bridenthal, Claudia Koonz and Susan Stuard (eds), *Becoming Visible: Women in European History* (Lawrenceville, NJ, Houghton Mifflin, 1987), pp. 499–533: 500–1.

4 The definitive discussion of the relationship between fascism and authoritarian conservatism is Martin Blinkhorn, *Fascists and Conservatives: The Radical Right and the Establishment in Twentieth-Century Europe* (Cambridge, Cambridge University Press, 1990).

minorities, and were somewhat more likely to value the families and property of all ethnic groups.

Authoritarian conservatives were less concerned than fascists to integrate women into politicised formations. Where they did establish women's organisations, they did not usually grant them a monopoly over the representation of women, and often they were happy to work with existing women's organisations. The conservative wing of the women's movement, including conservative feminists, retained some room for manoeuvre and indeed might have been strengthened by the prevalence of familialist ideology. In Poland, as Dobrochna Kałwa shows, the Piłsudski dictatorship's women's group, the Union of Women's Civic Work, was part of a loose hierarchy of political and non-political bodies supporting the regime, with the Non-Party Bloc for Co-operation with the Government at the summit. Likewise the French Vichy dictatorship, which gave much space to big business, the Church and army, mobilised women in a section of the main veterans' organisation, a body loosely linked to the regime. Mary Vincent's depiction of the Primo de Rivera dictatorship in Spain is illustrative of the nature of authoritarian conservative regimes in general. Primo identified the nation with a restrictive view of citizenship, defined in male and military terms, and counterpoised it to the 'people'. Just as men gallantly protected women, so citizens protected the people and women were supposed to occupy a secondary role. The same military definition of citizenship could perhaps be found in many other dictatorships of the period.

Fascism operated differently, in that it claimed to prioritise the nation, defined in populist terms, over all other interests.[5] Fascists did not, of course, pursue the national interest as disinterestedly as they pretended, for their ideals were actually constructed from a range of common prejudices, including gender prejudices. They regarded capitalism as more compatible with the national interest than socialism, for example, and most believed that the national interest required the political primacy of virile values. Nevertheless, fascists held that the re-making of the nation, the defeat of ethnic, socialist and feminist enemies, required displacement of old-style conservatism. Where the national interest was thought to require it, they were prepared to override in the name of the people the propertied, military, religious, administrative and familial interests so dear to authoritarian conservatives. So little concerned with the family *per se* were fascists, that

5 Kevin Passmore, *Fascism: A Very Short Introduction* (Oxford, Oxford University Press, 2002).

in the interests of the race they were often prepared to promote single motherhood.[6]

Fascism promised to bring to power a new elite, said to be drawn from the people and motivated by service to the nation. Certain conceptions of manhood figured strongly, for there was no better way for a man to prove his devotion to his country than through war service (unless he was a Jew), so veterans figured strongly amongst fascist leaders. The same gendered images were used to dismiss traditional conservatism as effeminate, sterile or impotent. Feminine images were used to signify the ideals *for* which men fought: veterans waged war on behalf of their wives and children, just as fascists defended women and children against Jews and communists (both often depicted as rapists). Women were therefore seen as essentially passive, and closely associated with domesticity. Mara Lazda cites a Latvian newspaper article of 1941: 'For what is the honour of the fighter and victor for the man, is the honour of mother for the women'.

Historians have long recognised that this simple attribution of gender roles did not work clearly in practice. The vehicle for the new elite was the mass party, conceived as an organic expression of the popular will, and contrasted with the unrepresentative cliques which allegedly controlled both the left and the established right. Fascist commitment to mobilisation of the people, conceived as an agglomeration of families, not individuals, together with the desire to win over as many voters as possible and nationalise all aspects of life, led to the incorporation of women in fascist movements. Whereas authoritarian conservatives worked with semi-autonomous women's movements, fascists organised women within the party itself. The women's sections of the Hungarian Party of National Unity (NPU), for example, were urged to press for the integration of rival bodies, and if persuasion failed they were to ensure that 'separate activities cease and that all kinds of welfare activities are initiated and carried out by the NPU'. The role envisaged for the women's sections fitted into the party's broader ambition to '*become the organiser of all manifestations of the nation's life* and thus through improving economic, moral, and intellectual circumstances [to] *develop into the Hungarian nation's vital organisation*'.[7] This was part of a broader project

6 Michael Burleigh and Wolfgang Wipperman, *The Racial State: Germany 1933–1945* (Cambridge, Cambridge University Press, 1991), pp. 252–3.

7 Party circulars, quoted in József Vonyó, 'Women in Hungary in the 1930s: the role of women in the Party of National Unity', *East Central Europe*, 20–30 (1993–96), 201–18: 210, 212, emphasis in the original.

designed to nationalise, or politicise, all areas of social life.

Because it prioritised the nation above all else, fascism was intrinsically hostile to feminism, as it was to socialism, for they put some other criteria before the nation. Yet absolute hostility to feminism was compatible with a more nuanced attitude towards specific demands advanced by the various components of the women's movement. Fascism was not repressive in a straightforward sense, for many fascists acknowledged that various groups, most notably employers and workers, and possibly also men and women, might have opposing interests, but they would not allow these conflicts to undermine the nation. Fascists hoped that by mobilising women (like workers) as a semi-autonomous component of an authoritarian party – occasionally within corporatist bodies too – they could both preserve the essential gender hierarchy and permit women to express their special concerns in an atmosphere where the national interest remained paramount. This one-sided compromise demanded some limited concessions from men (and employers). So just as fascists blamed 'selfish' capitalists for forcing workers to express their legitimate interests through socialism, so fascists sometimes counterpoised themselves to a mythical man who allows women *no* freedom and therefore provoked the excesses of feminism.

Women's position within fascist parties was not therefore one of *total* subordination, but of *relative* disempowerment. They had fewer choices open to them than women in democratic societies, and even than women in authoritarian conservative regimes. Yet so long as they were part of the ethnically and politically acceptable part of the nation they could negotiate and contest their position within the party.

This discussion of the position of women in authoritarian conservative and fascist movements suggests that the concepts conventionally used to understand generic fascism must be rethought. While both fascism and authoritarian conservatism are unequivocally positioned on the extreme right because of their uncompromising hostility to the left, both engaged in an implicit dialogue with their enemies. Authoritarian conservatives conducted a dialogue with semi-autonomous women's groups, while fascists combined repression with containment of opposition within the mobilised party. In seeking to destroy what it opposed 'at its roots', the extreme right effectively acknowledged the discourses it professed to oppose, and admitted them, in an attenuated and distorted form, into the extreme right.

Fascism is especially difficult to understand in terms of the usual binary oppositions, for it is engaged in the task of restoring order in the nation through the sweeping away of those normally believed to be the guardians of order. Fascism is not pro-feminist, any more than it is pro-socialist or pro-homosexual, but it is not surprising that some radicals – from revolutionary syndicalists in Italy to homosexual opponents of bourgeois morality such as Ernst Röhm in Germany – should have been attracted to fascism, especially once alternative outlets for subversion had been removed. Members of the women's movement, including feminists, were no exception. But by placing their hopes in fascism, feminists, like socialists and other radicals, abandoned much of what they had once held dear.

The women's movement, feminism and the crisis of liberalism

The question of continuities between the women's movement, feminism and the extreme right was at the centre of the Koonz–Bock exchanges.[8] Koonz held that there were strong continuities between the difference feminism of the pre-Nazi women's movement and the Nazi ideal of separate male and female spheres.[9] In her view only liberal feminism represented a genuine defence against fascism. Bock denied any such continuity between difference feminism and Nazism on the grounds that Nazism was not familialist. What light does international comparison cast upon this dispute?

Before we can answer this question, further definitional issues must be raised. First, we might agree that the minimum criteria for qualification as a feminist is the belief that *all* women are, perhaps in varying degrees, subordinate to men, and the commitment (in theory if not necessarily in practice) to ending that subordination for *all* women. Secondly, it is helpful to distinguish four types of women's movement, of which the first three were feminist. Unfortunately from the point of view of clarity, they were not linked to political movements in a one-to-one manner:

1 Socialist women contended that women could be free only when capitalism had been destroyed or substantially reformed. From a strict point of view those who espoused this view were not femi-

---

8 See Introduction, pp. 1–6.
9 Koonz's argument has something in common with that of Susan Kingsley Kent, in 'Gender reconstruction after the First World war', in Harold L. Smith (ed.), *British Feminism in the Twentieth Century* (Aldershot, Elgar, 1990), who argues that British New Feminism, perhaps unintentionally, helped trap women in traditional maternal roles.

nists, for they saw class as more important than gender and often denied that bourgeois women were exploited.

2 Some feminists saw women as fundamentally the same as men. They fought for *equality* before the law, the vote and equal access to higher education and the professions. Their political sympathies went to reformist socialists or liberal parties of the centre left or centre right.

3 A third group emphasised *differences* between the sexes. They demanded that women's special aptitudes (usually for motherhood and caring) should be valued and protected equally to male capacities. These 'difference feminists' were less interested in the vote, though some demanded it on the grounds that the maternal voice should be heard in elections. Their political sympathies ranged from liberalism, through moderate conservatism, to the nationalist right.

4 The non-feminist component of the women's movement was often of a religious bent. It shared difference feminists' belief that men and women should occupy separate spheres, and that maternity deserved state or charitable protection. They differed from difference feminists in their refusal to demand equality for women with men. They wished to strengthen the place of domesticity within a still-patriarchal order.

International comparison shows that while the conservative women's movement had the greater affinities with fascism, feminists of any persuasion were capable of turning to the extreme right. The numbers of women concerned varied, as did the degree to which their principles required revision.

Liberal feminism and the crisis of liberal democracy

Koonz's contention that only equality feminism provides a firm defence against the attraction of extreme-right values is hard to test, for it is not always easy to determine the precise nature of the feminism of those in whom we are interested. Even more significantly, in the early twentieth century it was less easy than today to distinguish equality from difference feminism, for the great majority of feminists believed men and women to possess different aptitudes – the notion that women would bring a more caring element to the electorate was, for example, a common justification for female suffrage.[10]

10 Karen Offen, 'Defining feminism: a comparative historical approach', *Signs*, 14 (1988), 119–57.

Only in Britain did a genuinely significant equality feminism exist. Even there it had never been uncontested, and Eleanor Rathbone's 'New Feminism' made considerable headway in the 1920s. Some liberal feminists, as Martin Durham reminds us, did turn to the BUF. Mary Allen, a former suffragette, claimed that the BUF represented the continuation of the pre-war struggle. We are not well enough informed about the type of liberal feminism formerly espoused by such figures to test Koonz's argument on that score. But, to anticipate a later point, it is significant that women in British fascist organisations engaged in tasks that can scarcely be construed as an extension of their maternal and caring natures: they carried out 'special patrols' and learned infantry drill and ju jitsu. True, this could be legitimated as a continuation of exceptional women's wartime auxiliary service, but there might be a distorted echo of equality feminism here too.

In most of Europe feminists hardly thought in terms of abstract rights at all.[11] We are obliged, therefore, to examine the itinerary of a more vaguely defined group of liberal feminists – women who had been associated with liberalism and reformist socialism in Western Europe. In Italy several such feminists were found in early Fascist women's groups. Subsequently, historic feminist organisations accommodated themselves to the regime and were repressed only in 1938. In Germany, Martha Voß-Zeitz and others moved from the left-liberal German Democratic Party to the radical *völkisch* wing of the German National People's Party (DNVP), and later sympathised with the Nazis.

It might be significant that liberal feminists were not attracted to the fascist movements or authoritarian conservative dictatorships of France and Spain. In these countries both fascism and authoritarian conservatism were highly Catholic in nature, and so left-wing feminists' long-standing anticlericalism caused them to be suspicious of them. British, German and Italian fascism, in contrast, was more heterodox in its religious and political make-up, and it was easier for leftists to see it as a reformulation of the radical tradition. In Britain and Italy a significant part of the fascist leadership had originated on the left, while the Nazis proved adept at picking up voters from all parties except the communists and Catholics.

Fascist movements everywhere presented themselves as radical alternatives to the *status quo*, and in countries where women had the vote, they were often anxious to reassure women voters fascists they

11 Victoria De Grazia, *How Fascism Ruled Women: Italy 1922–1945* (Berkeley, CA, University of California Press, 1992), p. 23.

were not simply reactionaries. The Nazis consciously set out to address their weakness among women. They made positive noises about women's work, and promised not to endanger the gains made by women. In Spain, whereas the conservative Primo de Rivera dictatorship had not mobilised women, all right-wing parties set up women's sections following the establishment of the Republic and female franchise in 1932. Martin Durham quotes one British fascist to the effect that while the BUF admired Italian and German natalist policies, they were not for import into Britain, 'which has advanced further along the road of equality and justice for the sexes'. An openly misogynist position was more likely to be adopted in Romania and Yugoslavia, where women did not have the vote.

Fascist promises to respect women's gains may have attracted some feminists who were disappointed by liberal and socialist records on women's rights. In Britain some feminists who opted for fascism had been personally disillusioned by the lack of change following from the introduction of female suffrage. The three ex-suffragettes who occupied senior positions in the BUF had all failed in bids to be elected to Parliament, and felt that they had been contemptuously treated by established parties. In Sweden Sigrid Gillner, a former suffrage campaigner and socialist, joined the Swedish National Federation because she was disappointed at the meagre fruits of enfranchisement.[12] In Italy, the Liberal regime had never shown much interest in women's organisations, and in spite of favourable noises from the established parties women's suffrage had still not become a reality by the time Mussolini came to power.[13] In Germany, female suffrage had been introduced, but the Social Democratic Party – the main defender of liberal principles in that country – had become markedly less favourable to women's issues in the inter-war period.[14] In these circumstances, it was possible for some to conceive of fascism as fulfilling promises broken by liberal democracy.

This is all the more understandable given that the universalist

12 Lena Berggren, 'Upper-class women and politics: the Swedish National Federation and its female members 1930–1945', unpublished paper.
13 De Grazia, *How Fascism Ruled Women*, pp. 18–20.
14 Adelheid von Saldern, 'Modernisation as challenge: perceptions and reactions of German Social Democratic women', in Hulmut Gruber and Pamela Graves (eds), *Women and Socialism, Socialism and Women: Europe Between the Wars* (New York and Oxford, Berghahn, 1998), pp. 95–134. For an excellent analysis of liberal-feminist disillusion see Elizabeth Harvey, 'The failure of feminism? Young women and the bourgeois feminist movement in Weimar Germany 1918–1933', *Central European History*, 28 (1995), 1–28.

values espoused by liberal feminists turn out on close analysis to have contained some explicit exclusions. Some liberal feminists in Germany and Britain had defended the property franchise. Many feminists had shared the racist assumptions underlying imperialism, and were strongly nationalist. In Britain relations between British and Irish suffragists became distant after the Easter Rising. Some feminists used women's participation in war work as a justification for demanding the vote, and many were deeply affected by wartime nationalism – one could point to the Pankhursts in Britain or to those women who had joined Italian fascism via the Interventionist movement.[15]

Another reason for the shift to the right was that some older feminists were suspicious of what they saw as the selfish individualism of younger girls, and shared ambient prejudices against the 'modern girl' and indeed against the permissiveness of individualistic liberal-capitalist society. The liberal individualism of the women's movement had always been tempered by a concern with the contribution women might make to attaining social cohesion. These sentiments sometimes led to a predilection for moral order, authority and nationalism.

Moreover, liberal feminism had always contained a strong element which advocated collaboration between women and men in their separate spheres. Thus Norah Elam, a member of the BUF, claimed to follow the suffragettes in understanding the need for co-operation between men and women 'within the corporate body of the state'. Many Italian feminists saw the Fascist National Organisation for Mother and Child as the realisation of their own demands for better treatment of unmarried mothers – something long resisted by the Church.[16]

Before concluding, it must remembered that whatever their *post hoc* justifications, the women in question had not shifted their allegiance unproblematically from liberalism to fascism. In Italy, for example, approval of fascist family policies made it no easier to swallow fascist policies on female employment. Feminists actually changed their minds on important issues. Above all, they had abandoned any universalist scruples.

From democratic nationalism to the extreme right

Feminists in the new states that had been carved out of the multinational Russian and Austro-Hungarian empires followed a rather

---

15 Julie M. Gottlieb, *Feminine Fascism: Women in Britain's Fascist Movement, 1923–1945* (I. B. Tauris, London and New York, 2000), p. 151.

16 De Grazia, *How Fascism Ruled Women*, pp. 59–68.

different path to the extreme right. Often regimes issuing from democratic nationalist movements mutated into authoritarian dictatorships during the inter-war years. This happened largely because the drive to create homogenous national states seemed to be threatened by peasant, working-class and ethnic minority unrest and by feminism. In Eastern Europe, as in the west, inter-war conflicts exposed the potentially exclusionary nature of democracy. Those who had once condemned multinational states in the name of the universal principle of self-determination became persecutors of minorities in their turn.

Since the Eastern European women's movement was largely integrated into nationalist movements, it is not surprising that it should have participated in nationalism's rightwards movement. The Council of Latvian Women, discussed by Mara Lazda, exemplified the ambiguities of liberal-democratic nationalism. It combined support for 'equal rights of men and women' with participation in the campaign for strengthening of the Latvian ethnic nation. Predictably, the Council supported the Ulmanis dictatorship, which had also moved from liberal to exclusive nationalism. Dobrochna Kałwa shows that the Union of Women's Civic Work in Poland travelled a similar route.

Although the circumstances were somewhat different in Hungary, which was not a new nation-state, but a truncated old one, the women's movement also moved from liberalism to the (semi) authoritarian and racist right. Under the pressure of inter-war social and ethnic conflicts, the right wing of the Hungarian women's movement fought off demands for restrictions on women's enrolment in universities by supporting proposals for a *numerus clausus* for Jews instead. The Hungarian Women's Association, formed in 1918, ditched the universalist liberal principles of Hungarian feminism, and claimed that its own feminism was 'as Hungarian as Hungarian wheat'.

It was not inevitable that nationalist women's movements should turn to the authoritarian right – Croatian Woman is one that did not, probably because it remained in opposition to the authoritarian multinational Yugoslav state. Nevertheless, the various examples considered under this heading do share one common feature. Many of the women who participated in authoritarian conservative organisations did not set out as reactionary anti-feminists, but as partisans of universal liberal and/or democratic principles. As such, they possessed something in common with liberal feminists in Britain, Sweden, Italy and Germany. In both cases sympathy for the extreme right can be seen both as a repudiation of liberal principles and as the realisation of exclusionary subtexts in the liberal tradition.

The major difference between east and west, perhaps surprisingly, was that in some Eastern European countries highly conservative and nationalist women's movements, as committed to the doctrine of separate spheres as any movement in the west, usually did not turn to fascism. The attempts of the Hungarian NPU to mobilise women were disappointing. Efforts by party leader and Prime Minister from 1932, Gyula Gömbös, to involve the anti-Semitic and nationalist Hungarian Women's Association in the NPU also failed. The NPU was obliged to abandon its campaign to monopolise welfare work, and adopted a more tolerant strategy which had more in common with that of authoritarian conservatism.[17] Likewise, the Romanian Astra movement developed no links with the extreme right, even though it espoused a populist, ethnic and even biologically defined nationalism – Astra wanted to raise the birth-rate of native Romanian women, and worried about intermarriage between Romanians and Hungarians. The Croatian Ustaša attempted to set up a women's section, which it was intended would play a part in welfare provision, but faced resistance from Catholic women's organisations to the politicisation of their organisations. Neither did conservative Serbian women's movements turn to fascism. It might be objected that fascism was relatively unimportant in Serbia, but we should not assume that political ideologies can exist only if men espouse them. The absence of a strong male fascist movement in Serbia does not invalidate the point that separate spheres ideology, even when coupled with nationalism, did not necessarily lead to sympathy with fascism.

In the present state of research it is not easy to explain why women in these Eastern European movements were happy to continue providing welfare through existing organisations rather than espouse fascism. It is possible that fascism's often clandestine mode of action in Romania and Croatia did not facilitate the organisation of welfare, but the obstacles were probably not insuperable. One might also point to the exceptionally rural and patriarchal nature of Southern European society. Melissa Bokovoy shows that the Croatian Ustaša believed that men belonged not to the family in the conventional sense, but to the national family, and they conceived Croatian history in terms of patrilineal descent. Yet such views were not necessarily representative of society as a whole, for in Croatia women had played a very important role in the largely liberal-democratic Croat Peasant Party.

---

17 Vonyó, 'Women in Hungary in the 1930s', pp. 215–16.

Perhaps the most convincing available explanation is that fascism in Eastern Europe, which was much more radical than its western counterparts, was unable, with some exceptions, to attract so many of the bourgeois women who were the backbone of social service. Especially in Romania and Hungary, where the non-native bourgeoisie was not numerous, fascist plans for the expropriation of Jewish property may have frightened both male and female members of the bourgeoisie.

Non-feminist women's organisations

Conservative, non-, or anti-feminist women's organisations shared wider conservative antipathy to the rise of unitary, democratic, nation-states. In the inter-war years some such movements had become a little more flexible in that they often accepted the right to vote, with qualifications such as extra votes for fathers of families. But they remained committed to separate male and female spheres within a hierarchical and patriarchal society. This ideology is said by Koonz to have predisposed German women's organisations to Nazism.

Conservative women's groups had little difficulty in living with conservative movements and regimes of various types, including authoritarian ones. In Yugoslavia the movements affiliated to the Yugoslav Women's Union (YWU) identified themselves with the Serbian royal family, and participated in the monarchy's attempt to create a Yugoslav consciousness 'from above' through administrative homogenisation. In Germany the women's movement was dominated by conservative organisations to a greater extent than elsewhere in Western Europe. They shared the anti-democratic policies of much of the right, and were especially engaged in using welfare to loosen the grip of socialism on the proletariat. In Spain and France, Catholic women's groups were closely related to conservative movements of several different shades, including the Francoist and Vichy dictatorships.

The readiness of conservative women's organisations all over Europe to back authoritarian conservatism confirms, as Kirsten Heinsohn argues for Germany, that they contributed to the undermining of democracy all over Europe. There were also many women who moved from conservative women's organisations to fascism. Given that both advocated domesticity for women, it is tempting to regard this as a natural progression. The process was actually rather complex.

We have seen that in crucial respects authoritarian conservatism differed from fascism: the former's religious nature and its belief in the autonomy of the family made it suspicious of fascist schemes for

regulating the domestic sphere and monopolising women's representation. And although conservative women's groups rejected liberal
universalism, their religiosity potentially limited their discriminatory
tendencies. The turn to fascism therefore required certain changes in
priorities. Kirsten Heinsohn provides us with an insight into the
impact of the rise of Nazism on *völkisch* women's groups in
Germany. While all the organisations she considers espoused separate
spheres ideology, there was much disagreement on its meaning.
Radicals within the DNVP women's group demanded the abolition of
separate women's committees on the grounds that they represented a
concession to the bourgeois women's movement, which allegedly put
separate interests before the well-being of the *volk*. Women would
still carry out gender-specific tasks, but alongside and under the
apprenticeship of men. The action of both men and women would be
subordinated to the national good. The New Land Movement, in
contrast, espoused a radical separatism, going as far as to advocate
women's municipal councils. The Nazis had no fixed policy towards
women, but they did oppose the versions of separate spheres advocated by the *völkisch* radicals. That separate spheres could be
interpreted so variably by different groups suggests that there was no
automatic affinity between movements which espoused the idea. Both
the *völkisch* radicals and the Nazis stressed the primacy of the ethnic
nation, but the former wished to reconcile the national imperative with
a degree of independence for women in their own sphere.

So did liberal feminism provide a greater barrier to fascism than
difference feminism? Given that genuine equality feminism was so
uncommon in early-twentieth-century Europe, we can reach no certain
conclusion on that score. We might even wonder whether the question is meaningful – it is perhaps tantamount to lamenting that early-
twentieth-century feminists weren't more like their granddaughters. It
is, however, possible that, as Karen Offen suggests, the crisis of feminism in the 1930s might have been caused partly by equality
feminists' inability to acknowledge the sexual differences created by
women's experience of maternity and by the gendered structure of the
labour movement. This view is supported by the research of Elizabeth
Harvey, which suggests that the bourgeois feminist movement in
Germany lost the support of young women because it remained
committed to achieving equality in employment and education at a
time when jobs were scarce.[18]

18 Offen, *European Feminisms*, p. 282. This view is supported by, for example,
Harvey, 'The failure of feminism'.

This is not to deny the greater affinities between difference feminism and the dominant tendencies within the extreme right, for we have seen plenty of evidence of the attraction between the two. But this should not obscure the fact that the interpretation of separate spheres espoused by the conservative women's movement could differ radically from that of the extreme right, especially that of fascists, or that some difference feminist movements, even quite nationalist ones, did not embrace fascism.

The most convincing conclusion would seem to be that no form of feminism *automatically* functioned as a barrier to engagement in the far right, and no form of feminism *automatically* prepared the way for the far right either. In a sense this is a banal point, for it is possible to find potential continuities and discontinuities between any two political ideologies, especially if elements of them are extracted from context. What is most important from our point of view is that the extreme right, fascism in particular, drew both from those who started from an anti-feminist position and from those who saw in the extreme right a means to realise the hopes once encapsulated in feminism and liberal democracy. In the former case participation in the extreme right reinforced explicitly exclusionary dispositions; in the latter case it revealed latent discriminatory tendencies within democratic movements.

Agency and empowerment

The malleability of separate spheres ideology supports Claudia Koonz's contention, reaffirmed by many others since, that it could be used as a source of empowerment by women within patriarchal extreme-right movements. Koonz's argument, moreover, has the merit of breaking down the binary opposition between structure and agency, for it assumes that structures can be simultaneously constraining and empowering. Even where women seem to be vectors of a patriarchal structure agency is present, in that reproduction of the traditional family requires much knowledge of childbirth and child-raising, education systems, markets and the nature of social relations more generally. It even involves an element of choice, if only between family and social ostracism. At the other end of the scale, those who consciously set out to modify the structures of the world they inhabit rely on structure: they may attempt to use patriarchal structures for their own ends, and the women's movement renders agency effective. The degree of agency, the nature of the available choices, consciousness of agency and the outcomes of actions vary historically and are a matter for historical investigation.[19] It is useful to distinguish several possibilities concerning women in the extreme right:

1 that women consciously pursued *feminist* agendas – that they sought to undermine or overthrow patriarchy;
2 that women sought consciously to maximise their sphere of action within a basically patriarchal framework;
3 that women unconsciously undermined patriarchy in spite of their commitment to it in principle.

A useful way to proceed is to compare the position of women in authoritarian conservative and fascist movements and regimes. In both, separate spheres ideology, along with class, religious and national/racial identities, acted simultaneously as a constraint upon and a source of empowerment for women. Yet the range of possibilities open to women differed in the two types of regime. In the former, class and religion, along with an exacerbated nationalism in Eastern Europe, provided means by which some women could maximise the scope of the domestic sphere. In the latter, although class and other forms of identity remained subtly important and no less important for that, militants mentally prioritised national and/or racial identities and these heavily structured ideas of separate spheres.

Another crucial way in which the options open to women varied was that whereas authoritarian conservatism did not abolish civil society, fascism sought to monopolise and nationalise all forms of social and political expression. In so doing fascists undermined the boundaries between public and private, whereas authoritarian conservatives aimed to preserve the family from political intervention.

Women in conservative authoritarianism: Western Europe
Some authoritarian conservative movements set up their own women's groups, while others allied with autonomous bodies. In either case women participated on condition that they regarded the family, as well as the rights of the upper classes, army, Church and other conservative interests, as sacrosanct. The prevailing conception of separate spheres was therefore conditioned by the need to defend conservative 'interests' more generally. So while separate spheres ideology destined women for the domestic sphere, the position of

19 I rely here on Anthony Giddens, *The Constitution of Society: Outline of the Theory of Structuration* (Polity, London, 1984).

bourgeois women who were members of religious groups was more advantageous than those who were not.

Women in conservative organisations did not think of themselves only as women, but as *bourgeois* and/or *Christian* women. This reminds us that the women's movement was not defined only by gender, but by other forms of social differentiation too. Perry Willson is doubtless right to say that many women sympathised with the extreme right simply because they shared their class's hostility to democracy. Particularly significant is that wealthy bourgeois and especially aristocratic families saw themselves as naturally entitled to participate in government as families of a particular class. Husbands and wives engaged in politics together, in a manner differentiated by gender. In nineteenth-century France, Italy and Spain, aristocratic Catholic women, through patronage of elementary confessional schools, were in the forefront of resistance against secularising states. In the inter-war years this form of female engagement remained most evident in aristocratic organisations like the monarchist Renovación Española in Spain. The more heterogenous CEDA, which carried the flag of the largely anti-republican right under the Republic, was also based on family and class ties. All over Europe analogous assumptions were present more subtly in the conviction of middle-class social workers, even though they had rarely given birth themselves, that their class qualified them to teach child-raising to working-class mothers. Domestic qualities were assumed to reside naturally in aristocratic and bourgeois women.

Conservative women conceived the domestic sphere positively, for it gave them, as mistresses of large households with servants, many advantages. As sponsors of charitable works they participated in a project for the moralisation of the working class and inculcation into the population of national cultures through education and child-raising. The idea that class conflict could be assuaged by the allegedly feminine values of compassion and reconciliation gave women a key role in welfare action, while the very disinterest of men in practical welfare work helped create space for women activists to organise own activities. Cheryl Koos and Daniella Sarnoff show how Vérine's activities in the education of parents led her to support the Vichy dictatorship's family and gender policies. Since conservative women's movements consciously discriminated between women on the grounds of class and religion, historians should be cautious in describing them as feminist (although contemporaries often did). Nevertheless, welfare work represented an empowerment strategy for some women.

This was all the more possible because autonomous women's organisations continued to exist in such regimes. Mary Vincent shows that this was the case under Primo de Rivera's dictatorship in Spain. The regime demanded the restoration of traditional gender roles – in practice this meant restriction of women's access to academic education, leaving them to act out the symbolic role as 'mothers of the nation' in military parades, and to participate in charitable activities. Yet the autonomy of the Church from government control permitted the small army of nuns who had traditionally provided welfare to carry on their work. In Spain the idea of religious vocation represented an alternative to marriage and motherhood as a suitable social role for women.

Women in conservative authoritarianism: Eastern Europe

Carol Lilly's analysis of the Serbian case shows that the position of women was similar in at least one of the Eastern European conservative dictatorships. The royal regime did not outlaw all opposition, and in Croatia, as Melissa Bokovoy shows, national separatists dominated the women's movement. The various organisations affiliated to the Yugoslav Women's Union (YWU) constituted a significant element in the loose constellation of bodies supporting the royal dictatorship. Although the women concerned unreservedly agreed that their social role was determined by their 'essential' nature, the autonomy of women's organisations permitted some discussion of the meaning of domesticity. In the YWU, birth control, women's paid employment and the vote were all debated – within the framework of the interests of the family. Like conservative women in Western Europe, YWU members saw themselves as intrinsically more moral and more religious than men, and therefore as uniquely qualified to propagate the principles of harmony within the nation. On this basis they demanded the right to be consulted in the elaboration of social legislation, perhaps through a corporatist framework which would recognise institutionally women's special aptitudes.

The Yugoslav women's organisation differed from its western counterparts in the greater saliency of nationalism, a product of the explicit threat to the unity of the state posed by Croatian nationalists. But nationalism was still muted by the YWU's commitment to the creation of a Yugoslav identity focusing on the royal family, rather than a popular cultural or ethnic nationalism. Class, together with royal links, was as important as nationalism in defining the female sphere and in providing women with leverage.

This class–nation nexus was perhaps clearest in Hungary, as described by Mária Kovács. Although the fascist opposition became more important in the 1930s, the Hungarian government was largely dominated by the landed magnates and capitalists of the Christian National Party, who ruled through a restricted franchise and manipulation of the rural electorate. The regime was also nationalist, seeking to restore Hungary's diminished position through economic modernisation and assimilation of ethnic minorities into Hungarian culture. The government, however, stopped short of condoning the anti-Semitism of the semi-fascist Gyula Gömbös and the open fascism of the Arrow Cross. Women associated with the Christian Nationals, organised in the National Association of Hungarian Women, were more favourably inclined to anti-Semitism. They fought off demands for restrictions on women's right to university education by supporting the far right's demands for restrictions on Jewish enrolment in universities. In effect, they exploited the nationalism of Hungarian politics in order to defend the right to higher education of upper-class women. But while they sympathised with the extreme right's anti-Semitism, they did not accept its radical hostility to the ruling class. Concern for class prerogatives may have influenced the National Association's indifference to overtures from Gömbös in the 1930s.

In Poland, the Piłsudski dictatorship was based primarily upon the army, which saw itself as the embodiment of the nation, and was backed increasingly by the landowning class. The middle- and upper-class women of the Union of Women's Civic Work (UWCW) participated in the coalition supporting the dictatorship partly as members of their class, but as elsewhere in Eastern Europe class was intimately connected to nation. As mothers or potential mothers and as educators of children, Polish women were bearers of the national culture. Borrowing Bakhtin's concept of the carnivalesque, Dobrochna Kałwa argues that the extensive participation of women in nationalist movements had traditionally represented a sort of 'symbolic inversion' of the oppression of the partition powers in Poland, and this provided women with some autonomy within a patriarchal system.

Women's activity was nevertheless still determined by gender. This became clear after the Great War. Women gained the vote in independent Poland, but not because politicians had accepted women's right to equality. Nationalist leaders still espoused a traditionalist vision of 'Mother Pole', but the primacy of the national interest now demanded mobilisation of women on the hustings and in the polling booth. Whilst men saw this action as a necessary evil, the UWCW argued that since women were inherently more moral than men it was their duty to call to order the petty world of male politicians. In effect they redefined political action in terms of separate spheres ideology, and through their actions they both undermined and reaffirmed conventional views of women. Kałwa argues that since women were incorporated into Polish nationalist movements primarily to provide electoral troops, they were subordinate to the political priorities of the parent movement, and found it difficult to assert a 'women's agenda'. Although the women of the UWCW had much in common with women in the more fascistic National Democrats, they were unable to co-operate with them in pursuit of women's issues.

Women in fascist organisations

Fascists declared the primacy of the nation, usually defined racially, over all other sources of allegiance. All groups and individuals were either to be harnessed to the national cause or eliminated from society. Only by adapting their conceptions of separate spheres to this priority could women hope to play a part in fascist regimes.

Feminism was an anathema to fascists, for it seemed to put loyalty to women above loyalty to the nation – hence fascists' depiction of feminism as part of an international Jewish and/or communist conspiracy. Those women who turned to fascism in order to further agendas inspired by liberal feminism were disappointed, as were those who sought to pursue the more ambiguous goals of radicals in the conservative women's organisations. In Italy, the Fascist Party (PNF) quickly established control over the women's groups that had sprung up more or less spontaneously around the movement, in which feminists were prominent. By 1926 Italian fascism had become explicitly anti-feminist, and suffragists had been expelled from the party. The party felt safe in expanding female activity only once women's sections had been effectively rendered leaderless. That autonomous 'feminist' movements survived until 1938 in Italy testifies more to the incomplete fascistisation of the regime than to any positive feeling towards feminism in the PNF. In Germany, too, feminists and other agitators were edged out. Martha Voß-Zeitz, for example, was rejected by Nazis because of her feminist past. Even when radicals attempted to rework demands for equality in terms of racial doctrine, this cut no ice.

As a self-proclaimed anti-bourgeois, radical movement, allegedly standing outside normal politics, fascism attracted a rainbow coalition of radicals, including feminists, at a time when the parties upon which radicals had traditionally relied were in crisis. That feminists, like other radicals, were disappointed by fascism did not mean that fascist radicalism was merely rhetorical. Rather its radicalism was political rather than socialist or feminist in form. The majority's radicalism resided in a desire to sweep away the establishment in order to restore order, yet it regarded conventional gender relations as an essential part of an ordered society. What is more, fascists saw the establishment as corrupted by 'femininity', so how could they dilute their own movement – the very antidote to feminisation – by admitting women to it on an equal basis? Mussolini said in 1924:

> Women must obey. My opinion of the role of women in the state is opposed to feminism. If I were to give women the vote, people would laugh at me; in a state like ours they ought not to count. Do you know how the Anglo-Saxons will end? In the Matrichiart.[20]

The radicalism of Italian Fascism consisted in a 'manly' national revolution directed against 'feminine' socialists and conservatives.

If women were to join fascist movements they would have to do so on terms appropriate to their 'proper' position in society. All of the fascist movements considered in this volume possessed separate women's groups, all of them were institutionally subordinate to the male parts of their organisations, and all were subject to petty restriction. The BUF women's section, for example, was deprived of its own newspaper on the grounds that it might foster a separate existence for women. With few exceptions, male fascists were indifferent, not to say hostile, to women members. Women were usually underrepresented as a proportion of total members, and few were influential at the peak of the fascist party.

In power, fascists eliminated or 'co-ordinated' autonomous women's organisations and reduced the range of choices available to active women. In so doing fascism not only opposed feminism, but severely weakened the empowerment strategies of conservative women's organisations. Kirsten Heinsohn shows, for instance, that the strategies of the *völkisch* radicals were rejected by the Nazis, and that some conservative women were alarmed at Nazi subordination of women's groups to the authority of the party.

All the same, millions of women did join fascist organisations in these conditions, and many of them did attempt to widen the space

20 Benito Mussolini, 'Maccina e donna', cited in Renate Bridenthal, Claudia Koonz and Susan Stuard (eds), *Becoming Visible: Women in European History* (Boston, Houghton Miflin, 1987), p. 505.

available to them. This was possible because fascists saw the nation as a hierarchy of co-operating groups. As our definitional discussion suggested, in spite of its opposition to feminism, fascism accepted that women might have separate interests and even that certain male attitudes were outdated. Fascists' views should not be mistaken for feminist, but they did represent an implicit recognition of the force of feminism in modern society and that repression alone could not deal with it. Fascists were prepared to allow for the expression of separate interests so long as they did not conflict with national priorities – for example for a numerous, healthy and ethnically valuable population. Separate interests were acceptable so long as conflicts were resolved in accordance with the national interest as defined by fascists. Fascism therefore combined destruction of feminism with an attempt to shift the terms of *dialogue* with women to a ground where women were weaker and more closely controlled. The mobilisation of women's groups within an authoritarian party, supposedly the exclusive interpreter of the national interest, represented one means of achieving this goal. Corporatism was another: Mosley, for example, wanted women to be represented as mothers in the corporate state, rather than by professional women politicians who supposedly knew nothing about motherhood.

Motherhood, then, *could* justify a very wide role for women. Judging by the limited extent to which maternal corporations were actually set up, many men doubted that motherhood *should* be interpreted in this way. Women within fascist movements fought a double battle against feminism and unenlightened male fascists, as the following 1937 quotation from Nora Torulf of the quasi-fascist Swedish National Federation illustrates:

> A new view is needed, one which radically breaks free from the those women's groups where outdated currents of thought have led to deadlock. ... We who fight for this idea demand respect for woman both as an independent individual and as a wife and mother, and we demand this from men as well as from women themselves. We know that this battle has to be fought not only against today's representatives of an outmoded women's radicalism, but just as much against the reactionary male phalanx who still more or less perceive woman as the being created from Adam's rib whose sole purpose is to delight men.[21]

Fascism was based on the premise of female inferiority and on hostil-

---

21 Quoted in Berggren, 'Upper-class women and politics'. See also her forthcoming monograph on the Swedish National Federation.

ity to feminism, but the precise role of women in actual movements depended on complex struggles between unequals in particular contexts.

The fascist concept of the private sphere was, in fact, fundamentally ambiguous. Antoine Rédier and Cornelieu Codreanu defined women's position especially narrowly and condemned the 'modern woman' for venturing out of the domestic sphere. Yet fascist ultranationalism meant that motherhood became a national duty, and was therefore politicised. The consequences were unpredictable. On the one hand, politicisation justified state intervention in reproduction, and reduced women's control over their own lives. On the other hand, as Cheryl Koos and Daniella Sarnoff show, disruption of the public/private dichotomy enabled Marie-Thérèse Moreau and others to claim that 'The life of the *patrie* is that of a *grande famille* and there is no firm divider between these two domains'. Typically, Moreau both reaffirmed and undermined the public/private distinction. Likewise, Mara Lazda shows that the Nazi-controlled Latvian press participated in a project for control of maternity, but also, coupled with assumptions about the ethnic Latvian nation, this same ideology provided right-wing Latvian women with a source of solidarity which fed into resistance movements, and ultimately had to be curbed by the Nazis.

Motherhood's flexibility as a concept had long been used by the women's movement to justify intervention in society. Welfare work had traditionally been seen as an extension of caring duties for married women, or as a substitute for motherhood for single women. The researches of Koonz and De Grazia showed that maternalism, through its connection with welfare, both defined women's position in fascist movements in Germany and Italy and permitted them to contest it. The essays in this book suggest that similar arguments can be applied to most of Western Europe. In South-Eastern Europe, welfare appears to have played a less significant role in fascist organisations, and this had certain consequences for women's activism.

Let us deal with the west first, where all the fascist movements considered possessed significant welfare sections. In this respect there was a major continuity between fascism and the conservative women's movement, authoritarian and democratic. As in conservative movements the appeal to women's 'essentially' caring nature, increasingly coupled with technical qualifications, permitted women to carve out a sphere of influence of their own. Welfare workers were formally subordinate to doctors, and from one perspective they implemented male-defined policy. But the sheer scale of welfare organisations in the two fascist regimes and in fascist movements in Spain and France meant that direct supervision of women was difficult. There were always some women who defined the reach of social work more broadly, and in a context where the boundaries of the social and political had become blurred, this reach was potentially very broad indeed.[22]

The outcome of such struggles varied. In Italy, some small victories were won. Although the party endeavoured to maintain male control over women's sections, female national inspectors were eventually appointed to deal with the massive administrative tasks in these complex organisations. After 1940 women gained seats on PNF provincial directories and in local corporations, and were granted their own central committee. In Germany, social workers lobbied without success to increase their role in the diagnosis of 'asociability', yet their protestations of inadequate power *vis-à-vis* doctors masked their participation in a powerful network. In France, Lucienne Blondel became secretary general of the Solidarité Française's newspaper – perhaps in spite of her agitation for equality for women before the law. Struggles of this type continued in fascist movements and regimes as they had in others.

There was nothing either new or specific to fascism about using welfare to domesticate the working class or as part of a project for nationalisation of the masses. Welfare services expanded in Germany and Italy during the 1930s under the twin stimuli of depression and war, just as they did in other countries. Middle-class women, young and single professionals, together with middle-class housewives, ran these welfare services, just as they did those of non-fascist governments and parties. As we have seen, class origin, together with formal training, legitimated intervention in the lives of working-class women, and to some extent men.

There were, however, some important discontinuities between authoritarian conservatism and fascism, in that the class component of welfare was institutionalised differently. In conservative women's organisations middle-class women were empowered at the price of constituting poor women as the clients for their services. In fascist movements this happened too, but the hierarchy was formalised and harnessed to a more exclusive nationalism in a context where nothing,

22 Elizabeth Heinemann, *What Difference Does a Husband Make? Women and Marital Status in Nazi and Postwar Germany* (Berkeley, University of California Press, 1999), pp. 28–9.

not even the family, was considered to be beyond the reach of the political and national. In Hungary, whereas conservative women's organisations and political parties had restricted recruitment to the middle and upper classes, Gömbös's NPU set out to include the lower classes too.[23] But women within the party were not organised on an equal basis. Rather class hierarchies were reproduced within the party, so whilst all party members were advantaged compared to non-members, class hierarchy was reaffirmed within the party. Perry Willson shows how in Italy PNF secretary Achille Starace campaigned to mobilise each section of the population, defined by class and gender, within the party. While middle-class women joined the Fasci Femminili, peasant women joined the Massaie Rurali and working-class women joined the SOLD – a division which betrayed an implicit assumption that only the women of the first organisation were truly women. Relations between the organisations were hierarchical. Welfare workers, often recruited from the first organisation, attempted to teach peasant women the virtues of Taylorist housework practices. Bourgeois members of the Fasci Femminili were more empowered by participation in the fascist project than poor peasant women in the Massaie Rurali.

Fascism did not, however, simply reaffirm surreptitiously pre-existing class hierarchies. In conservative women's groups class and religion alone had been sufficient to entitle women to meddle in the lives of others. Charity was meant to establish a human bond between members of classes who were equal before God, if not economically. During the inter-war years paper qualifications increasingly legitimated class superiority. In fascist organisations welfare work was explicitly politicised. In Hungary, the NPU instructed women to convince the population that only the NPU could effectively deliver aid, by, for example, wearing party armbands on home visits.[24] Fascists too expected many of their welfare workers to be formally trained, but they placed as much emphasis upon ideology as upon technical knowledge. They trained social workers themselves in classes where knowledge of party dogma was paramount. Trainees in the French PSF's school, for example, were asked in an examination: 'Do you agree that a holiday camp directed according to the principles outlined in this course can contribute to national renovation such as the PSF desires it?' There can be little doubt what the answer was, yet

---

23 Vonyó, 'Women in Hungary in the 1930s', p. 204.
24 Ibid., p. 210.

course organisers affected surprise when one candidate copied her response from a party circular.[25]

This example confirms the greater importance of nationalism in fascist welfare work. Women used the notion of welfare *service* to claim some of the prestige attached to war veterans within fascist movements. Just as male leaders of fascist movements used their war records to justify their claim to incarnate the nation, many women held that their war service as nurses or welfare workers gave them a special national role too. Note, for example, Elisa Majer Rizzioli, a former Red Cross nurse who in 1924 was appointed inspector of Fascist women's groups in Italy. Such women remained subordinate to male veterans, but their position in relation to non-combatant men and those who were not party members was more ambiguous.

This reminds us that discursive distinctions between the genders made by fascists did not fully coincide with the biological categories of male and female. Cheryl Koos and Daniella Sarnoff show that Antoine Rédier regarded many French men as unmanly: left-wing politicians were depicted as effeminate, or 'old grandmothers'. Extreme-right men, in contrast, were strong and powerful 'true men'. Women, too, were divided between the idealised mother and the hated 'modern woman'.

It followed that some women – so long as they were acceptable in political and national terms (and implicitly in terms of class too) – could exercise greater power than certain categories of men. This was most evident in the racialised nature of women's activities in fascist organisations, for they assisted in the implementation of policies that discriminated against both men and women of ethnic minorities. The Croix de Feu in France refused aid to the families of immigrant workers. Women in the Hungarian NPU were encouraged to produce handcrafted goods in order to help free the nation from Jewish influence and 'international cartels'.[26] Italian pro-natalist policies were meant to raise the birth-rate of the ethnic Italian population, not of its German or Slav minorities.

The British fascist Boulton argued that racial degeneration was manifested in the blurring of sexual boundaries, a view which was typical of the pseudo-scientific ideas which informed political opinion – not just on the far right – in this period. It implied that only higher races were differentiated by gender, a conviction that was taken to its

25 Archives Nationales, 451 AP Fonds La Rocque 174, Letter from Hirsch to de Préval, 9 July 1937.
26 Vonyó, 'Women in Hungary in the 1930s', p. 208.

logical conclusion in Nazi Germany, where only Aryan (sometimes only middle-class Aryan) women were deemed fit to inhabit a separate domestic sphere. Many lower-class Aryan men and women were sterilised on the grounds that they were racially unfit for fatherhood or motherhood. Non-Aryans were killed.

This prioritisation of the racial conception of the nation possessed implications for women in the master race too. Dagmar Reese has shown that young women regarded their experience in the League of German Girls (BDM) positively, because the movement did not preach domestic virtues, but gave them opportunities for initiative as part of a racial-generational community.[27] Here, racial ideas met with different expectations of married and single women, common across Europe. They were underpinned by the belief that many women were unavoidably denied the joys of motherhood because of the deaths of so many men during the Great War, and reinforced by women's expectation of participating in the emergent consumer economy.

To return to the question of race, we can agree with Michael Burleigh and Wolfgang Wipperman that the Nazis' 'racially-motivated antifeminism represented a significant departure from traditional Christian-Conservative antifeminism'.[28] With the obvious proviso that the fanaticism with which the Nazis' endeavoured to construct their biological racist dystopia sets them apart, the conclusion is nevertheless valid for all fascist movements and regimes, in that ultra-nationalism, usually with a racist component, and entangled with other forms of difference, exercised a major influence on the position of women in all such movements.

Women's empowerment in fascist regimes entailed, therefore, abandonment of solidarity with women of lower classes and 'inferior' races. Those few women's groups that still called themselves feminist did not do so without qualification. The Italian Teresa Labriola championed 'Latin feminism', which rejected the idea of universal rights as foreign. In 1938 Italian women's organisations expelled Jews.

In Western Europe, only Britain departed partially from the pattern described above, in which separate spheres doctine, class assumptions and welfare were harnessed to a racist project. Welfare was certainly important in the BUF, and differences between men and women were

27 Dagmar Reese, 'Emanzipation oder Vergesellschaftung: Mädchen im "Bund Deutscher Mädel"', in Hans-Uwe Otto and Heinz Sünker (eds) *Politische Formierung und soziale Erziehung im Nationalsozialismus* (Frankfurt, Suhrkampf, 1991), pp. 203–25.
28 Burleigh and Wipperman, *The Racial State*, p. 306.

assumed to be natural. Yet the notion that women were essentially passionate rather than rational was detached from their caring role as mothers or pseudo-mothers and used to justify tangentially related activity. Women played a role in the dissemination of electoral propaganda and some ran for office. Women were used quite extensively as electoral propagandists in other countries (Poland, Spain, France). But in Britain the balance was different, for only there were separatist arguments expressed alongside demands for equal rights.

Separate spheres ideology was no less pervasive in South-Eastern Europe than in Western, and the women's movement was just as involved in welfare work. Yet welfare work did not become fascistised in the way that it did in the west. Neither Serb nor Croat fascism attracted many women, while women in the Romanian Iron Guard did little other than produce handcrafted items for sale at fundraisers. The Hungarian NPU attempted without success to create women's sections intended to be concerned largely with welfare work.

In a context where social service was not available as a source of empowerment, ambitious women found their options restricted. The prevailing discourse in Eastern Europe as a whole was highly military. We know little about the implications of this for women in the Hungarian Arrow Cross, but the Romanian case, as described by Maria Bucur, is perhaps paradigmatic. The Iron Guard applied military expectations to women: women's sections were 'fortresses' and their aim was 'to give new Romania a new woman, an experienced and decisive soldier like the [new] man'. On the face of it, this breaks radically with accepted views of women's place in society in that it masculinises them. The purpose of this rhetorical inversion of normal gender roles was probably to establish the status of the Iron Guard as a radical alternative to a more conservative Romanian government – another case of the 'inversion' of gender roles evoked by Dobrochna Kałwa, and a reminder that gendered metaphors can be used to legitimate both authority and resistance to it.

Yet the notion of military hierarchy fixed women in a location subordinate to the male leadership, and there is little sign that the Iron Guard expected women to occupy anything other than such a position. Welfare represented a time-honoured means for women to intervene socially in a relatively autonomous domain. Military discourses offered no such opportunity, in spite of their apparent radicalism. In Romania, Nicoleta Niculescu wanted to participate in paramilitary and sabotage activities, but she was very much the exception. If women in such movements wanted to play the soldier, they had to break with all conventional expectations of women's behaviour, and few were willing to pay this price. This point is reinforced by the failure of the Swedish pro-Nazi movement, the Kristina Gyllenstierna, to become a mass movement. The historical Kristina Gyllenstierna was famous for having successfully led the defence of Stockholm against the Danes in the sixteenth century while carrying out the duties of a model mother. Coupled with the myth of the Valkyria, Gyllenstierna offered a potential role model to women. But most women preferred the rather more traditionalist Swedish National Federation, which was more concerned with welfare politics.[29]

Conclusion

In the introduction to this volume we posed a number of questions for comparative evaluation (see page 6). First, we have seen that the extreme right, especially fascism, was able to win recruits from a wide range of women's organisations, feminist and non-feminist. Fascism was an inherently contradictory phenomenon and feminists were capable of being attracted to it for its supposed radical egalitarian or for its perceived familialist reformism. Whether or not the women in question remained feminist once within the extreme right is another matter altogether.

This brings us to the question of whether the extreme right was intrinsically anti-feminist. We have seen that because they did not abolish civil society authoritarian conservative movements and regimes left some space for feminist movements, especially of a conservative persuasion. The position concerning fascist movements is more controversial. One critic of current trends in the historiography of women, gender and fascism has claimed that to emphasise the ambiguities of the extreme right's attitude towards women and to stress the roles played by women within fascist movements, as many of the contributors to this volume have, carries the danger of uncritical acceptance of fascist claims that their movements 'objectively' represented women's interests. The dominant tendency in fascist movements, he argues, was explicitly anti-feminist.[30] Yet one cannot resolve the problem of fascism and feminism simply by counting examples of feminist and anti-feminist measures proposed or implemented by fascist movements. To attempt to do so is to assume that

29 Berggren, 'Upper-class women and politics'.
30 Dave Renton, 'Women and fascism: a critique', *Socialist History*, 20 (2001), 71–81.

it is possible to establish an ahistorical standard of women's 'objective interests' and evaluate specific measures on this basis. Any attempt to do so comes up against the fact that feminists – and others – disagree fundamentally on what women's interests are. So we cannot assume that a proposal to extend female access to employment or to welfare benefits, for example, is 'objectively' feminist. All we can say is that feminists must believe that most women are oppressed by men and aspire to liberate them from this oppression, whilst proposing practical strategies designed to achieve this end. By this standard neither fascist movements nor the women who belonged to them were feminists. Fascists advocated measures to be applied only to women of a particular national or racial group or political persuasion and this meant rejection of the universalism essential to feminism. Fascists sought to incorporate *some* women into the national community by isolating specific issues from feminism, thereby achieving the goal of undermining feminism.

Contained within the answer to the second question is an answer to the third. Authoritarian conservatives were nearly always maternalist and pro-family, and their intervention in gender relations was limited by this fact. Fascists, in contrast, were concerned with protecting only ethnically, nationally and politically acceptable families, and in the name of the national imperative they were ready to intervene in the lives even of those families they favoured.

Fourthly, the contributions to this volume show that whilst patriarchal structures, discourses and practices in extreme-right movements bore heavily upon women, those who joined conservative women's groups or fascist parties were not completely without power. Authoritarian conservatives preached the inviolability of the family, and the very freedom of the family from regulation permitted women a position from which they could criticise prevailing ideas about the family. Conservative women could use separate spheres ideology, coupled with assumptions of class superiority, fortified by religious and nationalist beliefs, to pursue their own agendas. Fascists politicised women within the party itself, and through their abolition of civil society deprived them of any alternative position from which to intervene in the wider world. Whilst class remained important, women had to combine separate spheres ideology with racial and national priorities if they were to hope for influence. In both types of movement women were able to negotiate their positions only from a position of relative weakness. They could pursue their own goals only by reaffirming the extreme right's conviction that women were essentially irrational, compassionate, religious and/or maternal.

Fifthly, running through the answer to all these questions is evidence of the mutual construction of gender relations and other forms of difference. Neither separate spheres ideology nor maternalism can be understood in isolation from national, racial, political, religious or class discourses. Feminists who joined fascist movements abandoned solidarity with women deemed unacceptable because of their race, religion, class, lifestyle or sexuality.

These considerations also suggest that the binary oppositions – traditional/modern, radical/reactionary, victim/victimiser – usually used to understand the extreme right must be rethought. Extreme right-wing movements, like the right more generally, are not simply binary opposites of the left. Applying Bakhtin's understanding of literary texts to political conflict, we might say that the extreme right does not simply oppose the left. It might crush the political representatives of the left – that is why the extreme right is extreme – but it also engages in dialogue with the left, modifying its own discourse to anticipate the reactions of, and win over, those it opposes.[31] In other words, the extreme right assumes the agency of those it opposes. This is all the more important because the extreme right itself includes groups which are assumed (rightly or wrongly) to be 'normally' represented by the left – workers' and women's groups, for example. So in dialoguing with the left, the extreme right creates dialogue within itself too. Even the ultra-patriarchal Rédier was forced, against his better judgement, to accept the creation of a women's section within his Légion. In Spain women's sections were created in the Falange because of women's pressure. From the point of view of fascist leaders, women's sections within the party seemed to bring the feminist danger right into the heart of the party. Hence their efforts to control them.

In sum, the extreme right (like the right) differs from the left in the nature of the relationship and balance of power between the heterodox elements which make up its constituency. If we understand the extreme right as not absolutely differentiated from the left, comprising groups unequally endowed with power, and positioned in various ways in relation to the prevailing class, gender, religious, ethnic and other divisions in a given society, then the problems addressed by this book become easier to comprehend. It is no longer

---

31 M. M. Bakhtin, *The Dialogic Imagination*, ed. Caryl Emerson and Michael Holquist (Austin, University of Texas Press, 1981).

surprising that women from so many backgrounds, feminist and anti-feminist, left and right, should have been attracted to the extreme right, and neither is it surprising that the extreme right should have proved so inhospitable to women.

Index